Wallace A. Bartlett

Digest of Trade-Marks for Machines, Metals, Jewelry, and the Hardware and Allied Trades

With a Synopsis of the Law and Rractice relating to Trade-Marks

Wallace A. Bartlett

Digest of Trade-Marks for Machines, Metals, Jewelry, and the Hardware and Allied Trades
With a Synopsis of the Law and Rractice relating to Trade-Marks

ISBN/EAN: 9783337135805

Printed in Europe, USA, Canada, Australia, Japan

Cover: Foto ©ninafisch / pixelio.de

More available books at **www.hansebooks.com**

DIGEST OF TRADE-MARKS

(Registered in the United States)

for

MACHINES, METALS, JEWELRY,

and

THE HARDWARE AND ALLIED TRADES,

with a

SYNOPSIS OF THE LAW AND PRACTICE RELATING TO TRADE-MARKS.

by

WALLACE A. BARTLETT,

Solicitor of Patents,

Author of Weapons of War, Digest of Cartridges, Progress in the Arts, &c.

Washington, D. C.
Gibson Bros., Printers.
1893.

Entered according to act of Congress, in the year 1893, by
WALLACE A. BARTLETT,
in the Office of the Librarian of Congress at Washington.

INTRODUCTORY.

Patents do not receive the liberal construction by the courts which was accorded a few years ago. This is within the experience of every practitioner whose practice takes in a number of circuits.

The Patent Office, following the courts, refuses to grant patents for small improvements. The objection that an alleged improvement is a "mere mechanical expedient not involving invention" is now often raised against devices which a few years ago would have been patented without objection.

The manufacturer who knows that his wares are better than similar goods made by others believes there must be some reason for it. He thinks he is entitled to recognition for the improvement he has made. This recognition he finds it more and more difficult to get by means of the patent law, although the statute has not been changed in any important particular for more than thirty years.

While the courts have been restricting patents, they have come to recognize more clearly the right of the honest producer to his business reputation, and the duty of the Government to protect the people from fraud. Hence trade-mark protection has grown more valuable, and there is a very evident disposition in the courts to protect this class of property.

The writer, who has devoted more than twenty years to patent practice, as an examiner in the U. S. Patent Office, and as a practitioner before the Office and expert in the courts, has of late been constrained to advise many clients to devote less attention to patents for minor improvements, and more to maintaining their business reputation, as they may do under the trade-mark law.

In England the value of trade-mark protection, under the "Statute of Monopolies," has long been recognized. More than five times as many marks are registered in England as in the United States. The importance of trade-mark protection is not yet fully realized in America.

Most American manufacturers have some distinguishing mark by which their goods are known. Too often they are careless about the use of their marks, or about infringement.

In adopting a new mark the manufacturer should be careful that it is original, appropriate, and not too nearly like that of a competitor.

When a mark has been long used, the owner should insist that no other dealer use one so near like it as to deceive.

The following compilation has been made to enable manufacturers and dealers in machines, metals, and hardware and analogous trades to know the relation they bear toward each other in the matter of the marking of their goods.

My thanks are due to the examiner of the class of trade-marks, and his assistants in the Patent Office, for their courtesy and kind suggestions during the progress of this work, which, small as it seems, required a vast amount of research, comparison, and investigation.

The essential features of the trade-mark have been given in the compilation. The intention is to make the work a key, or ready reference index. The Patent Office furnishes a copy of any trade-mark for ten cents, so that, having found the lead, further information in any case need not be expensive.

W. A. BARTLETT.

TRADE-MARKS.

THE LAW AND PRACTICE.

A trade-mark is a symbol which indicates the origin of goods, wares, or merchandise, and distinguishes these goods from others not marked or otherwise marked.

The right of possession in a trade-mark is a natural right, founded on the inherent principle of justice which gives to the producer that which he produces. The courts recognize trade-marks as property, and trade-marks may be protected at law or in equity in the same manner as other property.

The United States statutes give special protection to trade-marks registered in the United States Patent Office, under the provisions of the act of March 3, 1881, which act is as follows:

AN ACT to authorize the registration of trade-marks and protect the same.

Be it enacted by the Senate and House of Representatives of the United States in Congress assembled, That the owners of trade-marks used in commerce with foreign nations or with the Indian tribes, provided such owners shall be domiciled in the United States or located in any foreign country or tribes, which, by treaty, convention, or law, affords similar privileges to citizens of the United States, may obtain registration of such trade-marks by complying with the following requirements:

First. By causing to be recorded in the Patent Office a statement specifying name, domicile, location, and citizenship of the party applying; the class of merchandise, and the particular description of goods comprised in such class to which the particular trade-mark has been appropriated; a description of the trade-mark itself, with fac-similes thereof, and a statement of the mode in which the same is applied and affixed to goods, and the length of time during which the trade-mark has been used.

Second. By paying into the Treasury of the United States the sum of twenty-five dollars, and complying with such regulations as may be prescribed by the Commissioner of Patents.

SEC. 2. That the application prescribed in the foregoing section must, in order to create any right whatever in favor of the party filing it, be accompanied by a written declaration verified by the person, or by a member of a firm, or by an officer of a corporation applying, to the effect that such party has at the time a right to the use of the trade-mark sought to be registered, and that no other person, firm, or corporation has the right to such use, either in the identical form or in any such near resemblance thereto as might be calculated to deceive; that such trade-mark is used in commerce with foreign nations or Indian tribes, as above indicated; and that the description and fac-similes presented for registry truly represent the trade-mark sought to be registered.

Sec. 3. That the time of the receipt of any such application shall be noted and recorded. But no alleged trade-mark shall be registered unless the same appear to be lawfully used as such by the applicant in foreign commerce or commerce with Indian tribes, as above mentioned, or is within the provision of a treaty, convention, or declaration with a foreign power; nor which is merely the name of the applicant; nor which is identical with a registered or known trade-mark owned by another, and appropriate to the same class of merchandise, or which so nearly resembles some other person's lawful trade-mark as to be likely to cause confusion or mistake in the mind of the public, or to deceive purchasers. In an application for registration the Commissioner of Patents shall decide the presumptive lawfulness of claim to the alleged trade-mark; and in any dispute between an applicant and a previous registrant, or between applicants, he shall follow, so far as the same may be applicable, the practice of courts of equity of the United States in analogous cases.

Sec. 4. That certificates of registry of trade-marks shall be issued in the name of the United States of America, under the seal of the Department of the Interior, and shall be signed by the Commissioner of Patents, and a record thereof, together with printed copies of the specifications, shall be kept in books for that purpose. Copies of trade-marks and of statements and declarations filed therewith, and certificates of registry so signed and sealed shall be evidence in any suit in which such trade-marks shall be brought in controversy.

Sec. 5. That a certificate of registry shall remain in force for thirty years from its date, except in cases where the trade-mark is claimed for and applied to articles not manufactured in this country, and in which it receives protection under the laws of a foreign country for a shorter period, in which case it shall cease to have any force in this country by virtue of this act at the time that such trade-mark ceases to be exclusive property elsewhere. At any time during the six months prior to the expiration of the term of thirty years such registration may be renewed on the same terms and for a like period.

Sec. 6. That applicants for registration under this act shall be credited for any fee or part of a fee heretofore paid into the Treasury of the United States with intent to procure protection for the same trade-mark.

Sec. 7. That registration of a trade-mark shall be *prima facie* evidence of ownership. Any person who shall reproduce, counterfeit, copy, or colorably imitate any trade-mark registered under this act and affix the same to merchandise of substantially the same descriptive properties as those described in the registration shall be liable to an action on the case for damages for the wrongful use of said trade-mark at the suit of the owner thereof; and the party aggrieved shall also have his remedy according to the course of equity to enjoin the wrongful use of such trade-mark used in foreign commerce or commerce with Indian tribes, as aforesaid, and to recover compensation therefor in any court having jurisdiction over the person guilty of such wrongful act; and courts of the United States shall have original and appellate jurisdiction in such cases without regard to the amount in controversy.

SEC. 8. That no action or suit shall be maintained under the provisions of this act in any case when the trade-mark is used in any unlawful business or upon any article injurious in itself, or which mark has been used with the design of deceiving the public in the purchase of merchandise, or under any certificate of registry fraudulently obtained.

SEC. 9. That any person who shall procure the registry of a trade-mark, or of himself as the owner of a trade-mark, or an entry respecting a trade-mark, in the office of the Commissioner of Patents, by a false or fraudulent representation or declaration, orally or in writing, or by any fraudulent means, shall be liable to pay any damages sustained in consequence thereof to the injured party, to be recovered in an action on the case.

SEC. 10. That nothing in this act shall prevent, lessen, impeach, or avoid any remedy at law or in equity which any party aggrieved by any wrongful use of any trade-mark might have had if the provisions of this act had not been passed.

SEC. 11. That nothing in this act shall be construed as unfavorably affecting a claim to a trade-mark after the term of registration shall have expired; nor to give cognizance to any court of the United States in an action or suit between citizens of the same State, unless the trade-mark in controversy is used on goods intended to be transported to a foreign country, or in lawful commercial intercourse with an Indian tribe.

SEC. 12. That the Commissioner of Patents is authorized to make rules and regulations and prescribe forms for the transfer of the right to use trade-marks and for recording such transfers in his office.

SEC. 13. That citizens and residents of this country wishing the protection of trade-marks in any foreign country, the laws of which require registration here as a condition precedent to getting such protection there, may register their trade-marks for that purpose as is above allowed to foreigners, and have certificate thereof from the Patent Office.

Approved March 3, 1881.

Also act of August 5, 1882, as follows:

AN ACT relating to the registration of trade-marks.

Be it enacted by the Senate and House of Representatives of the United States of America in Congress assembled, That nothing contained in the law entitled "An act to authorize the registration of trade-marks and protect the same," approved March third, eighteen hundred and eighty-one, shall prevent the registry of any lawful trade-mark rightfully used by the applicant in foreign commerce or commerce with Indian tribes at the time of the passage of said act.

Approved August 5, 1882.

Under the provisions of the act of October 1, 1890, goods bearing infringing trade-marks are absolutely excluded from importation. The following circular from the Treasury Department explains the nature of the proceedings necessary to secure such protection:

TREASURY DEPARTMENT,
OFFICE OF THE SECRETARY,
Washington, D. C., October 31, 1890.

To Officers of the Customs and Others:

The circular of the 10th instant, No. 92, concerning "trade-marks," is hereby withdrawn, and in lieu thereof the following is prescribed:

The attention of officers of the customs and others is invited to the following provision of section 7 of the act of October 1, 1890, viz:

"SECTION 7. That on and after March first, eighteen hundred and ninety-one, no article of imported merchandise which shall copy or simulate the name or trade-mark of any domestic manufacture or manufacturer shall be admitted to entry at any custom-house of the United States. And in order to aid the officers of the customs in enforcing this prohibition, any domestic manufacturer who has adopted trade-marks may require his name and residence and a description of his trade-marks to be recorded in books which shall be kept for that purpose in the Department of the Treasury, under such regulations as the Secretary of the Treasury shall prescribe, and may furnish to the Department fac-similes of such trade-marks; and thereupon the Secretary of the Treasury shall cause one or more copies of the same to be transmitted to each collector or other proper officer of the customs."

Applications for the recording of names or trade-marks in this Department will mention the name and residence of the domestic manufacturer, and furnish a description of the mark and the names of the ports to which the fac-similes should be sent. No such name or trade-mark will be received unless accompanied by the proper proof of ownership, which must consist of the affidavit of the owner or one of the owners, certified by a notary public or other officer entitled to administer oaths and having a seal.

On the receipt by a customs officer of any such fac-similes, with information from the Department that they have been recorded therein, he will properly record and file them, and will exercise care to prevent the entry at the custom-house of any article of foreign manufacture copying or simulating such mark.

No fees are charged for recording trade-marks in the Department and custom-houses.

A sufficient number of fac-similes should be forwarded to enable the Department to send one copy to each port named in the application.

O. L. SPAULDING,
Assistant Secretary.

The acts of July 8, 1870, and August 14, 1876, gave original jurisdiction to the federal courts in matters of registered trade-marks used in domestic commerce. This law was declared unconstitutional by the Supreme Court in 1879 (Trade-Mark Cases, 10 Otto, 82).

As the purpose of a trade-mark is merely to distinguish the origin of the goods, it should properly be a mere mark or symbol. A trade-mark should not be a description of the goods, as any other person has a right to describe his goods in suitable terms.

A trade-mark should not be merely the name of the manufacturer, as another man of the same name cannot generally be prevented from using his name in connection with his wares.

A trade-mark should not be merely the name of the town in which the goods are made, as others in the same town might have a right to use it, or others in another town of the same name.

There have been exceptions to these general rules, and courts have sustained trade-marks which consisted of a firm name (Rogers Co. *v.* Rogers & Spur Co., 11 Fed. Rep. 495), or geographical name (Blackwell *v.* Dibrell, 3 Hughes, 151), on the ground that long use of such a mark gave vested right; or that the infringement of such a mark was calculated to deceive or injure the public.

As a general rule, the longer a trade-mark has been in use, the better title has the owner of such mark; and in seeking to register a trade-mark, the length of use is in favor of the applicant.

There is no rule of law precluding the use of an elaborate picture or engraving, or a lengthy treatise, or a chapter of the Bible or of the Revised Statutes, as a trade-mark. But as the very elaboration is apt to defeat its object; a simple figure, word, letter, phrase, or symbol is generally preferred for a trade-mark.

In registering a trade-mark in the U. S. Patent Office the applicant is required to state the essential feature of the trade-mark. He may also show and describe matters which may be used alternatively as part of the mark. In the compendium hereto attached it is intended to give only the essential feature of the trade-mark in each case.

Before a trade-mark can be registered the applicant is required to state the class of merchandise to which the mark applies, and the particular description of goods to which the mark has been appropriated. (Sec. 1, law of 1881.)

Trade-marks registered under the old law, declared unconstitutional, can be re-registered to the same parties without additional fee. (Sec. 6, act of 1881.)

Transfers of trade-marks may be recorded in the Patent Office, but the record of transfers is not compulsory.

A trade-mark need not be an original device or design. It need only be exclusive in its application to the particular goods of the maker or dealer.

A happy selection of a word or phrase frequently gives great value to a mark, in a business way. Thus "Phonograph" is a name to which proprietary rights attach. "He pays the freight." is not only an advertising catch phrase, but an excellent trade-mark. The mark

I X L, used to distinguish certain lines of goods, has become valuable in such connection.

The registration of a trade-mark is *prima facie* evidence of ownership, and infringement by colorable imitation gives the owner the right to proceed in equity against the infringer.

Trade-marks do not apply to mere abstractions. A man may not register a trade-mark which is not used on some article of merchandise, nor even for a proposed future use of a mark on merchandise. Use only gives right to monopoly.

In filing trade-marks for registration the Patent Office now requires that a facsimile be furnished on card-board, 10 x 15 inches in size, with an inch margin, the mark being executed in black, so that photolithographic copies may be produced.

Note, that the term of a trade-mark is thirty years, and that it may be extended for a second similar term.

In the Patent Office, trade-marks are classified in 77 classes. This classification is artificial, but the best now existing.

The intention of the present compilation is to present such marks as are used in the machine, metal, and hardware trades, and on articles or devices closely connected to the machine, metal, hardware, jewelry, or carriage trades. Where marks are marginal or are applied to several classes of goods, the designation will generally give a sufficient indication as to the particular line of goods to which the mark applies.

Following the Patent Office classification, and excluding other lines of trade, the following index gives the general outline of the marks herein presented:

INDEX OF CLASSES.

Agricultural Implements (Class 1) includes machines and tools used on the farm and plantation.

Cleaning and Polishing Metal (Class 12) includes, also, grinding implements and devices.

Cutlery and Edge Tools (Class 17) includes most cutting implements and flat table-ware.

Fire-arms (Class 24) includes, also, ammunition, explosives, torpedoes, and the like.

Household Articles (Class 32) includes refrigerators, coolers, and devices analogous thereto.

Iron and Steel (Class 34) includes, also, metals and alloys in early manufactured stages.

Jewelry and Plated Ware (Class 35) includes, also, ornamental articles of metal.

Lamps and Lanterns (Class 36) includes the metallic parts of lighting devices, but excludes glass.

Laundry Articles (Class 38) includes washing machines, wringers, &c., (not soaps or chemicals).

Locks and Hardware (Class 40) includes miscellaneous hardware not otherwise classified.

Machines (Class 41) embraces steam-engines, textile, paper, metal, and wood working machines, and generally machines not otherwise classified.

Needles and Pins (Class 47) includes, also, safety-pins, needle-threaders, &c.

Machine Packing (Class 50) includes, also, belting, hose, boiler coverings, and the like.

Sewing Machines and Attachments (Class 58) embraces, also, parts of such machines.

Stoves and Heaters (Class 66) embraces, also, parts of stoves, furnaces, &c.

Surgical Implements (Class 68) includes, also, electrical appliances, many but not all being used in surgery.

Time-keeping Instruments (Class 70) includes clocks and watches, &c., and parts thereof.

Vehicles (Class 76) includes carriages, wagons, sleighs, cycles, cars, &c.

PATENTS.

United States patents are granted for four things only: Arts, machines, manufactures, and compositions of matter.

An art, under the patent practice, is generally a process or method of doing something. It may be a chemical process.

A machine is an assemblage of mechanical elements, and is generally intended to work on other material.

A manufacture is a thing ready for use.

A composition of matter is something made up of more than one element.

To be patentable, invention must have been employed in the production of any one of these patentable things, and the thing must be useful.

A design patent applies only to the ornamentation of manufactures (made things).

The Government fee on filing an application for patent is $15; after allowance, but before issue of the patent, $20 additional; total $35. Patents run 17 years from date of issue.

The Government fee for a design is $10, $15, or $30, according to the term desired ($3\frac{1}{2}$, 7, or 14 years).

Patents are granted in most foreign countries to citizens of the United States on the same terms as to their own citizens.

In most foreign countries there is an annual tax on all patents. There is no such tax in the United States.

A caveat is a partial disclosure of an invention admitted to be incomplete. It is therefore not reliable evidence of the completion of an invention.

COPYRIGHTS.

A trade-mark cannot be registered by the Librarian of Congress under the Copyright Law, as was formerly done. Copyrights apply only to books, maps, charts, dramatic and musical compositions, or works of the fine arts, such as engraving, painting, statuary, &c.

The printed title or description of a copyrighted work must be filed with the Librarian of Congress before publication of the work. Two copies of the book, map, or similar subject of copyright must be delivered or mailed to the Librarian of Congress not later than the day of publication, under penalty of fine.

The Government fee for recording a copyright claim is fifty cents, and fifty cents additional for a copy of the record.

No copyright is valid unless notice is given by inserting in each copy of the publication the notice prescribed by law.

The term of a copyright is twenty-eight years, and it may be extended for fourteen years, by a proper showing made during the last six months of the original term.

Copyrights are assignable, and the assignment must be recorded with the Librarian of Congress.

Citizens of foreign countries which extend the benefit of their copyright laws to citizens of the United States on the same terms as to their own citizens may obtain copyright protection in the United States.

The copyright law does not cover prints and labels nor inventions in the mechanic arts.

PRINTS AND LABELS.

Under the act of June 18, 1874, owners of prints and labels may register the same in the Patent Office on payment of the fee of $6.

A label is construed to be a device or representation borne by a vendible commodity. A print is a device not borne by such commodity, but in some way relating thereto (e. g., as an advertisement thereof).

A label cannot be registered in the Patent office, if it bear a device capable of sequestration as a trade-mark, until after the registration of such device as a trade-mark.

A label proper is generally the description of the goods or wares to which the label is applied, and may contain directions for preparation, production or use.

The statute provides no specific remedy in case of the infringement of a registered print or label. It is believed that the law will soon be amended in this particular.

The prints referred to in the act relating to prints and labels differ from the prints referred to in the copyright law, in that the latter are supposed to be purely esthetic, and to have no connection with mere trade, while the former are based entirely on considerations of trade, although artistic excellence is not prohibited.

TRADE-MARKS
FOR
AGRICULTURAL IMPLEMENTS.
(CLASS 1.)

Embracing machines and implements used in tillage, harvesting and curing crops, such as plows, harrows, diggers, mowers, reapers, thrashers, scythes, rakes, hoes and spades, cotton pickers and gins, and the like. (See also Class 17, Cutlery and Edge Tools; Class 40, Locks and Hardware; Class 41, Machines; Class 73, Tools and Devices.)

Words and phrases constituting the marks alphabetically arranged. Number, date, and registrant given after mark.

AA.—9953. January 16, 1883. Plows and analogous implements. Collins Company, Collinsville, Conn.
A1XX.—1240. April 29, 1873. Rake and other handles. Smith & Montross, Galien, Mich.
Acme.—11,645. November 11, 1884. Lawn Mowers. Blair Manufacturing Company, Springfield, Mass.
Acme.—12,819. December 1, 1885. Pulverizing Harrows, Clod-Crushers, and Levelers. Nash & Bro., Millington, N. J.
Adriance (and design).—5480. January 8, 1878. Reapers and Mowers. Adriance, Platt & Co., Poughkeepsie, N. Y.
Advance.—12,170. April 21, 1885. Threshing Machines and Engines. Case & Williard Thresher Co., Battle Creek, Mich.
Ajax.—10,661. October 23, 1883. Agricultural and Mechanical Tools. Henry W. Peabody & Co., Boston, Mass.
A. J. N.—124. January 3, 1871. Hay Elevators, &c. Aaron J. Nellis, Pittsburg, Pa.
Allen's Improved Victor.—1753. April 28, 1874. Plows. Higganum Manufacturing Co., Higganum, Conn.
Alliance.—16,296. February 26, 1889. Plows. Cealy Billups, Norfolk, Virginia.
Alton Pitts.—3222. December 14, 1875. Threshing Machines. Alton Agricultural Works, Alton, Illinois.
Amber.—7384. June 3, 1879. Cane-Mills. Deere, Mansur & Co., St. Louis and Kansas City, Mo.
American (with eagle).—1606. January 27, 1874. Plows. Carr & Hobson, New York, N. Y.
American.—5810, April 2, 1878. Horse Hay Rakes. Benj. C. Taylor, Dayton, Ohio.
American Crown.—7513. July 15, 1879. Hoes. Moritz & Keidel, Baltimore, Md.
Americus.—7709. September 30, 1879. Cider Mills. Whitman Agricultural Co., St. Louis, Mo.

Anchor (design).—2024. October 13, 1874. Shovels, spades, &c. B. Rowland & Co., Philadelphia, Pa.

Antrim.—4724. June 12, 1877. 8,337. June 14, 1881. Shovels, Spades, and Scoops. Ames & Sons Corporation, North Easton, Mass.

Aspinwall.—16,131. January 1, 1889. Potato Planters and Diggers. Aspinwall Manufacturing Co., Three Rivers, Mich.

As ye sow, so shall ye reap.—18,247. July 29, 1890. Grain Drills. Helen M. Kirkpatrick, Macedon, N. Y.

Banner.—15,040. December 20, 1887. Horse Hay-Rakes. Ohio Iron Wheel Co., Hamilton, Ohio.

B D.—11,541. September 30, 1884. Plows. Arabella G. Starke, Richmond, Va.

Big Bonanza.—5449. December 18, 1877. Agricultural Implements and Machines. Collins Company, Collinsville, Conn.

Blizzard.—19,390. April 21, 1891. Hay Knives. Hiram Holt Co., East Wilton, Me.

Blue Diamond Hoe.—3355. January 18, 1876. Cast-Steel Hoes. F. J. Fischer, Hamilton, Ohio.

Bolmes.—7039. February 18, 1879. Hoes. Semple & Birge Manufacturing Co., St. Louis, Mo.

Bonanza.—5448. December 18, 1877. 8832. November 15, 1881. Agricultural Implements and Machines. Collins Company, Collinsville, Conn.

Boss.—12,014. March 10, 1885. Plows and Plow Castings. Wrenn, Whitehurst & Co., Norfolk, Va.

Boy.—12,113. April 7, 1885. Plows. Arabella G. Starke, Richmond, Virginia.

Briggs, The.—11,891. February 3, 1885. Cultivator. Burton Handle Co., Burton, Ohio.

Brown Gin, The.—1570. December 9, 1873. Cotton Gin. Brown Cotton Gin Company, New London, Conn.

Buckeye.—7214. April 22, 1879. Lawn Mowers. Mast, Foos & Co., Springfield, Ohio.

Buckeye.—1075. December 3, 1872. 2362. April 13, 1875. 8191. May 17, 1881. Reaping and Mowing Machines. Adriance, Platt & Co., Poughkeepsie, N. Y.

Buffalo Pitts.—308. June 6, 1871. 2797. August 3, 1875. Thrashing Machine. James Brayley, Buffalo, N. Y.

Buffalo (and design).—216. April 11, 1871. Thrashing Machines. James Brayley, Buffalo, N. Y.

Cadet.—20,243. October 20, 1891. One-Horse Steel Plows. B. F. Avery & Sons, Louisville, Ky.

Cast Cast-Steel.—849. June 4, 1872. Edge Tools and Agricultural Implements. Collins Company, Collinsville, Conn.

C. & H.—7147. April 1, 1879. 8278. May 31, 1881. Plows. Carr & Hobson, New York, N. Y.

C. C. S.—850. June 4, 1872. 11,346. July 22, 1884. Edge Tools and Agricultural Implements. Collins Company, Collinsville, Conn.

Centennial.—5185. October 2, 1877. Plows. Ames Plow Co., Boston, Mass., and New York, N. Y.

Centennial Medal.—4646. May 15, 1877. Grain Seeders. Farmers' Friend Manufacturing Co., Dayton, O.

Ceres (and design).—1241. April 29, 1873. Harvesting Machines. D. M. Osborne & Co., Auburn, N. Y.

Challenger.—3213. December 7, 1875. Thrashing Machine. Knapp, Burrell & Co., Portland, Oregon.

Charter Oak.—2853. August 24, 1875. Plows. Higganum Manufacturing Co., Higganum, Conn.

Champion (cancelled by said Co.)—428. August 22, 1871. Harvesters. Harris Manufacturing Co., Janesville, Wis.

Champion.—1705. March 31, 1874. Plows. J. Lane Reed & Co., Dayton, O.

Champion.—2945. September 21, 1875. Thrashers and Separators. Alton Agricultural Works, Alton, Ill.
Champion.—4092. October 31, 1876. Smut and Separating Machines. James H. Redfield, Salem, Ind.
Champion.—7135. March 25, 1879. Corn Planter. Beedle & Kelly, Troy, Ohio.
Champion.—8174. February 22, 1881. Agricultural Forks. Auburn Manufacturing Co., Auburn, N. Y.
Champion.—14,356. May 3, 1887. Lawn Mowers. Mast, Foos & Co., Springfield, Ohio.
Champion.—1127, 1128, 1129. February 11, 1873. 3164, 3185, 3186. November 30, 1875. Harvesting Machines, Implements, Parts, etc. Whiteley, Fassler & Kelly, Springfield, Ohio.
Champion Hoe.—4931. July 24, 1877. Hoes. Union Manufacturing Co., Lockport, N. Y.
Chilled (and design).—1275. May 20, 1873. Plows. James Oliver, South Bend, Ind.
Chrystal (and design).—4197. December 12, 1876. Plows. Merrell & Wilder, South Toledo, O.
Clarinda Breaker.—3189. November 30, 1875. Plows. Wm. K. Harrell, Thomas B. Chamberlain, and Dewitt C. Chamberlain, Clarinda, Iowa.
Clipper.—1149. February 25, 1873. Plows. E. Remington & Sons, Ilion, N. Y.
Coleman, Eagle Works.—20,628. January 19, 1892. Machines, Plows, Bolts, Etc. Upson Nut Co., Unionville, Conn.
Collins.—9955. January 16, 1883. 10,006. January 30, 1883. Certain Earth Working Tools. Collins Co., Collinsville, Conn.
Collins & Co.—9956. January 16, 1883. Certain Earth Working Tools. Collins Co., Collinsville, Conn.
Collins & Co. Hartford Cast Steel.—523. November 7, 1871. Plows. Collins Co., Collinsville, Conn.
Collins & Co. Hartford Cast Cast-Steel.—11,345. July 22, 1884. Plows, etc. Collins Company, Collinsville, Conn.
Collins & Co., Hartford.—7644. September 2, 1879. 9954. January 16, 1883. Earth Working Tools. Collins Company, Collinsville, Conn.
Columbia.—19,356. April 14, 1891. Forks, Hoes, Rakes, etc. Iowa Farming Tool Co., Fort Madison, Iowa.
Continental.—15,852. September 11, 1888. Lawn Mowers. Loyd & Supplee Hardware Co., Philadelphia, Pa.
Coronet.—9989. January 30, 1883. Agricultural Implements. Henry W. Peabody & Co., Boston, Mass.
Cotton Bloom (and design).—1908. July 28, 1874. Cotton Gins. Sanborn Manufacturing Co., Mystic River, Conn.
Creedmore.—7051. February 25, 1879. Scythe Snaths, etc. Semple & Birge Manufacturing Co., St. Louis, Mo.
Crescent (and design).—8288. May 31, 1881. Hoes. G. T. Lane, Troy, N. Y.
Crucible.—21,771. September 29, 1892. Agricultural Implements. Iowa Farming Tool Co., Fort Madison, Iowa.
Cyclone.—19,619. June 2, 1891. Dust Conveyers for Thrashing Machines. William S. Miller, Meyersdale, Pa.
Daisy.—10,704. November 6, 1883. Single Wheel Reapers. McCormick Harvesting Machine Company, Chicago, Ill.
Damascus Blade.—563. November 28, 1871. Scythes. Dunn Edge Tool Co., West Waterville, Me.
Deadwood.—6484. August 20, 1878. Shovels and Scoops. Ezra H. Linley, St. Louis, Mo.
Diamond Iron. 1951. September 1, 1874. Plows, etc., of hard metal. Lawrence & Chapin, Kalamazoo, Mich.

Dixie.—14,225. March 29, 1887. Hoes. Iowa Farming Tool Company, Fort Madison, Iowa.
Dixie.—11,025. March 18, 1884. Plows. Arabella G. Starke, Richmond, Va.
Dixie (and design).—12.413. July 14, 1893. Plow. Arabella G. Starke, Richmond, Va.
Dynamicut.—18,524. October 14, 1890. Plows and Edge Tools. Collins Company, Collinsville, Conn.
Eagle.—6368. July 16, 1878. 10,801. December 25, 1883. Cotton Gins. Eagle Cotton Gin Co., Bridgewater, Mass.
Electric.—8600. August 30, 1881. Agricultural Implements. James H. Barley, Sedalia, Mo.
Empire.—4595. May 1, 1877. Harvesters and Mowers. John F. Seiberling, Akron, Ohio.
Eureka.—6995. February 4, 1879. 8731. October 18, 1881. Smut Machines, Magnetic Separators, etc. Howes, Babcock & Ewell, Silver Creek, N. Y.
Eureka (and design).—18,136. July 8, 1890. Post Hole Diggers. Wm. H. Rhodes, Chicago, Ill.
Excelsior.—7010. February 4, 1879. Hay and Manure Forks, etc. Stafford & Holden Manufacturing Co., Barre, Vt.
Excelsior.—13,260. May 4, 1886. Shovels and Spades. John Dunn, New York, N. Y.
Excelsior Shovels and Spades, New York.—3257. December 21, 1875. Shovels and Spades. John Dunn, Orange, N. Y.
Farmer.—3037. October 12, 1875. Plows. David Burel Smith, Bastrop, Louisiana.
Farmers' Friend.—4764. June 26, 1877. Grain Seeders. Farmers' Friend Manufacturing Co., Dayton, Ohio.
Farmers' Friend, Perfected.—14,092. February 22, 1887. Plows. Chas. Edgar Hunter. Fredericksburg, Va.
Farmers' Friend, Perfected.—1539. November 25, 1873. Plows. Hunter & Frost, Fredericksburg, Va.
Farquhar.—6883. December 17, 1878. Farm and Agricultural Implements, etc. Arthur B. Farquhar. York, Pa.
Fearless.—9254. April 4, 1882. Thrashing Machine. Gear, Scot & Co., Richmond, Ind.
Fearless.—10,226. May 1, 1883. Thrashers and Separators. Minard Harder, Cobleskill, N. Y.
Fine Cutlery Steel.—562. November 28, 1871. Scythes. Dunn Edge Tool Co., West Waterville, Me.
Fire Fly.—14,860. November 1, 1887. Agricultural Implements. Samuel L. Allen & Co., Philadelphia, Pa.
Flying Dutchman.—11,315. July 8, 1884. Plows. Moline Plow Co., Moline, Ill.
G. A. L. E.—8049. September 28, 1880. Plow. Gale Manufacturing Co., Albion, Mich.
Garza (and design).—19,439. May 5, 1891. Shovels, Axes, Hatchets, etc. Struller, Meyer & Schumacher, New York, N. Y.
Geiser, The.—7546. July 22, 1879. Grain Separators, Cleaners, etc. Geiser Manufacturing Co., Waynesborough, Pa.
Gem.—15,929. October 2, 1888. Plows and Plow Castings. Wrenn, Whiteburst & Co., Norfolk, Va.
Girl.—14,363. May 10, 1887. Plows and the like. Cealy Billups, Norfolk, Virginia.
Globe.—8503. July 19, 1881. Plows, Harrows, and Cultivators. Alexander Speer & Sons, Pittsburg, Pa.
Globe Plow Works.—1949. August 25, 1874. Plows, Harrows, and Cultivators. Alexander Speer & Sons, Pittsburg, Pa.
Golden Crown.—1535. November 18, 1873. Agricultural Implements. L. M. Rumsey & Co., St. Louis, Mo.

Gold Metal, S. K. & Co.—1017. October 1, 1872. Agricultural Implements. Soule, Kretsinger & Co., Fort Madison, Iowa.
Gold—O—Basis.—4824. July 3, 1877. Agricultural Implements. Manny & Co., St. Louis, Mo.
Gowanda.—14,772. September 20, 1887. Plows and Plow Points. Gowanda Agricultural Works Co., Gowanda, N. Y.
Granger.—4138. November 21, 1876. Axes, Hatchets, and Hoes. William C. Kelley, Louisville, Ky.
Great American.—15,853. September 11, 1888. Lawn Mowers. Lloyd & Supplee Hardware Co., Philadelphia, Pa.
Guanaco (and design).—13,346. June 1, 1886. Agricultural Implements. John Dunn, New York, N. Y.
Harvester.—774. April 16, 1872. Corn Knife. Greenwoods Scythe Co., New Hartford, Conn.
Harvest Victor.—843. June 4, 1872. Scythes. Beardsley Scythe Co., West Winsted, Conn.
Hobson's American Eagle.—17,873. May 6, 1890. Plows. Hobson & Co., New York, N. Y.
Hoosier.—8247. May 24, 1881. Grain Seeding Machines. Hoosier Drill Co., Richmond, Ind.
Hoosier Drill.—4650. May 15, 1877. Seed and Grain Drills. Joseph Ingels, Irvington, Indiana.
Hurlburt's North Star.—2049. November 3, 1874. Plows. E. E. Lumnus & Co., Boston, Mass.
Hustler.—17,052. September 24, 1889. Thrashing Machines. Eagle Machine Works Co., Indianapolis, Ind.
Imperial.—14,883. November 1, 1887. Straw Stacking Machines. Newark Machine Co., Columbus, Ohio.
Invincible.—5565. January 22, 1878. Threshing Machines. Roberts, Throp & Co., Three Rivers, Mich.
Iron Age.—5601. February 5, 1878. Cultivators. E. S. & F. Bateman, Spring Mills, N. J.
I X L.—788. April 23, 1872. Mowing, Reaping, and Harvesting Tools. Greenwoods Scythe Co., New Hartford, Conn.
I X L.—4726. June 12, 1877. 8335. June 14, 1881. Shovels, Spades, and Scoops. Oliver Ames & Sons Corporation, North Easton, Mass.
I. X. L., Neblett & Goodrich.—7042. February 18, 1879. Cotton Gins. Printup, Brother & Pollard, Augusta, Ga.
Joe George Plow.—1009. September 2, 1872. Plows. Springfield Iron Works, Springfield, Mo.
Jones * Plow.—627. January 9, 1872. Plows. Bouton, Whitehead & Co., Naperville, Ill.
Jumbo.—16,511. April 23, 1889. Hay Elevators or Carriers. Manias G. Grosscup, Milwaukee, Wis.
Kaiser.—18,787. January 6, 1891. Plows and Cultivators. Mansur & Tebbetts Implement Co., St. Louis, Mo.
Kentucky Plow Co.—18,595. November 4, 1890. Plows. B. F. Avery & Sons, Louisville, Ky.
King of the Field.—753. April 9, 1872. Mowing, Reaping, and Harvesting Tools. Greenwoods Scythe Co., New Hartford, Conn.
King of the Harvest.—3187. November 30, 1875. Grain Separators. O. K. Wood & Co., West Chazy, N. Y.
Knickerbocker.—8669. September 27, 1881. Lawn Mowers. Carr & Hobson, New York, N. Y.
La Cruz Colorado (and design).—15,722. July 24, 1888. Edge Agricultural Tools, etc. A. W. Wills & Son, Birmingham, England.
Lane's Crescent Planter's Hoe Co. (and design). 1940. July 24, 1877. Hoes. Geo. T. Lane, Troy, N. Y.
Ladow.—8295. May 31, 1881. Agricultural Implements. Wheeler & Melick Co., Albany, N. Y.

La Victoria.—2267. March 2, 1875. Cotton Working Machines. R. H. Allen & Co., New York, N. Y.
Leader.—7226. April 22, 1879. Horse Hay Rake. Ithaca Agricultural Works, Ithaca, N. Y.
Lightning.—9583. August 1, 1882. Hay Knives. Hiram Holt & Co., East Wilton, Me.
Lion.—6251. June 18, 1878. Hay Rakes. A. N. Miner & Co., Belmont, New York.
Lonc*—2924. September 7, 1875. 8505. July 19, 1881. Plows. Alexander Speer & Sons, Pittsburg, Pa.
L W.—15,928. October 2, 1888. Plows and Plow Castings. Wrenn, Whitehurst & Co., Norfolk, Va.
Magnolia.—1410. August 19, 1873. Cotton Gins. Gillett Gin Manufacturing Co., Amite City, La.
Maid of the South.—892. July 16, 1872. 2750. July 20, 1875. Corn and Wheat Mills. H. D. Coleman, New Orleans, La.
Malta, Malta.—13,781. November 2, 1886. Plows. Brown Manly Plow Co., Malta and Columbus, Ohio.
Meadow King.—3575. April 11, 1876. Harvesters. Gregg & Co., Trumansburg, N. Y.
Minneapolis.—22,150. December 6, 1892. Harvesters and Harvester Binders. Walter A. Wood Harvester Co., St. Paul, Minn.
Minnesota Chief.—6481. August 13, 1878. Thrashing Machines. Seymour, Sabin & Co., Stillwater, Minn.
Minnie.—21,153. May 17, 1892. Harvesters and Harvester Binders. Walter A. Wood Harvester Co., St. Paul, Minn.
Missouri.—38. November 1, 1870. Corn Planter. David W. Hughes, Palmyra, Mo.
Monarch.—4304. January 23, 1877. Plows. J. Lane Reed & Co., Dayton, Ohio.
Monitor.—2892. August 31, 1875. Seed Sowers and Cultivators. Van Brunt & Davis, Horicon, Wis.
Monitor, S. T. Ferguson.—3066. October 19, 1875. Plows. Monitor Plow Works, Minneapolis, Minn.
Montgomery's Rockaway.—5689. February 26, 1878. Wheat Fans. E. Whitman, Sons & Co., Baltimore, Md.
N.—2304. March 23, 1875. Plows and the like. B. F. Avery & Sons, Louisville, Ky.
N. D.—9957. January 16, 1883. Plows and Analogous Implements. Collins Co., Collinsville, Conn.
N. E. (and crossed arrows) 4722. June 12, 1877. Shovels, etc. Oliver Ames & Sons Corporation, North Easton, Mass.
New Departure.—3440. February 22, 1876. Cultivators. Pattee Bros. & Co., Monmouth, Ill.
New Manny, F. G., The.—3774. June 13, 1876. Combined Reapers and Mowers. Freeman Graham, Rockford, Ill.
North Bend.—7541. July 22, 1879. 8384. June 21, 1881. Plows. Alexander Speer & Sons, Pittsburg, Pa.
North Star.—2049. November 3, 1874. Plows. E. E. Lummus & Co., Boston, Mass.
Norwegian.—4145. November 21, 1876. Plows, etc. J. Thompson & Co., Beloit, Wis.
O—2302. March 23, 1875. Plows and the like. B. F. Avery & Sons, Louisville, Ky.
O-K.—10,620. October 9, 1883. Spades, Shovels, and Scoops. Oliver Ames & Sons, North Easton, Mass.
Oliver's South Bend Plow.—3515. March 14, 1876. Plows. South Bend Iron Works, South Bend, Ind.
Oliver, The.—16,350. March 5, 1889. Plows. South Bend Iron Works, South Bend, Ind.

O. R. O.—18,613. November 11, 1890. Agricultural Implements, etc. Graham, Hinkley & Co., New York, N. Y.
Oscillator.—5355. November 20, 1877. Thrashing Machines and Separators. Eagle Machine Works, Indianapolis, Ind.
Our Best.—773. April 16, 1872. Mowing, Reaping, and Harvesting Tools. Greenwoods Scythe Co., New Hartford, Conn.
P.—2303. March 23, 1875. Plows and the like. B. F. Avery & Sons, Louisville, Ky.
Palmetto.—7760. October 28, 1879. Plows. Cox & Poynter, Maysville, Kentucky.
Partridge Fork, The.—786. April 23, 1872. 2692. June 22, 1875. Agricultural Forks. Franklin P. Shumway, Leominster, Mass.
Pennsylvania (and design).—11,494. September 16, 1884. Shovels, Spades, etc. Hussey, Binns & Co., Pittsburg, Pa.
Perry, The.—13,908. December 21, 1886. Spring Tooth Harrows. G. B. Olin & Co., Canandaigua, N. Y.
P. G. W.—123. January 3, 1871. Agricultural Implements. Hall & Speer, Pittsburg, Pa.
Pigmy.—6817. November 26, 1878. Cast-Iron Plows. B. F. Avery & Sons, Louisville, Ky.
Pirate.—18,436. September 16, 1890. Plows. Mast, Burford & Burwell Co., St. Paul, Minn.
Planet, Jr.—12,765. November 17, 1885. Agricultural Implements. S. L. Allen & Co., Philadelphia, Pa.
Planter.—6335. July 9, 1878. Cotton Presses. Kingsland, Ferguson & Co., St. Louis, Mo.
Pony.—1770. May 5, 1874. Plows and the like. B. F. Avery & Sons, Louisville, Ky.
Post Capital City.—13,771. November 2, 1886. Straddle Row Cultivators. Chas. W. Post, Springfield, Ill.
President.—4795. July 3, 1877. 8299. May 31, 1881. Lawn Mowers. Carr & Hobson, New York, N. Y.
Prong Joy Hill Hoe.—2293. March 16, 1875. Prong Hoes. Reisig & Hexamer, New Castle, N. Y.
Quaker City.—7890. May 4, 1880. Lawn Mowers. Lloyd, Supplee & Walton, Philadelphia, Pa.
Queen Bee.—11,762. December 9, 1884. Combined Shelling and Grinding Mills. C. M. Wilcox & Wm. Jay Hopkins, Whitewater, Wis.
Queen of the Harvest.—3188. November 30, 1875. Grain Separators. O. K. Wood & Co., West Chazy, N. Y.
Queen of the Meadow.—751. April 9, 1872. Mowing, Reaping, and Harvesting Tools. Greenwoods Scythe Co., New Hartford, Conn.
Razor-edge Hoe (and design).—21,013. April 19, 1892. Hoes. Geo. B. Durell, Harriman, Tenn.
R. S.—5710. March 5, 1878. Plows. H. C. Shaw Plow Co., Stockton, California.
Red Jacket.—20,974. April 12, 1892. Plows. Deere & Co., Moline, Illinois.
Red Racer.—749. April 9, 1872. Mowing, Reaping, and Harvesting Tools. Greenwoods Scythe Co., New Hartford, Conn.
Rex.—20,043. August 18, 1891. Lawn Mowers. Willard & Lape, Syracuse, N. Y.
Richibucto.—13,259. May 4, 1886. Shovels and Spades. John Dunn, New York, N. Y.
Richibucto.—15,383. April 24, 1888. Agricultural Implements. Thomas Drysdale & Co., New York, N. Y.
Rival.—20,936. April 5, 1892. Lawn Mowers. Chadborn & Coldwell, Manufacturing Co., Newburgh, N. Y.
Rockaway.—7032. February 18, 1879. Grain Fans. Joseph Montgomery, Baltimore, Md.

Rockford Ideal.—21,826. October 4, 1892. Plowshares. L. A. Weyburn Co., Rockford, Ill.

Roland.—7852. March 16, 1880. Plows. Ezra B. Whitman, Baltimore, Maryland.

Sam'l Johnston, The.—11,390. August 5, 1884. Harvesting Machines. Samuel Johnston & Co., Rockport, N. Y.

Series.—1694. March 31, 1874. Plows. B. F. Avery & Sons, Louisville, Kentucky.

Silver Eagle.—1752. April 28, 1874. Plows. Higganum Manufacturing Co., Higganum, Conn.

Smoothing Harrow and Broad Cast Weeder.—635. January 16, 1872. Harrows. J. J. Thomas & Co., Geneva, N. Y.

Solid.—22,055. November 22, 1892. Hay Carriers. Joseph C. Porter, Ottawa, Ill.

Solid Comfort.—14,202. March 29, 1887. Sulky Plows. Economist Plow Co., South Bend, Ind.

South Bend Chilled Plow.—3514. March 14, 1876. Plows. South Bend Iron Works, South Bend, Ind.

Southern Cross.—2050. November 3, 1874. Plows. E. E. Lummus & Co., Boston, Mass.

Spading.—19,074. February 24, 1891. Harrows and Pulverizers. D. S. Morgan & Co., Brockport, N. Y.

Splendid Lawn Mower, The.—17,881. May 6, 1890. Lawn Mowers. Rogers Fence Co., Springfield. Ohio.

Standard.—9421. May 30, 1882. Grain Machinery. Edmands Manufacturing Co.. Hamilton, Ohio.

Star of the West.—752. April 9, 1872. Mowing, Reaping, and Harvesting Tools. Greenwood's Scythe Co., New Hartford, Conn.

Star Rake (The * Rake).—3507. March 14, 1876. Horse Hay-Rakes. Dayton Machine Co., Dayton, Ohio.

Strawsonizer.—20,481. December 22, 1891. Pneumatic Distributer for Sowing Grain, etc. Geo. F. Strawson, Newbury, England.

Sure Will the Harvest Be.—20,447. December 8, 1891. Seeders and Grain Drills. Dowagiac Manufacturing Co., Dowagiac, Mich.

Telegraph.—13,082. March 2, 1886. Hay, Fodder, and Straw Cutters. Willson Bros. & Co., Harrisburg, Pa.

Teru-Teru.—14,978. November 29, 1887. Farm Implements and Vehicles. Thomas Drysdale & Co., New York, N. Y.

Texas Ranger.—3433. February 22, 1876. Plows. Deere & Co., Moline, Ill.

Thomas Drysdale Y Cia.—13,474. July 6, 1886. Agricultural Implements, etc. Thos. Drysdale & Co., Buenos Ayres, Argentine Republic.

Tiny Tim.—6818. November 26, 1878. Steel Plows. B. F. Avery & Sons, Louisville, Ky.

Tip Top.—750. April 9, 1872. Mowing, Reaping, and Harvesting Tools. Greenwood's Scythe Co., New Hartford, Conn.

Triumph.—11,758. December 9, 1884. Reaping, Mowing, and Grain Binding Machines. D. S. Morgan & Co., Brockport, N. Y.

Tuttle.—2855. August 24, 1875. Hoes, Forks, Rakes, etc. Tuttle Manufacturing Co., Naugatuck, Conn.

T. Waldron.—20,822. March 8, 1892. Agricultural Implements. Firm of Isaac Nash, Belbroughton, England.

Universal.—15,223. February 21, 1888. Furrow Plows. Universal Plow Co., Canton, Ohio.

Universal.—16,942. August 20, 1889. Cheek-Row Corn Planters. H. P. Deuscher Co., Hamilton, Ohio.

U. T. K. (in monogram).—1622. February 10, 1874. Agricultural Implements. Jackson & Childs, Utica, N. Y.

Vibrator.—1702. March 31, 1874. 8488. July 19, 1881. Thrashing Machines. Nichols, Shepard & Co., Battle Creek, Mich.

Vibrator.—6823. November 26, 1878. Corn Shellers. Kingsland, Ferguson & Co., St. Louis, Mo.
Victor.—7327. May 20, 1879. 8628. September 6, 1881, Clover Machines. Hagerstown Agricultural Implement Manufacturing Co., Hagerstown, Md.
Warrior.—1824. June 9, 1874. Mowing and Reaping Machines. Frank Bramer, Little Falls, N. Y.
Washoe.—10,775. December 11, 1883. Picks and other Adze-eye Tools. Washoe Manufacturing Co., Newark, N. J.
W. B. (and arrow).—4725. June 12, 1877. Shovels, etc. Oliver Ames & Sons' Corporation, North Easton, Mass.
Western Dutchman.—754. April 9, 1872. Mowing, Reaping, and Harvesting Tools. Greenwood's Scythe Co., New Hartford, Conn.
Western Star.—591. December 19, 1871. Pitchforks. Bouton, Whitehead & Co., Naperville, Ill.
West's Improved Ladow (and design).—15,455. May 15, 1888. Cultivators. A. Baldwin & Co., New Orleans, La.
White Metal.—2312. March 23, 1875. Plows. B. F. Avery & Sons, Louisville, Ky.
Wisconsin Farmer.—4624. May 15, 1877. Agricultural Implements. Wm. Frankfurth & Co., Milwaukee, Wis.
76.—9486. June 27, 1882. Plows. Francis A. Barrows, Castleton, Vt.

COMPILED BY
WALLACE A. BARTLETT,
Patent Attorney,
WASHINGTON, D. C.

TRADE-MARKS
FOR
AGRICULTURAL IMPLEMENTS.
(CLASS 1.)

Designs or Figures showing the essential feature claimed as the Mark.

 91. December 6, 1870. Corn Planter. Pope & Baldwin, Quincy, Ill.

 131. January 10, 1871. Agricultural Implements. Batcheller Manufacturing Co., New York, N. Y.

 144. January 24, 1871. Corn Planter. James Selby & Co., Peoria, Ill.

 155. February 14, 1871. Plows and Agricultural Implements. John C. Bidwell, Pittsburg, Pa.

 216. April 11, 1871. 2798. August 3, 1875. Threshing Machine. James Brayley, Buffalo, N. Y.

 217. April 11, 1871. Plows. Bucher, Gibbs & Co., Canton, Ohio.

 251. May 9, 1871. Plows and Cultivators. Moline Plow Co., Moline, Ill.

 571. December 5, 1871. Cutters for Harvesters. Sweet, Barnes & Co., Syracuse, N. Y.

 819. May 14, 1872. 2512. May 11, 1875. Plows, Cultivators, etc. Wiard & Hough, East Avon, N. Y.

 1067. November 26, 1872. Cotton Gins. Welcome G. Clemons, Columbus, Ga.

 1241. April 29, 1873. Harvesting Machines. D. M. Osborne & Co., Auburn, N. Y.

1262. May 13, 1873. 12,414. July 14, 1885. Cutters, &c., for Harvesting Machines. Walter A. Wood Mowing and Reaping Machine Co., Hoosick Falls, N. Y.

1275. May 20, 1873. Plows. James Oliver, South Bend, Ind.

1410. August 19, 1873. Cotton Gins. Gillett Gin Manufacturing Co., Amite City, La.

1535. November 18, 1873. Agricultural Implements. L. M. Rumsey & Co., St. Louis, Mo.

1606. January 27, 1874. Plows. Carr & Hobson, New York, N. Y.

1622. February 10, 1874. Agricultural Implements. Jackson & Childs, Utica, N. Y.

1908. July 28, 1874. Cotton Gins. Sanborn Machine Co. Mystic River, Conn.

1933. August 18, 1874. Agricultural Implements. Keystone Manufacturing Co., Sterling, Ill.

2024. October 13, 1874. Shovels, Spades, and Scoops. B. Rowland & Co., Philadelphia, Pa.

2260. February 23, 1875. Cotton Presses. Mrs. Thomas C. Nisbet, Macon, Ga.

2699. July 6, 1875. Agricultural Implements. George W. & M. Strouse, Avon, N. Y.

3098. October 26, 1875. Plows, Agricultural Implements, etc. Watt & Call, Richmond, Va.

3285. December 28, 1875. 12,399. July 7, 1885. Mowers, Reapers, etc. Walter A. Wood Mowing & Reaping Machine Co., Hoosick Falls, N. Y.

3406 and 3407. February 8, 1876. 3458. February 22, 1876. 8833. November 15, 1888. Earth-Working Tools of all kinds, Axes, etc. Collins Co., Collinsville, Conn.

3434. February 22, 1876. Plows and Cultivators. Deere & Co., Moline, Ill.

3505. March 7, 1876. 8425. July 5, 1881. Thrashing Machines. Aultman & Taylor Co., Mansfield, Ohio.

3543. March 28, 1876. Hoes. D. & H. Scovil, Higganum, Conn.

3889. August 1, 1876. Parts of Thrashing Machines, etc. James Brayley, Buffalo, N. Y.

4197. December 12, 1876. Plows. Merrell & Wilder, South Toledo, Ohio.

4722. June 12, 1877. 8339. June 14, 1881. Shovels, Spades, and Scoops. Oliver Ames & Sons' Corporation, North Easton, Mass.

4723. June 12, 1877. 8336. June 14, 1881. Shovels, Spades, and Scoops. Oliver Ames & Sons' Corporation, North Easton, Mass.

4725. June 12, 1877. 8338. June 14, 1881. Shovels, Spades, and Scoops. Oliver Ames & Sons' Corporation, North Easton, Mass.

4907. July 17, 1877. Grain Seeders. Farmers' Friend Manufacturing Co., Dayton, Ohio.

4940. July 24, 1877. Iron and Cast-steel Hoes. George T. Lane, Troy, N. Y.

5304. November 13, 1877. Grain Cleaners. C. Duprez et Cie., Rheims, France.

5480. January 8, 1878. 9024. January 17, 1882. Reaping and Mowing Machines. Adriance, Platt & Co., Poughkeepsie and New York, N. Y.

8288. May 31, 1881. Hoes. George Tibbits Lane, Troy, N. Y.

8325. June 7, 1881. Plows. Carr & Hobson, New York, N. Y.

8504. July 19, 1881. Plows. Alexander Speer & Sons, Pittsburg, Pa.

8505. July 19, 1881. Plows. Alexander Speer & Sons, Pittsburg, Pa.

10,516. August 14, 1883. Shovels, Scoops, and Spades. Groom Shovel Co., St. Louis, Mo.

10,579. September 11, 1883 Agricultural Machinery. Russell & Co., Massillon, Ohio.

10,726. November 20, 1883. Hoes. Iowa Farming Tool Co., Ft. Madison, Iowa.

11,494. September 16, 1884. Shovels, Spades, and Scoops. Hussey, Binns & Co., Pittsburg, Pa.

11,644. November 11, 1884. Agricultural Forks. Batcheller & Sons Co., Wallingford, Vt.

12,413. July 14, 1885. Plows. Arabella G. Starke, Richmond, Va.

13,314. May 18, 1886. Hoes. Iowa Farming Tool Co., Fort Madison, Iowa.

13,345. June 1, 1886. 13,346. June 1, 1886. Agricultural Implements, and Edge Tools. John Dunn, New York, N. Y.

13,437. June 22, 1886. 13,438. June 22, 1886. Agricultural Implements and Edge Tools. John Dunn, New York, N. Y.

13,474. July 6, 1886. Cutlery, Hardware, and Agricultural Implements. Thos. Drysdale & Co., Buenos Ayres, Argentine Republic, and New York, N. Y.

13,508. July 20, 1886. Pulverizing Harrows, Clod-Crushers, Levelers, etc. Nash & Bro., Millington, N. J.

13,781. November 2, 1886. Plows. Brown-Manly Plow Co., Malta and Columbus, Ohio.

15,035. December 20, 1887. Cotton Gins. Eagle Cotton Gin Co., Bridgewater, Mass.

15,455. May 15, 1888. Cultivator. A. Baldwin & Co., New Orleans, La.

15,705. July 24, 1888. Harvesting Machines and Parts thereof. Aultman, Miller & Co., Akron, Ohio.

15,722. July 24, 1888. Edge, Agricultural and Mining Tools, etc. A. W. Wills & Son, Birmingham, England.

15,723. July 24, 1888. Edge, Agricultural, Mining Tools, etc. A. W. Wills & Son, Birmingham, England.

15,733. July 31, 1888. Fodder Cutters and their Attachments. Smalley Manufacturing Co., Manitowoc, Wisconsin.

18,136. July 8, 1890. Post Hole Diggers. William H. Rhodes, Chicago, Ill.

19,439. May 5, 1891. Shovels, Axes, Hatchets, etc. Struller, Meyer & Schumacher, New York, N. Y.

20,474. December 22, 1891. Seeders and Grain Drills. Dowagiac Manufacturing Co., Dowagiac, Mich.

Razor Edge Hoe. 21,013. April 19, 1892. Hoes. Geo. B. Durell, Harriman, Tenn.

22,073. November 29, 1892. Plows. South Bend Iron Works, South Bend, Ind.

TRADE-MARKS
FOR
Cleaning and Polishing Preparations.
(CLASS 12.)

Embracing materials, tools, and devices for cleaning, burnishing, abrading, or blacking metals, but not common soaps or paints.

Words or phrases constituting the marks arranged alphabetically. Number, date, and ownership given after mark.

A. B. C.—4530. April 10, 1877. Stove Polish. S. S. Myers, Philadelphia, Pa.

Adamant.—14,920. November 8, 1887. Emery Wheels. Jas. P. Sweney, St. Louis, Mo.

Adamanta.—4429. March 6, 1877. Abrasive Cloth, etc. Freeman K. Sibley, Waltham, Mass.

Anchor (and design).—3092. October 26, 1875. Stove Polish. Simon S. Meyers, Philadelphia, Pa.

Argentala.—17,063. September 24, 1889. Polish for Jewelry, etc. Reed & Barton, Taunton, Mass.

Asbestolio.—17,997. June 3, 1890. Cleaning and Polishing Soap. United Asbestos Co., London, England.

Bar Keeper's Friend.—17,313. December 24, 1889. Polish for Metals, Wood, Glass, etc. Geo. W. Hoffman, Indianapolis, Ind.

Belle City.—11,671. November 11, 1884. Stove Polish. Wood Bros., Racine, Wis.

Bessemer.—14,281. April 12, 1887. Anti-Rust Compound. John F. Nolan, San Francisco, Cal.

Blazer (and design).—17,247. December 10, 1889. Stove Polish. Frederick W. Anderson, Worcester, Mass.

Bonanza.—6811. November 19, 1878. Stove and Shoe Polish. George A. Hyers, Chicago, Ill.

Brilliant (and design).—13,401. June 15, 1886. Stove Polish, etc. Edward D. Ransom, Albany, N. Y.

Buckeye.—18,802. January 6, 1891. Copper Polish. John Grether, Akron, Ohio.

Burnishine.—18,703. December 16, 1890. Metal Polish. John C. Paul, Chicago, Ill.

Callustro.—17,541. February 18, 1890. Polishing Powder and Soap. Callustro Co., San Francisco, Cal.

Carburet of Iron.—6486. August 20, 1878. Graphite for Stove Polish, etc. Joseph Dixon Crucible Co., Jersey City, N. J.

Centennial.—3252. December 14, 1875. Stove Polish. Charles E. Teets, New York, N. Y.

Cera-Carbo.—10,772. December 11, 1883. Water-Proof Stove Polish. B. F. Meyers, J. W. Hayford & G. S. Yingling, Tiffin, Ohio.

Challenge.—4353. February 13, 1877. Stove Blacking. Edward Baxter, Cold Spring, N. Y.

Champion.—15,167. February 7, 1888. Wash for cleaning Jewelry. A. W. Isaacs, Chicago, Ill.
Ching Chong (and design).—9723. October 17, 1882. Cleaning Silver, etc. Bean & Rabe, Philadelphia, Pa.
Cinderella.—11,940. February 10, 1885. Stove Polish, etc. Daniel W. Raymond, Middletown, Conn.
Climax.—12,524. August 18, 1885. Stove Polish. Jane Taylor, Fall River, Mass.
Coaline.—6784. November 12, 1878. Cleaning and Polishing Preparation. N. T. Folsom & Co., Boston, Mass.
Color-King.—20,930. April 5, 1892. Polish for Wood and Metal Work. Manley & Turner, Elmira, N. Y.
Coral Cream.—7575. August 12, 1879. Polishing Fluid. Baxter & Hughson, Cold Spring, N. Y.
Corundite.—13,538. August 3, 1886. Emery Wheels. New York Belting and Packing Co., New York, N. Y.
Crow (and design).—19,113. March 3, 1891. Stove Paste Polish. Harry C. Bomhard, Milwaukee, Wis.
Crown.—14,815. October 11, 1887. Stove Polish. W. H. Colebrook & Co., Syracuse, N. Y.
Crumbs of Comfort.—18. November 1, 1870. Stove Blacking. Henry A. Bartlett & Co., Philadelphia, Pa.
Dalmore Hone.—12,443. July 28, 1885. Grinding, Sharpening, and Polishing Articles. John C. Montgomerie, Dalmore, Ayr Co., Scotland.
Diamond.—1375. July 22, 1873. Stove Polish. Fletcher & Dwyer, Lynn, Mass.
Diamond (and design).—9573. July 25, 1882. Cleaning Paste. A. E. Jeaneret, Boston, Mass.
Dome.—3558. April 4, 1876. Stove Polish. Edward James & Sons, Plymouth, England.
Ebony.—17,767. April 15, 1890. Stove Polish. Buffalo Polish Co., Buffalo, N. Y.
Electric.—12,475. August 4, 1885. Stove Polish. Phœnix Plumbago Mining Co., Philadelphia, Pa.
Electric Brilliant.—11,566. October 14, 1884. Stove Polish. Electric Brilliant Stove Polish Manufacturing Co., Richmond, Ind.
Electron.—15,792. August 21, 1888. Cleansing and Abrasive Soap. Electron Manufacturing Co., Philadelphia, Pa.
Electro Silicon.—1267. May 13, 1873. Polishing Material. Coffin, Reddington & Co, New York, N. Y.
Elektrik.—11,045. March 25, 1884. Prepared Whiting. Arthur Buel, New York, N. Y.
Eureka.—16,521. April 23, 1889. Cleaning and Polishing Stones. J. J. Murphy and J. W. Mosier, Louisville, Ky.
Excelsior.—7961. July 6, 1880. Corundum. Alden Emery Co., Boston, Mass.
Extra Plymouth Rock Stone.—20,131. September 15, 1891. Scythe Stones. Chas. E. Strong, Huntington, Mass.
Fire King.—2833. August 24, 1875. Stove Polish. H. A. Bartlett & Co., Philadelphia, Pa.
Genuine Lamoille.—14,716. August 30, 1887. Whetstones. A. F. Pike Manufacturing Co., Pike Station, N. H.
Glacial.—13,020. February 9, 1886. Silica Cleaning and Polishing Preparations. Plymouth Silica Co., Plymouth, Mass.
Glassine.—17,992. June 3, 1890. Cleaning and Polishing Preparations. Glassine Co., Boston, Mass.
Golden Polisher.—2721. July 6, 1875. Polishing Compound. Streeter & Riker, New York, N. Y.
Gold Gloss.—6565. September 10, 1878. Polishing Compound. Henry S. Zeigler, Philadelphia, Pa.

Good Luck.—13,252. April 27, 1886. Stove Polish. John Peter Wallgren, Orono, Me.
Green Mountain.—14,714. August 30, 1887. Whetstones. A. F. Pike Manufacturing Co., Pike Station, N. H.
Gritty Diamond Pearl.—14,715. August 30, 1887. Whetstones. A. F. Pike Manufacturing Co., Pike Station, N. H.
Housekeepers' Friend.—5781. March 19, 1878. Glossing and Polishing Solution. Wm. B. Wolf, Baltimore, Md.
Indian Pond, Red End.—14,658. August 2, 1887. Whetstones. A. F. Pike Manufacturing Co., Pike Station, N. H.
Infallible.—19,970. August 4, 1891. Polish for Metal. Geo. W. Hoffman, Indianapolis, Ind.
I polished up the handle of the big front door (and design).—12,025. March 17, 1885. Cleaning and Polishing Preparation. Plymouth Silica Co., Plymouth, Mass.
Iron-clad.—21,110. May 10, 1892. Stove Polish. Douglas & Kingsland, Middletown, Conn.
Ivory.—19,148. March 10, 1891. Metal Polish. Caledonia Mining and Manufacturing Co., Lancaster, Pa.
I. X. L.—6350. July 9, 1878. Stove Polish. I. X. L. Stove Polish Co., Grand Rapids, Mich.
Kalmoid.—17,764. April 15, 1890. Emery Wheels and Grinding Machinery. Tanite Co., Stroudsburg, Pa.
Keystone.—6401. July 23, 1878. Stove Polish. Phœnix Plumbago Mining Co., Philadelphia, Pa.
Klenzer.—16,883. July 30, 1889. Silver Polish. Jones & Dudley, Jersey City, N. J.
Lady's Friend.—21,061. May 3, 1892. Stove Polish. Chas. H. Curfew, Providence, R. I.
Leatherol.—19,974. August 4, 1891. Cleaning and Polishing Preparations. Leatherol Co., New York, N. Y.
Lightning.—18,179. July 15, 1890. Stove Blacking. Sherman S. Jewett & Co., Buffalo, N. Y.
Lightning Polish.—859. June 11, 1872. Polish for Metals. Frank J. Tinkham, New York, N. Y.
Little Giant.—21,471. July 19, 1892. Scouring and Cleaning Powder. Thomas Armstrong, Baltimore, Md.
Lusterine.—5648. February 12, 1878. Polish for Metals and Glass. John P. Haines, New York, N. Y.
Magic.—6415. July 30, 1878. 13,075. March 2, 1886. Stove Polish. Phœnix Plumbago Mining Co., Philadelphia, Pa.
Mau Tau.—21,007. April 19, 1892. Polish for Wood, Glass, and Metal. Robert A. Schultz, Oak Park, Ill.
Matchless.—14,497. June 7, 1887. Compound for Polishing and Cleaning Metal. Matchless Metal Polish Co., Chicago, Ill.
Mexoline.—19,549. May 19, 1891. Metal Polish. Matchless Metal Polish Co., Chicago, Ill.
Michigan Tripoli (and design).—3941. August 22, 1876. Polish. Eureka Mining and Manufacturing Co., Detroit, Mich.
Mirror.—6211. June 11, 1878. Stove Polish. Shadrach T. Smith, Kasson, Minn.
Montgomeriestone.—12,442. July 28, 1885. Grinding and Sharpening Articles. J. C. Montgomerie, Dalmore, Ayr Co., Scotland.
New England.—4951. July 24, 1877. 8662. September 20, 1881. Flint, Sand, and Emery Papers, etc. Wiggin & Stevens, Malden, Mass.
New Era.—12,311. June 23, 1885. Stove Polish. Randall H. Wetherell, Hoboken, N. J.
Nickline.—7139. April 1, 1879. Metal Polish. Herman Behr & Co., New York, N. Y.
Nixey.—17,149. October 29, 1889. Black Lead. Wm. G. Nixey, London, England.

Opaline.—18,446. September 23, 1890. Composition for Cleaning Metals, Glass, etc. Frank R. Hay, Johnstown, Pa.
Overton's.—16,768. July 2, 1889. Plate Powder. Overton, London, England.
Parlor.—5198. October 2, 1877. Stove Polish. Joseph Dixon Crucible Co., Jersey City, N. J.
Peerless.—13,701. October 5, 1886. Metal Polish. George A. Haws, New York, N. Y.
Pencil.—5197. October 2, 1877. Stove Polish. Joseph Dixon Crucible Co., Jersey City, N. J.
Phospho.—15,672. July 10, 1888. Compound for Cleaning, etc. Keystone Chemical Co., Philadelphia, Pa.
Prestoline.—18,905. January 27, 1891. Polishes and Cleaners for Metals. Wm. J. Ladd, New York, N. Y.
Pride.—9044. January 24, 1882. Stove Enamel. Benj. D. Milliken, Boston, Mass.
Pyn-ka.—20,674. February 2, 1892. Polishing Paste, etc., for Jewelers. The Pyn-ka Syndicate, Liverpool, England.
Quick Shine.—18,634. November 18, 1890. Stove Polish. Hiram W. Weeks, Philadelphia, Pa.
Rainbow.—4365. February 13, 1877. Metal Polish. Quérard & Co., New York, N. Y.
Raven.—4407. February 27, 1877. Stove Polish. N. H. Parker & Co., Boston, Mass.
Red Seal.—4117. November 14, 1876. Stove Polish. Joseph N. Birch, New York, N. Y.
Red Star (and star printed in red).—1441. September 2, 1873. 14,565. June 28, 1887. Powder for Cleaning Metal. John A. Wright & Co., Keene, N. H.
Rising.—3394. February 1, 1876. 8397. June 21, 1881. Black Lead or Plumbago. Morse Bros., Canton, Mass.
Rosy Red.—14,740. September 6, 1887. Oil Stones and Whetstones. A. F. Pike Manufacturing Co., Pike Station, N. H.
Royal.—21,253. June 7, 1892. Polish for Metals. Noble & Streeter, New York, N. Y.
Ruby.—13,203. April 20, 1886. 13.451. June 29, 1886. Abrasive Paper. Herman Behr & Co., New York, N. Y.
Russian.—14,161. March 8, 1887. Stove Blacking Paste. G. H. West, Chelsea, Mass.
Sacosa.—15,292. March 20, 1888. Compounds for Cleaning and Polishing Metals. Coffin, Redington & Co., New York, N. Y.
Salamander (and design).—2949. September 21, 1875. Stove Polish. H. A. Bartlett & Co., Philadelphia, Pa.
Salamander.—9245. March 28, 1882. Plumbago Crucibles, etc. Patent Plumbago Crucible Co., Battersea, Surrey county, England.
Sandilene (monogram).—3723. May 30, 1876. Polishing. Theodore R. White, Philadelphia, Pa.
Sapolio.—18,502. October 7, 1890. Scouring Compound. Enoch Morgan's Sons' Co., New York, N. Y.
Sapopolitum.—4836. July 10, 1877. Cleaning and Polishing Compound. Albert C. Emerick, Toledo, Ohio.
Savogran S.—4529. April 10, 1877. Cleaning Compound. Masury, Young & Co., Boston, Mass.
Scourene.—11,757. December 9, 1884. Compounds for Cleaning, etc. Melville Strong, New York, N. Y.
Semper Paratus (and design).—19,449. May 12, 1891. Metal Polish. Ames & Son, Albany, N. Y.
Silver Comet, The.—15,614. June 26, 1888. Liquid Stove Polish. Isaac H. Reddie, Boston, Mass.
Silver Dust.—11,341. July 15, 1884. Metal Polishing Powder. James T. White, Philadelphia, Pa.

Silver Glance Stove Polish.—1838. June 16, 1874. Stove Polish. Hoppings, New York, N. Y.
Silverine.—10,329. June 5, 1883. Preparation for Cleaning Jewelry. Eugene H. Hartshorn, Boston, Mass.
Silver Ore Lacquer.—12,907. December 29, 1885. Stove Polish. Gilbert M. Richardson, New York, N. Y.
Silvo.—21,338. June 21, 1892. Silver Polish. Wm. H. Lewis, Philadelphia, Pa.
Society Polish.—14,873. November 1, 1887. Polish for Metals. Robert F. S. Heath, Camden, N. J.
Solar.—17,256. December 10, 1889. Stove Polish. William J. Rigby, Philadelphia, Pa.
Starbright.—5608. February 5, 1878. Stove Polish. Geo. F. Gantz, New York, N. Y.
Starine.—21,673. August 23, 1892. Metal Polish. Samuel Kidder, Boston, Mass.
Star-Light.—21,947. November 8, 1892. Silver Polish. Purl C. Plasterer, Fort Wayne, Ind.
Suffrage.—5072. August 21, 1877. Stove Polish. Henry D. Atwood, Taunton, Mass.
Sun.—8396. June 21, 1881. Black Lead or Plumbago. Morse Bros., Canton, Mass.
Sunbright.—17,852. May 6, 1890. Soap and Polishing Compound. Simon Greenbaum, Chicago, Ill.
Sunnyside (and design).—1845. June 23, 1874. Stove Polish. Strow, Wile & Co., Philadelphia, Pa.
Sun (or Rising Sun).—1042. Oct. 29, 1872. 2,534. May 18, 1875. Prepared Plumbago. Morse Bros., Canton, Mass.
Surprise.—16,442. April 2, 1889. Cleaning and Polishing Compound. Emma J. Austin, Carthage, N. Y.
Tam o' Shanter.—12,441. July 28, 1885. Grinding and Sharpening Articles. J. C. Montgomerie, Dalmore, county of Ayr, Scotland.
Tanite.—1047. October 29, 1872. Emery Wheels, etc. Tanite Company, Stroudsburgh, Pa.
Tid Bits.—10,216. April 24, 1883. Stove Polish. Henry A. Bartlett, Philadelphia, Pa.
Tripoline.—13,983. January 18, 1887. Articles for Cleaning and Polishing Metal. Frank C. Baker, Chicago, Ill.
Tripolio.—15,759. August 7, 1888. Polishing and Scouring Soap. Waters & Wrigley Manufacturing Co., Chicago, Ill.
Turkey (and design). 1537. November 25, 1873. Emery. Abbott & Howard, Boston, Mass.
Universum.—6356. July 16, 1878. Stove Polish. William Frankfurth & Co., Milwaukee, Wis.
Ve-To.—17,830. April 29, 1890. Materials for Polishing. John H. Piper, New York, N. Y.
Washee.—20,271. October 27, 1891. Cleaning Compound. Luise Dirksen, Brooklyn, N. Y.
White Diamond.—15,988. November 6, 1888. Metal Polishes. Matchless Metal Polish Co., Chicago, Ill.
White Giant.—17,860. May 6, 1890. Grinding Wheels of Corundum. Andrew L. Bush, Westfield, Mass.
White Mountain.—15,127. January 24, 1888. Whetstones. A. F. Pike Manufacturing Co., Pike Station, N. H.
White Rouge.—21,518. July 26, 1892. Polishing Preparation. Yucker & Levett Chemical Co., New York, N. Y.
Willoughby Lake.—3051. October 19, 1875. Scythe-Stones. J. C. Orne & Co., Westmore, Vt.
Woman's.—5132. September 11, 1877. Stove Polish. Henry D. Atwood, Taunton, Mass.
Zincine.—9099. February 7, 1882. Polishing Preparations. B. G. Seebach, Peru, Ill.

TRADE-MARKS
FOR
Cleaning and Polishing Preparations.
(CLASS 12.)

Designs or figures showing the essential feature claimed as the mark.

13. October 25, 1870. Polishing Preparation. Buffalo Magic Polishing Co., Buffalo, N. Y.

70. November 22, 1870. Detergent Powder. Jesse S. Smith, Waverly, N. Y.

109. December 20, 1870. 7534. July 22, 1879. Stove Polish. James L. Prescott, North Berwick, Me.

227. April 25, 1871. Stove Polish. Robt. E. Cherrington, South Boston, Mass.

466. October 3, 1871. Polish for Metal Ware. W. S. & T. S. Witherspoon & T. Werne, Fairview, W. Va.

641. January 30, 1872. Emery. Tully & Davenport, New York, N. Y.

805. May 7, 1862. Polishing Brick. T. T. Luscombe & Co., St. Louis, Mo.

890. July 16, 1872. Emery. Baeder, Adamson & Co., Philadelphia, Pa.

1061. November 12, 1872. Emery Wheels or Blocks. James Tyzick, St. John, Canada.

1441. September 2, 1873. Cleaning Powder. J. A. Wright & Co., Keene, N. H.

1537. November 25, 1873. Emery. Abbott & Howard, Boston, Mass.

1845. June 23, 1874. Stove Polish. Strow, Wile & Co., Philadelphia, Pa.

 2034. October 20, 1874. Emery Wheels and Grinders. Lehigh Valley Emery Wheel Co., Weissport, Pa.

 2073. November 17, 1874. Stove Polish. H. A. Bartlett & Co., Philadelphia, Pa.

 2074. November 17, 1874. Stove Dressing. B. F. Brown & Co., Boston, Mass.

 2129. December 22, 1874. Polish for Metal. D. D. Cornell, Hyde Park, Ill.

 2219. February 9, 1875. Stove Polish. C. H. Fischer & Co., New York, N. Y.

 2247. February 23, 1875. 10,634. October 16, 1883. Silver Polish. William E. Dunham, Fall River, Mass.

 2542. May 18, 1875. Plumbago or Graphite Lubricant. American Graphite Co., New York, N. Y.

  2908. September 7, 1875. Polishing Powder. Detroit Polish Co., Detroit, Mich.

 2949. September 21, 1875. Stove Polish. H. A. Bartlett & Co., Philadelphia, Pa.

  3092. October 26, 1875. Stove Polish. Samuel S. Miers, Philadelphia, Pa.

 3554. April 4, 1876. Burnishing Blacking. Nathaniel J. Downing, Lynn, Mass.

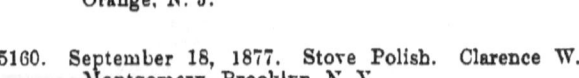 3723. May 30, 1876. Cleaning and Polishing Compound. Theodore R. White, Philadelphia, Pa.

3941. August 22, 1876. Polish. Eureka Mining and Manufacturing Co., Detroit, Mich.

4880. July 17, 1877. Stove Polish, etc. Geo. A. Moss, Orange, N. J.

5160. September 18, 1877. Stove Polish. Clarence W. Montgomery, Brooklyn, N. Y.

6084. May 14, 1878. Stove Polish. Henry S. Zeigler. Philadelphia, Pa.

CLEANING AND POLISHING. 21

6488. August 20, 1878. Stove Polish. J. C. Jacoby & Co., New York, N. Y.

7472. July 1, 1879. Scouring Crystals. John Dawson & Son, Philadelphia, Pa.

9573. July 25, 1882. Dry Paste for Cleaning Gold and Silver Plated Ware, etc. A. E. Jeaneret, Boston. Mass.

9723. October 17, 1882. Cleaning Silver, etc. Bean & Rabe, Philadelphia, Pa.

9858. December 5, 1882. Polishing Compound. Adalbert Vogt, Berlin, Germany.

9908. December 26, 1882. Stove Polish. Ignatius Schwarz, Chicago, Ill.

10,064. February 20, 1883. Stove Polish. Lustro Company, New York, N. Y.

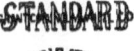
11,607. November 4, 1884. Grinding and Polishing Implements of Corundum or Emery. Grant Corundum Wheel Co., Chester, Mass.

11,671. November 11, 1884. Stove Polish. Wood Bros., Racine, Wis.

12,025. March 17, 1885. Silica Cleaning and Polishing Preparations. Plymouth Silica Co., Plymouth, Mass.

12,996. February 2, 1886. Polishing Powder for Metal. Glass, etc. Fischler & Co., Philadelphia, Pa.

13,044. February 23, 1886. Chamois Skin for Polishing Metal. Blakeslee & Darby, Cleveland, O.

13,401. June 15, 1886. Foundry Facings and Stove Polish. Edward D. Ransom, Albany, N. Y.

14,060. February 8, 1887. Stove Polish. Frederick H. Schweizer, Columbus, Ohio.

14,247. April 5, 1887. Putz Pomade. Albert Vogt & Co., Freiderichsburg, Prussia.

14,529. June 21, 1887. Preparation for Polishing Metal. Benj. Beddow & Sons, London, England.

TRADE-MARKS.

14,676. August 9, 1887. Whetstones. A. F. Pike Manufacturing Co., Pike Station, N. H.

15,135. January 31, 1888. Blacking or Polish for Stoves. Black Flag Stove Polish Co., Detroit, Mich.

15,725. July 24, 1888. Metal Polishing Preparation. Savage Bros., Washington, D. C.

16,340. March 5, 1889. Stove Polish. Gaylord M. Jackson, Los Angeles, Cal.

16,369. March 12, 1889. Metal Polishing Paste. Walter J. Ramsay, New Bedford, Mass.

16,456. April 2, 1889. Liquid Coating for Iron, Stone, Wood, etc. Léon Pupat, Romans, France.

17,247. December 10, 1889. Stove Polish. Frederick W. Anderson, Worcester, Mass.

17,510. February 11, 1890. Polish for Metals. Borsum Bros., New York, N. Y.

17,537. February 11, 1890. Liquid Metal Polish. Borsum Bros., New York, N. Y.

17,852. May 6, 1890. Soap and Polishing Compound. Simon Greenbaum, Chicago, Ill.

18,501. October 7, 1890. Scouring Compound. Enoch Morgan's Sons Co., New York, N. Y.

18,539. October 21, 1890. Stove Polish. William Connors, Troy, N. Y.

18,661. December 2, 1890. Polishing Soap. Joseph Pickering & Sons, Sheffield, England.

18,663. December 2, 1890. Polishing Soap. Joseph Pickering & Sons, Sheffield, England.

18,664. December 2, 1890. Polishing Soap. Joseph Pickering & Sons, Sheffield, England.

CLEANING AND POLISHING. 23

 19,082. February 24, 1891. Stove Polish. Jennie R. Stoeckel, New York, N. Y.

  19,113. March 3, 1891. Stove Paste Polish. Harry C. Lombard, Milwaukee, Wis.

 19,449. May 12, 1891. Metal Polish. Ames & Son, Albany, N. Y.

  19,630. June 2, 1891. Stove Polish. James B. Dyer, Brooklyn, N. Y.

 19,799. June 30, 1891. Stove Polish. Renzo T. Sargent, Clinton, Mass.

 19,987. August 4, 1891. Whiting for use on Equipments. Cassard & Neal, Baltimore, Md.

  21,031. April 26, 1892. Metal Burnishing Powder. Diamond Lustre Polish Co., Boston, Mass.

 21,136. May 17, 1892. Stove Polish. John D. Butz, Wilkes-Barre, Pa.

  21,820. October 4, 1892. Silver Polish. Electro Silicon Co., New York, N. Y.

 21,989. November 15, 1892. Polishing Powder. Daniel W. Curtis, Syracuse, N. Y.

COMPILED BY
WALLACE A. BARTLETT,
Patent Attorney,
Washington, D. C.

TRADE-MARKS

FOR

CUTLERY AND EDGE TOOLS.

(CLASS 17.)

Embracing axes, knives, shears, clippers, and the like; flat table ware, razors, &c. (See also Class 35, Jewelry; Class 40, Locks and Hardware; Class 68, Surgical Instruments; Class 73, Tools, &c.)

Words or phrases constituting the marks arranged alphabetically. Number, date, and registrant follow mark.

A A A 1.—14,026., February 1, 1887. Cutlery. Andrew J. Jordan, St. Louis, Mo.
A ✻ 1.—4190. December 5, 1876. Cutlery. Theile & Quack, Eberfeld, Germany.
Acme.—11,538. September 30, 1884. Knives, Razors, and Shears. Frederick Westpfal, New York, N. Y.
Adirondack.—21,899. October 25, 1892. Spoons, Forks, Knife Handles, etc. Ferdinand C. Lamy, Saranac Lake, N. Y.
Adolphus Cutlery Company.—19,701. June 16, 1891. Shears, Scissors, Cutlery, etc. Andrew J. Jordan, St. Louis, Mo.
A Luxury.—Razor Steel Scissors.—262. May 16, 1871. Scissors. Robt. J. Roberts, New York, N. Y.
American Horse.—22,050. November 22, 1892. Hair and Wool Clippers. American Shearer Manufacturing Co., Nashua, N. H.
An exquisite pleasure to shave with R. J. Roberts' Diamond-Edge Razors.—300. May 30, 1871. Razors. Robt. J. Roberts, New York, N. Y.
Antietam, Sept. 17, 1862 (and design).—19,792. June 30, 1891. Tableware, etc. E. A. Whitney & Co., Boston, Mass.
Appomattox, Apr. 9, 1865 (and design).—19,782. June 30, 1891. Tableware, etc. E. A. Whitney & Co., Boston, Mass.
Ark, The.—15,860. September 11, 1888. Cutlery and Edge Tools. Stacey Bros., Sheffield, England.
Arkansaw Traveler.—10,771. December 11, 1883. Cutlery and Edge Tools. Fones Bros., Little Rock, Ark.
Ascend.—14,419. May 17, 1887. Cutlery, Saws, Files, etc. Wm. Thomas Staniforth, Sheffield, England.
Atlas (and design).—8724. October 11, 1881. Cutlery. John Russell Cutlery Co., Turner's Falls, Mass.
Barbara Fritchie (and design).—19,788. June 30, 1891. Tableware, etc. E. A. Whitney & Co., Boston, Mass.
Barber's Favorite.—13,411. June 15, 1886. Razors and Razor Strops. Flagg Cutlery Co., New York, N. Y.
Bengall.—8945. December 29. 1881. Razors, Scissors, Pocket and Table Cutlery. Thomas Radley Cadman, Sheffield, England.

CUTLERY AND EDGE TOOLS. 25

Big Bonanza.—4210. December 19, 1876. Edge Tools. Collins Company, Collinsville, Conn.
Blizzard.—19,390. April 21, 1891. Hay Knives. Hiram Holt Co., East Wilton, Me.
Bonanza.—4211. December 19, 1876. Edge Tools. Collins Company, Collinsville, Conn.
B. Swift X.—5779. March 19, 1878. Edge Tools. Collins Company, Collinsville, Conn.
Bullion.—1673. March 17, 1874. Axes. Hubbard, Lippincott, Bakewell & Co., Pittsburg, Pa.
B4 ✳ Any.—755. April 9, 1872. 6953. January 14, 1879. 8766. October 25, 1881. Pocket and Table Knives, Scissors and Razors, etc. Frederick Ward & Co., Sheffield, England.
Captain's Well, The (and design).—19,959. August 4, 1891. Flat Ware. Horace G. Hudson, Amesbury, Mass.
C. C. S.—850. June 4, 1872. Edge Tools and Agricultural Implements. Collins Company, Collinsville, Conn.
Carbon.—10,765. December 4, 1883. Knives, Forks, and Spoons. Leonard F. Dunn, Niagara Falls, N. Y.
Challenge.—4309. January 23, 1877. Cutlery. Frederick Wiebusch, New York, N. Y.
Challenge (and design).—4418. March 6, 1877. Pocket Knives, etc. Joseph W. Gardner, Shelburne Falls, Mass.
Charter Oak.—1126. February 11, 1873. 1328. June 17, 1873. Axes and Hatchets, etc. Collins Company, Collinsville, Conn.
Climax.—21,472. July 19, 1892. Razors. Broch & Thiebes Cutlery Co., St. Louis, Mo.
Collins.—6112. November 7, 1882. 9789. May 21, 1888. Edge Tools. Collins Company, Collinsville, Conn.
Collins & Co.—9704. October 3, 1882. Edge Tools. Collins Company, Collinsville, Conn.
Collins & Co., Hartford.—7094. March 11, 1879. Edge Tools. Collins Company, Collinsville, Conn.
Columbian.—22,067. November 29, 1892. Hair Clippers. American Shearer Manufacturing Co., Nashua, N. H.
Columbia, The.—15,440. May 8, 1888. Spoons, Forks, Ladles, etc. G. I. Mix & Co., Yalesville, Conn.
Columbus.—20,482. December 22, 1891. Razors, Pocket-Knives, and Scissors. Graef & Schmidt, New York, N. Y.
Columbus and the Egg (and design).—19,779. June 30, 1891. Table Ware. etc. E. A. Whiting & Co., Boston, Mass.
Columbus Before the Queen (and design).—19,778. June 30, 1891. Table Ware, etc. E. A. Whiting & Co., Boston, Mass.
Cow Boy.—7980. July 20, 1880. 8775. October 18, 1881. Clasp Knives. Andrew J. Jordan, St. Louis, Mo.
Crown Ax.—840. May 28, 1872. Axes. Underhill Edge Tool Co., Nashua, N. H.
Cutler.—304. May 30, 1871. Axes. Douglas Ax Manufacturing Co., Douglas, Mass.
Cutlers to the American People.—19,091. February 24, 1891. Household Cutlery. Landers, Frary & Clark, New Britain, Conn.
Daisy (and design).—10,665. October 23, 1883. Razors. Frederick Aschener, New York, N. Y.
Damascene.—12,125. April 14, 1885. Razors. C. Klauberg & Bros., New York, N. Y.
D. E. T. Co.'s Clipper.—477. October 17, 1871. Edge Tools. Dunn Edge Tool Co., West Waterville, Me.
Diamond Edge.—108. December 13, 1870. 299. May 30, 1871. Cutlery. Robert J. Roberts, New York, N. Y.
Diamond Spear. 8898. December 6, 1881. Razors, Knives, and Scissors. William Brokhahne, New York, N. Y.

Discovery.—20,218. October 13, 1891. Table Ware, Jewelry, etc. William W. Dugin, Concord, N. H.
Dungeon Rock.—19,221. March 24, 1891. Spoons, Forks, and Flat Ware. H. M. Hill, Lynn, Mass.
Eagle Axe.—2763. July 20, 1875. Axes. Kloman, Park & Co., Pittsburg, Pa.
Echo.—14,939. November 15, 1887. Cutlery. Pauls Bros., New York, New York.
Eclipse.—14,073. February 15, 1887. Cutlery and Scissors. Hermann Boker & Co., New York, N. Y.
Edwards.—15,898. September 25, 1888. Metal Table Ware. Holmes & Edwards Silver Co., West Stratford, Conn.
1880 (eighteen eighty).—12,594. September 22, 1885. Table Ware and Cutlery. Pairpoint Manufacturing Co., New Bedford, Mass.
Electric.—1367. July 15, 1873. 8237. May 24, 1881. Razors and Cutlery. Friedmann & Lauterjung, New York, N. Y.
Electric.—12,707. October 27, 1885. Axes, Hatchets, Mattocks, etc. Chas. K. Hawkes, San Francisco, Cal.
Emperor.—18,007. June 10, 1890. Razors. Graef & Schmidt, New York, N. Y.
E. Sterling Inlaid.—18,163. July 8, 1890. Flat Metal Table Ware. Holmes & Edwards Silver Co., Bridgeport, Conn.
Eureka.—2285. March 9, 1875. Axes. Richard Patrick & Co., San Francisco, Cal.
Extra—K. B.—17,392. January 14, 1890. Knives, Shears, Razors, etc. Krusius Bros., New York, N. Y.
Federal.—14,320. April 26, 1887. Axes, Hatchets, etc. McLean Bros. & Rigg, New York, N. Y.
Fiddler.—7586. August 12, 1879. Table and Pocket Cutlery. Landers, Frary & Clark, New Britain, Conn.
Fort Sumter, April 12, 1861 (and design).—19,790. June 30, 1891. Table Ware, etc. E. A. Whitney & Co., Boston, Mass.
Fox.—11,333. July 15, 1884. Cutlery. Koeller & Schmitz Cutlery Co., Milwaukee, Wis.
French Toilet.—15,303. March 20, 1888. Hair Clippers and Cutters. McCoy & Sanders, New York, N. Y.
Gem.—15,591. June 12, 1888. Safety Razors. Henry B. Leach, Boston, Mass.
Gen. Putnam.—19,736. June 16, 1891. Spoons, Forks, and Table Ware. Geo. E. Shaw, Putnam, Conn.
Gettysburg, July, 1863 (and design).—19,789. June 30, 1891. Table Ware, etc. E. A. Whitney & Co., Boston, Mass.
Gowanda (and crown).—14,132. March 8, 1887. Chopping Axes. Nicholas, John P., & Andrew C. Romer, Gowanda, N. Y.
Granger.—4138. November 21, 1876. Axes, Hatchets, and Hoes. Wm. C. Kelley, Louisville, Ky.
Guanaco (and design).—13,845. June 1, 1886. Edge Tools. John Dunn, New York, N. Y.
H & B.—3516. March 14, 1876. 15,695. July 17, 1888. Pocket Cutlery. Humason & Beckley Manufacturing Co., New Britain, Conn.
Hamburg.—5603. February 5, 1878. 8848. November 15, 1881. Cutlery. William Brokhahne, New York, N. Y.
Hammer Brand.—13,009. February 9, 1886. Pocket and Table Cutlery. New York Knife Co., Walden, N. Y.
Harper's Ferry, October 17, 1859 (and design).—19,800. June 30, 1891. Table Ware, etc. E. A. Whitney & Co., Boston, Mass.
Hoosier Boy.—10,358. June 9, 1883. Axes. Henry D. Loveland, Lamar, Pennsylvania.
Hunt's.—303. May 30, 1871. 2852. August 24, 1875. Axes. Douglas Ax Manufacturing Co., Douglas, Mass.

CUTLERY AND EDGE TOOLS. 27

Hurd's Razor Blade.—3917. August 8, 1876. Axes. Lane & Gale, Troy, N. Y.
Hurd's Razor Blade.—8637. September 13, 1881. Axes, Hatchets, Adzes, etc. Geo. Tibbets Lane, Troy, N. Y.
Imperial.—20,507. December 29, 1891. Razors. Adolph Kastor & Bros., New York, N. Y.
Invincible.—21,079. May 3, 1892. Razors. Ransom & Randolph, Toledo, Ohio.
Iron City—John & Co.—6234. June 18, 1878. Axes. Kloman, Park & Co., Pittsburg, Pa.
I-X-L.—666. February 20, 1872. 6870. December 10, 1878. 8765. October 25, 1881. Cutlery. George Wostenholm & Son, Sheffield, England.
I X L.—7131. March 25, 1879. Axes. Boetticher, Kellogg & Co., Evansville, Ind.
John Grippin's.—15,074. January 3, 1888. Axes. E. F. Carpenter & Co., Jamestown, N. Y.
John G. Whittier (and design).—20,220. October 13, 1891. Table Ware, etc. Horace G. Hudson, Amesbury, Mass.
July 4, 1776 (and design).—19,784. June 30, 1891. Table Ware, etc. E. A. Whitney & Co., Boston, Mass.
La Cruz Colorado (and design).—15,722. July 24, 1888. Edge, Agricultural Tools, etc. A. W. Wills & Son, Birmingham, England.
Lightning.—9583. August 1, 1882. Hay-Knives. Hiram Holt & Co., East Wilton, Me.
Little Folks.—7034. February 18, 1879. Table Cutlery. John Russell Cutlery Co., Turner's Falls, Mass.
Lumberman's Pride.—7320. May 20, 1879. Axes. Henry S. Smith & Co., Grand Rapids, Mich.
Magic.—12,122. April 14, 1885. Knives. Eagle Pencil Co., New York, N. Y.
Magnetic.—9032. January 17, 1882. Razors. Pribyl Bros., Chicago, Illinois.
Malacca.—10,957. February 19, 1884. Tinned Spoons and Forks. G. I. Mix & Co., Yalesville, Conn.
March to the Sea (The) (and design).—19,781. June 30, 1891. Table Ware, etc. E. A. Whitney & Co., Boston, Mass.
Mascotte.—17,942. May 27, 1890. Razors. Ransom & Randolph, Toledo, Ohio.
M. B. Co.—20,828. March 15, 1892. Scissors. Milton Bradley Co., Springfield, Mass.
Mikado (The).—19,655. June 2, 1891. Knives, Scissors, Razors, etc. Frederick A. Clauberg, New York, N. Y.
Monarch.—13,789. November 9, 1886. Razors, Scissors, and Pocket Knives. McCoy & Sanders, New York, N. Y.
Monitor and Merrimac, March 9, 1862 (and design).—19,791. June 30, 1891. Table Ware, etc. E. A. Whitney & Co., Boston, Mass.
Monumental.—1773. May 5, 1874. Cutlery. Frederick Wiebusch, New York, N. Y.
New York Barber's Favorite.—13,583. August 17, 1886. Razors. Flagg Cutlery Co., New York, N. Y.
New York Cutlery Co.—3935. August 15, 1876. Cutlery. Rowe & Post, New York, N. Y.
NON-XLL.—17,160. November 5, 1889. Cutlery and Edge Tools. Joseph Allen & Sons, Sheffield, England.
O. K. (and design).—1504. October 21, 1873. Razors. Herman, Boker & Co., New York, N. Y.
Old Washoe.—9595. August 8, 1882. Pickaxes, Hatchets, Axes, etc. Henry H. Trenor, New York, N. Y.
Old Constitution. —19,770. June 30, 1891. Table Ware. John H. Hutchinson, Portsmouth, N. H.

Old Faithful.—16,246. February 5, 1889. Cutlery. Andrew J. Jordan, St. Louis, Mo.
Old Town Mill, 1650 (and design).—20,327. November 3, 1891. Plated Ware, etc. Wm. H. Saxton, Jr., New London, Conn.
Orchids.—14,254. April 5, 1887. Knives, Forks, Spoons, etc. Towle Manufacturing Co., Newburyport, Mass.
Oriental.—15,490. May 22, 1888. Metal Table Ware. Holmes & Edwards Silver Co., West Stratford, Conn.
Our Own.—1533. November 18, 1873. Cutlery. Isaac T. Meyer & Co., New York, N. Y.
O. V. B.—18,317. August 19, 1890. Knives, Scissors, Razors, etc. Hibbard, Spencer, Bartlett & Co., Chicago, Ill.
Owl (and design of owl).—14,227. April 5, 1887. Cutlery. C. B. Barker & Co., New York, N. Y.
Paragon.—9450. June 13, 1882. Cutlery. Fuller Bros., New York, N. Y.
Perfection.—16,973. September 3, 1889. Razors. T. Hessenbruch & Co., Philadelphia, Pa.
Pipe (and design).—8764. October 25, 1881. Razors. Geo. Wostenholm & Son, Sheffield, England.
President.—6854. December 3, 1878. Axes and Hatchets. W. H. Crossman & Bro., New York, N. Y.
President.—17,217. November 26, 1889. Pencil Sharpeners and Razor Strops. Geo. H. Coursen. Baltimore, Md.
Progress.—14,730. September 6, 1887. Cutlery. Alfred Field & Co., New York, N. Y.
Queen.—6894. December 17, 1878. 9946. January 9, 1883. Razors. Henry Sears & Co., Chicago, Ill.
Queen's Own.—5124. September 4, 1877. Razors. Nathan Joseph, San Francisco, Cal.
Queen's Own Co.—1146. February 25, 1873. Cutlery. Nathan Joseph. San Francisco, Cal.
Rangoon.—18,009. June 10, 1890. Razors. Henry Keidel, Baltimore, Md.
Razor Steel.—368. July 4, 1871. Cutlery. R. J. Roberts, New York, N. Y.
R. D.—12,323. June 16, 1885. Cutlery. Herman, Boker & Co., New York, N. Y.
Red Clipper.—1108. January 28, 1873. Pruning Shears. Christy & Hughes, Clyde, Ohio.
Red Mann Axe (The).—2961. September 21, 1875. Axes. J. Fearon Mann, Bellefonte, Pa.
Red Warrior.—5220. October 16, 1877. Axes. William Mann, Jr., & Co., Lewiston, Pa.
Ring.—8906. December 6, 1881. Razors, Knives, and Scissors. William Brokhahne, New York, N. Y.
River.—19,236. March 31, 1891. Shears, Scissors, Cutlery, etc. Andrew J. Jordan, St. Louis, Mo.
Riverside Tool Co.—21,622. August 16, 1892. Edge Tools. Harry C. Marshall. New York, N. Y.
R. King, Canton.—5681. February 26, 1878. 11,344. July 22, 1884. Edge Tools. Collins Company, Collinsville, Conn.
Rogers & Son (and design).—7157. April 8, 1879. Cutlery. Rogers & Son, Greenfield, Mass.
Rodgersine.—16,478. April 9, 1889. Cutlery and Plate. Joseph Rodgers & Sons, Sheffield, England.
Royal.—10,494. August 7, 1883. Shears and Scissors. Elyria Shear Co., Elyria, Ohio.
Royal Worcester.—20,976. April 12, 1892. Edge Tools and Cutlery. McKnight & Co., Wichita, Kansas.

CUTLERY AND EDGE TOOLS. 29

Sharps.—302. May 30, 1871. 2851. August 24, 1875. Axes. Douglas Ax Manufacturing Co., Douglas, Mass.

Sheridan's Ride (and design).—19,783. June 30, 1891. Table Ware, etc. E. A. Whitney & Co., Boston, Mass.

Signal.—19,143. March 3, 1891. Razors. John Sellers & Sons, New York, N. Y.

Signing the Emancipation Proclamation, January 1, 1863 (and design).—19,787. June 30, 1891. Table Ware, etc. E. A. Whitney & Co., Boston, Mass.

Solid Comfort.—13,410. June 15, 1886. Razors and Razor Strops. Flagg Cutlery Co., New York, N. Y.

Speed (and design).—2379. April 13, 1875. 7715. October 7, 1879. 8849. November 15, 1881. Cutlery. Wm. Brokhahne, New York, N. Y.

Standard.—10,495. August 7, 1883. Shears and Scissors. Elyria Shear Co., Elyria, Ohio.

Star Ax.—593. December 19, 1871. Axes. C. Gerber & Co., Toledo, Ohio.

Sterling—M. & B.—15,642. June 26, 1888. Metal Table Ware. Miller & Berry, Shelton, Conn.

Sultana.—15,663. July 3, 1888. Razors. Son Brothers & Co., San Francisco, Cal.

T. & Q. E. (and design).—4050. October 10, 1876. Cutlery. Theile & Quack, Elberfeld, Germany.

Tinned.—21,599. August 9, 1892. Meat Choppers and Presses. Enterprise Manufacturing Co. of Pennsylvania, Philadelphia, Pa.

Tonsorial Gem.—19,654. June 2, 1891. Razors, Strops, and Shears. Frederick A. Clauberg, New York, N. Y.

Tower.—16,024. November 20, 1888. Cutlery. August Vom Dorp, New York, N. Y.

Tuxedo.—18,693. December 9, 1890. Knives, Forks, Spoons, etc. Rogers & Bro., Waterbury, Conn.

Tyler & Co.—4741. June 12, 1877. Cutlery. Theile & Quack, Elberfeld, Germany.

Union.—15,720. July 24, 1888. Table, Pocket, and Toilet Cutlery, etc. Union Cutlery Co., Chicago, Ill.

U N X L D.—19,215. March 24, 1891. Cutlery, etc. Northfield Knife Co., Litchfield, Conn.

Victor.—12,417. July 21, 1885. Razors, Strops, Guards, etc. A. V. Brokhahne, New York, N. Y.

W. W. G.—20,726. February 16, 1892. Sheep Shears, Garden Shears, and Butcher Knives. Wm. Wilkinson & Sons, Sheffield, England.

Washoe.—4071. October 24, 1876. Edge and other Tools. Lathrop & Co., Newark, New Jersey.

Washoe.—10,775. December 11, 1883. Picks and other Tools. Washoe Manufacturing Co., Newark, N. J.

Watteau.—21,369. June 28, 1892. Flat and Table Ware, Jewelry, etc. Wm. B. Durgin, Concord, N. H.

West Branch.—17,287. December 17, 1889. Axes. Haynes, Pillsbury & Co., Bangor, Me.

Western.—14,662. August 2, 1887. Cutlery. Wiebusch & Hilger, New York, N. Y.

Wills.—15,625. June 19, 1888. Edge Tools. A. W. Wills & Son, Birmingham, England.

Wisconsin Farmer.—8378. June 21, 1881. Axes and Saws. Wm. Frankfurth & Co., Milwaukee, Wis.

Wisconsin Wood Chopper.—923. July 23, 1872. Axes. Biddle Hardware Co., Philadelphia, Pa.

Wood Chopper's Pride.—5901. April 23, 1878. Axes. Markley, Alling & Co., Chicago, Ill.

Worth.—17,125. October 22, 1889. Cutlery and Edge Tools. B. Worth & Sons, Sheffield, England.

W 1.—8687. September 27, 1881. Axes. Weed & Becker Manufacturing Co., New York, N. Y.
X L C R.—14,530. June 21, 1887. Cutlery, etc. W. Bingham & Co., Cleveland, Ohio.
Zeeck Pattern Axe.—10,131. March 20, 1883. Axes. Johnson Bros. & Lieper, Cincinnati, Ohio.
20th Century.—19,237. March 31, 1891. Cutlery, etc. Andrew J. Jordan, St. Louis, Mo.

COMPILED BY
WALLACE A. BARTLETT,
Patent Attorney,
WASHINGTON, D. C.

TRADE-MARKS
FOR
CUTLERY AND EDGE TOOLS.
(CLASS 17.)

Designs and figures showing the essential feature claimed as Trade-Mark.

43. November 1, 1870. Ax. Julius W. Meyer, St. Louis, Mo.

83. December 6, 1870. Ax. Boeticher, Kellogg & Co., Evansville, Indiana.

1504. October 21, 1873. Razors. Hermann Boker & Co., New York, N. Y.

1546. December 2, 1873. Hardware, Cutlery, Guns, Pistols, etc. Theophilus Hessenbruch, Philadelphia, Pa.

1880. July 14, 1874. 14,428. May 24, 1887. Cutlery. Herman Boker & Co., New York, N. Y.

2379. April 13, 1875. 8851. November 15, 1881. Cutlery. William Brokhahne, New York, N. Y.

2602. June 1, 1875. Chisels and Edge Tools. Buck Bros., Millbury, Mass.

2703. July 6, 1875. 1004. September 24, 1872. Cutlery and Surgical Instruments. Wilhelm Clauberg, Solingen, Prussia.

3406. February 8, 1876. 8830, 8831. November 15, 1881. Axes, Adzes, Augers, Tools, etc. Collins Co., Collinsville, Conn.

3704. May 23, 1876. Edge Tools. Ten Eyck Axe Manufacturing Co., Cohoes, N. Y.

4050. October 10, 1876. Cutlery. Theile & Quack, Elberfeld, Germany.

4418. March 6, 1877. Pocket and other Knives. Joseph N. Gardner, Shelburne Falls, Mass.

4593. May 1, 1877. 8594. August 23, 1881. Pen and Pocket Knives. John Russell Cutlery Co., Turner's Falls, Mass.

5602. February 5, 1878. 8850. November 15, 1881. Cutlery. Wm. Brokhahue, New York, N. Y.

5778. March 19, 1878. 9681. September 19, 1882. 9958. January 16, 1883. Edge Tools. Collins Company, Collinsville, Conn.

5779. March 19, 1878. 11,403. August 12, 1884. Edge Tools. Collins Co., Collinsville, Conn.

5782. March 26, 1878. Cutlery. Gustavus V. Brecht, St. Louis, Mo.

6111. May 21, 1878. 8829. Nov. 15, 1881. Edge Tools. Collins Co., Collinsville, Conn.

6386. July 23, 1878. Razors. George F. Creutzburg, Philadelphia, Pa.

6816. November 19, 1878. 8419. June 28, 1881. Cutlery. Joseph Rogers & Sons, Sheffield, England.

7157. April 8, 1879. Table Cutlery. Rogers & Son, Greenfield, Mass.

7349. May 20, 1879. 8681. September 27, 1881. Pocket Cutlery. John Russell Cutlery Co., Turner's Falls, Mass.

7667. September 9, 1879. Table and Pocket Cutlery and Butcher Knives. Frary Cutlery Co., Bridgeport, Conn.

8106. November 30, 1880. Razors, Knives, Surgical Instruments, etc. Gustav Knecht, Chicago, Ill.

8605. August 30, 1881. Knives, Scissors, Razors, etc. Lloyd, Supplee & Walton, Philadelphia, Pa.

8678. September 27, 1881. Axes. Weed & Becker Manufacturing Co., New York, N. Y.

8684. September 27, 1881. Axes. W. C. Kelly & Co., Louisville, Ky.

8723. October 11, 1881. Plated Silver Knives. John Russell Cutlery Co., Turner's Falls, Mass.

8724. October 11, 1881. Table, Butcher, and Hunting Knives. John Russell Cutlery Co., Turner's Falls, Mass.

8764. October 25, 1881. Razors. Geo. Wostenholm & Son, Sheffield, England.

CUTLERY AND EDGE TOOLS. 33

9182. March 7, 1882. Cutlery. John Wilson, Sheffield, England.

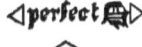
9258. April 4, 1882. Razors. William H. De Pew, New York, N. Y.

9516. July 4, 1882. Table, Butcher, and Hunting Knives. John Russell Cutlery Co., Turner's Falls, Mass.

9546. July 11, 1882. Cutlery and Edge Tools. James Veall, Sheffield, England.

9551. July 18, 1882. Edged Tools. Collins Co., Collinsville, Conn.

9916. December 26, 1882. Cutlery. Allan G. Lamson, Brooklyn, N. Y.

10,344. June 12, 1883. Cutlery. Gustavus V. Brecht, St. Louis, Mo.

10,375. June 26, 1883. Certain Edge Tools. Les Fils de Peugeot Frères, Valentigney, Doubs, France.

10,423. July 17, 1883. Razors. Charles F. Butcher, Sheffield, England.

10,560. August 28, 1883. Cutlery and Edge Tools. Hale Brothers, Sheffield, England.

10,665. October 23, 1883. Razors. Friederick Aschener, New York, N. Y.

10,909. February 5, 1884. Cutlery and Cutting Implements. Friedrich Wilhelm Beckmann, Solingen, Prussia, Germany.

11,333. July 15, 1884. Cutlery. Koeller & Schmitz Cutlery Co., Milwaukee, Wis.

11,430. August 19, 1884. Cutlery and Edge Tools. Edwin Murray Dickinson, Sheffield, England.

11,800. December 16, 1884. Knives, Forks, and Spoons. Gebrueder Noelle, Luedenscheid, Prussia, Germany.

12,392. July 7, 1885. Axes. Jennie C. O. Wetmore, Adrian, Mich.

12,627. October 6, 1885. Razors, Scissors, Shears, etc. Richard, Dinkelmann & Co., St. Louis, Mo.

34   TRADE-MARKS.

13,050. February 23, 1853. Pocket Knives, Shears, Scissors. etc. Flagg Cutlery Co., New York, N. Y.

13,088. March 9, 1886. Shears and Scissors. Henry Seymour Cutlery Co., Holyoke, Mass.

13,289. May 11, 1886. Spoons, Knives, Forks, etc. Chas. A. Hamilton, Waterbury, Conn.

13,400. June 15, 1886. Table, Pocket, and other Cutlery. Gebrüder Peters, Merscheid. near Solingen, Germany.

13,498. July 13, 1886. Pocket and Table Cutlery. New York Knife Co., Walden, N. Y.

13,506. July 20, 1886. Scissors, Pocket and Table Cutlery, Razors, etc. C. B. Barker & Co., New York, N. Y.

13,738. October 19, 1886. White Metal Table Ware. Potosi Silver Co., Birmingham, England.

13,739. October 19, 1886. White Metal Table Ware. Potosi Silver Co., Birmingham, England.

14,132. March 8, 1887. Axes. Romer & Romer, Gowanda, N. Y.

14,227. April 5, 1887. Scissors, Razors, Pocket Knives, etc. C. B. Barker & Co., New York, N. Y.

14,806 and 14,807. October 11, 1887. Cutlery and Edge Tools. James Dixon & Sons, Sheffield, England.

15,145. January 31, 1888. Pocket and Table Cutlery, Scissors, Razors, etc. Schmachtenberg Bros., New York, N. Y.

15,320. March 27, 1888. Pocket and Table Cutlery. Scissors, etc. Hubbell & Randall, New York, N. Y.

15,431. May 8, 1888. Metallic Table Ware. Holmes & Edwards Silver Co., West Stratford, Conn.

15,432. May 8, 1888. Metallic Table Ware. Holmes & Edwards Silver Co., West Stratford, Conn.

15,675 and 15,676. July 10, 1888. Knives, Razors, Scissors, etc., Engravers' Plates, Dies, and Tools. John Sellers & Sons, New York, N. Y.

15,747. August 7, 1888. Razors. William H. Hambleton, Philadelphia, Pa.

15,859. September 11, 1888. Cutlery and Edge Tools. Stacey Bros., Sheffield, England.

CUTLERY AND EDGE TOOLS. 35

 15,905. September 25, 1888. Cutlery and Edge Tools. A. F. Shapleigh Hardware Co., St. Louis, Mo.

16,081. December 11, 1888. Cutlery. August Vom Dorp, New York, N. Y.

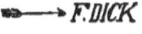 16,154. January 8, 1889. Butchers' Knives and Steels. Friedrich Dick, Esslingen, Wurtemberg, Germany.

 16,202. January 22, 1889. Cutlery. Graef & Schmidt, New York, N. Y.

 16,459. April 2, 1889. Shears. Henry Seymour Cutlery Co., Holyoke, Mass.

 16,762. July 2, 1889. Cutlery and Hardware. Brookes & Crookes, Sheffield, England.

 16,767. July 2, 1889. Cutlery. C. Lutters & Co., Solingen, Prussia, Germany.

17,542. February 18, 1890. Scissors, Knives, Axes, etc. Frederick A. Clauberg, New York, N. Y.

 17,700. March 25, 1890. Butchers' Knives and Steel Implements. Cattaraugus Cutlery Co., Little Valley, N. Y.

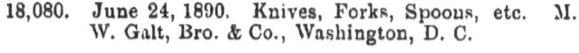 18,080. June 24, 1890. Knives, Forks, Spoons, etc. M. W. Galt, Bro. & Co., Washington, D. C.

 18,084. June 27, 1890. Axes. Kelly Axe Manufacturing Co., Louisville, Kentucky.

 18,144. July 8, 1890. Razors. Ransom & Randolph, Toledo, Ohio.

 18,795. January 6, 1891. Table Cutlery. American Cutlery Co., Chicago, Ill.

 18,906. January 27, 1891. Table Ware. Wm. H. Lyon, Newburg, N. Y.

19,222. March 24, 1891. Spoons, Forks, and Flat Ware. L. Kimball & Son, Haverhill, Mass.

 19,404. April 28, 1891. Spoons, Forks, and other Flat Ware. Albert Feldenheimer, Portland, Oregon.

 19,421. May 5, 1891. Knives, Forks, Spoons, etc. M. W. Galt, Bro. & Co., Washington, D. C.

19,480. May 12, 1891. Pocket Cutlery and Razors. Canton Cutlery Co., Canton, Ohio.

TRADE-MARKS.

19,659. June 2, 1891. Table Cutlery. Rand & Crane, Boston, Mass.

19,751. June 23, 1891. Table Ware. Wm. F. Newhall, Lynn, Mass.

19,778. June 30, 1891. Table and Flat Ware. E. A. Whitney & Co., Boston, Mass.

19,779. June 30, 1891. Table and Flat Ware. E. A. Whitney & Co., Boston, Mass.

19,781. June 30, 1891. Table Ware. E. A. Whitney & Co., Boston, Mass.

19,782. June 30, 1891. Table and Flat Ware. E. A. Whitney & Co., Boston, Mass.

19,783. June 30, 1891. Table and Flat Ware. E. A. Whitney & Co., Boston, Mass.

19,784. July 30, 1891. Table and Flat Ware. E. A. Whitney & Co., Boston, Mass.

19,785. June 30, 1891. Table and Flat Ware. E. A. Whitney & Co., Boston, Mass.

19,786. June 30, 1891. Table and Flat Ware. E. A. Whitney & Co., Boston, Mass.

19,787. June 30, 1891. Table and Flat Ware. E. A. Whitney & Co., Boston, Mass.

19,788. June 30, 1891. Table and Flat Ware. E. A. Whitney & Co., Boston, Mass.

19,789. June 30, 1891. Table and Flat Ware. E. A. Whitney & Co., Boston, Mass.

19,790. June 30, 1891. Table and Flat Ware. E. A. Whitney & Co., Boston, Mass.

19,791. June 30, 1891. Table and Flat Ware. E. A. Whitney & Co., Boston, Mass.

19,792. June 30, 1891. Table and Flat Ware. E. A. Whitney & Co., Boston, Mass.

19,800. June 30, 1891. Table and Flat Ware. E. A. Whitney & Co., Boston, Mass.

CUTLERY AND EDGE TOOLS. 37

19,959. August 4, 1891. Flat Ware. Horace G. Hudson, Amesbury, Mass.

20,220. October 13, 1891. Spoons, Knives, Forks, etc. Horace G. Hudson, Amesbury, Mass.

20,221. October 13, 1891. Spoons, Forks, Knives, etc. Horace G. Hudson, Amesbury, Mass.

20,270. October 27, 1891. Flat Ware and Jewelry. Montgomery Bros., Los Angeles, Cal.

20,273. October 27, 1891. Cutlery. Graef & Schmidt, New York, N. Y.

20,327. November 3, 1891. Flat and Table Ware. William H. Saxton, Jr., New London, Conn.

20,392. November 24, 1891. Cutlery and Edge Tools, etc. Joseph Allen, Sheffield, England.

20,393. November 24, 1891. Cutlery and Edge Tools, etc. Joseph Allen, Sheffield, England.

20,448. December 8, 1891. Knives, Forks, Spoons, etc. M. W. Galt, Bros. & Co., Washington, D. C.

20,610. January 19, 1892. Bread and Cake Knives. Christy Knife Co., Fremont, Ohio.

20,725. February 16, 1892. Knives, Forks, Scissors, etc. William Wilkinson & Sons, Sheffield, England.

20,771. February 23, 1892. Sheep Shears, Garden Shears, etc. Wm. Wilkinson & Sons, Sheffield, England.

20,953. April 5, 1892. Edge Tools, Cutlery, and Surgical Instruments, etc. Jacoby & Wester, New York, N. Y.

21,240. May 31, 1892. Knives, Forks, Scissors, etc. Firm of Gottlieb Hammesfahr, Solingen-Foche, Germany.

21,248. June 7, 1892. Shears, Scissors, and Pocket Knives. Hermann Boker & Co., New York, N. Y.

21,352. June 21, 1892. Razors. Firm of Alexander Coppel, Solingen, Germany.

21,478. July 19, 1892. Razors, Knives, etc. Hermann Boker & Co., New York, N. Y.

21,560. August 2, 1892. Knives, Scissors, and Forks. Graef & Schmidt, New York N. Y.

Metall und Eisen Zeitung.

(METAL AND IRON JOURNAL.)

A JOURNAL OF THE METAL, IRON, STOVE, HARDWARE AND HOUSE-FURNISHING TRADES.

PUBLISHED IN GERMAN AND ENGLISH,

On the 20th of Each Month.

Reaches the German Dealers, and is the only German paper in its line.

Size of printed page, 11 x 7¼ inches, divided into three advertising columns, 11 x 2¼ inches each.

ANNUAL SUBSCRIPTION, $1.00.

PUBLISHED BY

EUGENE A. SITTIG & SON,

Lake and Clark Streets,

CHICAGO.

The Bicycling World

and L. A. W. Bulletin.

 A medium which reaches all the cycling trade in the United States, and over 40,000 readers besides.

A medium unsurpassed for advertising any kind of goods.

It is issued weekly at 167 Oliver Street, Boston, by the Wheelman Company, to whom write for terms of advertising and sample copy.

The yearly subscription to this paper has been lately reduced to fifty cents, and the circulation is rapidly increasing in consequence.

 Address all communications to the Wheelman Company, 167 Oliver Street, Boston.

TRADE-MARKS

FOR

Fire-Arms, Ammunition, and Explosives.

(CLASS 24.)

Embracing guns, pistols, fireworks, explosives, &c.

Words or phrases constituting trade-marks arranged alphabetically. Number, date, and registrant follow mark.

Acme.—17,433. January 28, 1890. Shot-Guns. Hermann Boker & Co., New York, N. Y.
A. S. T. Co.–Hero.—318. June 6, 1871. Pistols. American Standard Tool Co., Newark, N. J.
Bang Up.—6859. December 3, 1878. Pistols and Guns. Graham & Haines, New York, N. Y.
Black Swan (and design).—16,263. February 12, 1889. Shot Cartridge. Chamberlin Cartridge Co., Cleveland, Ohio.
Blue Jacket.—1322. June 17, 1873. Pistols. Merwin, Hulbert & Co., New York, N. Y.
Blue Rock.—13,709. October 5, 1886. Flying or So-Called Bird Targets. Cleveland Target Co., Cleveland, Ohio.
C. C. C.—18,724. December 23, 1890. Cartridges. Creedmoor Cartridge Co., New Portage, Ohio.
C.—18,723. December 23, 1890. Cartridges. Creedmoor Cartridge Co., New Portage, Ohio.
Cassady.—11,251. June 10, 1884. Cartridges for Breech-Loading Fire-Arms. Winchester Repeating Arms Co., New Haven, Conn.
Climax (and design).—12,987. February 2, 1886. Safety Fuses. Climax Fuse Co., Avon, Conn.
Climax.—14,160. March 8, 1886. Cartridge Shells. United States Cartridge Co., Lowell, Mass.
Climax.—16,706. June 11, 1889. Revolvers, Shot-Guns, and Rifles. Hermann Boker & Co., New York, N. Y.
Club Gun.—2762. July 20, 1875. Double-Barrel Breech-Loading Guns. B. Kittredge & Co., Cincinnati, Ohio.
Continental (The).—14,477. May 31, 1877. Fire-Arms. A. Simonis, J. Janssen & Dumoulin Frères, Liége, Belgium.
Creedmoor.—2847. August 24, 1875. Rifle Powder. Paul A. Oliver, Wilkes-Barre, Pa.
Creedmoor.—18,759. December 30, 1890. Cartridges for Fire-Arms. Creedmoor Cartridge Co., New Portage, Ohio.
Crescent.—17,483. February 4, 1890. Shot-Guns and Rifles. Hermann Boker & Co., New York, N. Y.
Dead Shot.—6225. June 11, 1878. Gunpowder. American Powder Co., Boston, Mass.
Diamond.—11,006. March 11, 1884. Gunpowder. Curtis's & Harvey, London, England.

Diamond.—15,811. August 28, 1888. Gunpowder, Ammunition, and Explosives. Chas. W. Curtis, London, England.
Dynamite.—1582. December 23, 1873. Explosive Compound. Giant Powder Company and Atlantic Giant Powder Company, San Francisco, California.
Eagle.—10,628. October 16, 1883. Blasting Caps for Exploding Dynamite. Jacob H. Lau, New York, N. Y.
E. B., London.—6581. September 17, 1878. Cartridges and Percussion Caps. Eley Brothers, London, England.
E. B., Quality.—6790. November 12, 1878. Cartridges and Percussion Caps. Eley Brothers, London, England.
Eley Bros.—7233. April 22, 1879. Cartridges and Percussion Caps. Eley Brothers, London, England.
Falcon.—4302. January 23, 1877. Gunpowder. Oriental Powder Mills, Boston, Mass.
Field.—21,222. May 3, 1892. Paper Shot Shells. Union Metallic Cartridge Co., Bridgeport, Conn.
Giant.—18,062. June 24, 1890. Fire-Crackers. Edmund S. Hunt & Son, Weymouth, Mass.
Giant Powder.—1583. December 23, 1873. Explosive Compound. Giant Powder Co., and Atlantic Giant Powder Co., San Francisco. Cal.
Granite.—9907. December 26, 1882. Blasting Powder. Granite Powder Co., San Francisco, Cal.
Hercules.—1885. July 21, 1874. Powder. Joseph M. Millard, San Francisco, Cal.
Hero—A. S. T. Co.—318. June 6, 1871. Pistol. American Standard Tool Co., Newark, N. J.
International (The).—11,508 September 23, 1884. Sporting Guns. Hermann, Boker & Co., College Point, N. Y.
I X L.—12,156. April 21, 1885. Shot-Guns and Rifles. Hermann Boker & Co., New York, N. Y.
Junior.—18,478. September 30, 1890. Rifles. Merwin, Hulbert & Co., New York, N. Y.
Kangaroo.—16,391. March 19, 1889. Shot-Gun Cartridges. Chamberlin Cartridge Co., Cleveland, Ohio.
Lightning.—21,131. May 17, 1892. Paper Shot Shells. Von Lengerke & Detmold, New York, N. Y.
Mandan.—18,777. January 6, 1891. Cartridges for Fire-Arms. Creedmoor Cartridge Co., New Portage, Ohio.
Match.—8001. August 10, 1880. Shot-Guns. Winchester Repeating Arms Co., New Haven, Conn
Nitro.—21,765. September 20, 1892. Powder Measures and Rammers. Hartley & Graham Co., Bridgeport, Conn.
Nitro.—20,368. November 10, 1891. Shell Cartridges. Von Lengerke & Detmold, New York, N. Y.
Old Reliable.—3680. May 16, 1876. Guns, Pistols, etc. Sharps Rifle Co., Bridgeport, Conn.
Oriental.—4362. February 13, 1877. Gunpowder. Oriental Powder Mills, Boston, Mass.
Peters Popular.—16,191. January 15, 1889. Shot-Gun Cartridges. Peters Cartridge Co., Cincinnati, Ohio.
Quick Shot.—13,293. May 11, 1886. Gunpowder. King's Great Western Powder Co., Xenia, Ohio.
Quick Shot Cartridges.—16,193. January 15, 1889. Shot-Gun Cartridges. Peters Cartridge Co., Cincinnati, Ohio.
Rabbit.—16,390. March 19, 1889. Shot-Gun Cartridge. Chamberlin Cartridge Co., Cleveland, Ohio.
Ranger.—9824. November 21, 1882. Revolving Cylinder Pistols. Merwin, Hulbert & Co., New York, N. Y.
Red Star Blasting Supplies. 18,913. January 27, 1891. Fuses, Caps, etc. New York Powder Co., New York, N. Y.

Rendrock.—3139. November 16, 1875. Blasting Powder. J. R. Rand & Co., New York, N. Y.
Right.—3581. April 18, 1876. Pistols. Edward Palmer Boardman, Boston, Mass.
Rival.—11,540. September 30, 1884. Cartridges for Breech-Loading Fire-Arms. Winchester Repeating Arms Co., New Haven, Conn.
Rival.—17,432. January 28, 1890. Shot-Guns. Herman Boker & Co., New York, N. Y.
Semi-Hammerless.—9547. July 18, 1882. Fire-Arms. American Arms Co., Boston, Mass.
S. G.—11,249. June 10, 1884. Shells composed of Paper with a Metallic Base. Union Metallic Cartridge Co., Bridgeport, Conn.
Shotless.—16,152. January 8, 1889. Shot-Gun Cartridges. Peters Cartridge Co., Cincinnati, Ohio.
Smokeless.—21,341. June 21, 1892. Paper Shot Shells. Union Metallic Cartridge Co., Bridgeport, Conn.
Southerner.—1036. October 22, 1872. Pistols. Asa Farr, New York, New York.
Southern Sporting.—6094. May 21, 1878. Gunpowder for Sporting Purposes. Miami Powder Co., Xenia, Ohio.
Special, N. P. L.—19,058. February 17, 1891. Cartridge Shells and Wads. Creedmoor Cartridge Co., New Portage, Ohio.
Sportman's, The.—4500. March 27, 1877. Gun and Sporting Implements. Samuel Glover & Bern L. Budd, Fairfield Conn.
S. Q.—11,642. November 11, 1884. Cartridges for Breech-Loading Fire-Arms. Winchester Repeating Arms Co., New Haven, Conn.
S. W.—20,627. January 19, 1892. Fire-Arms. Smith & Wesson, Springfield, Mass.
Thunder.—8187. March 1, 1881. Explosive Compounds. Thunder Powder Co., San Francisco, Cal.
Trap.—8549. August 9, 1881. Shot-Guns. William W. Greener, Aston, England.
Trap.—18,251. July 29, 1890. Cartridge Shells and Primers. Union Metallic Cartridge Co., Bridgeport, Conn.
U.—14,134. March 8, 1887. Cartridges and Bullets. Union Metallic Cartridge Co., Bridgeport, Conn.
U. M. C.—10,967. February 26, 1884. Caps, Cartridges, Primers, etc. Union Metallic Cartridge Co., Bridgeport, Conn.
U. M. C. Club.—12,720. October 27, 1885. Cartridges. Union Metallic Cartridge Co., Bridgeport, Conn.
Union.—5915. April 23, 1878. Caps for Toy Pistols. Ernest H. Wander, New York, N. Y.
Union Metallic.—10,748. November 27, 1883. Pistol and Gun Caps, Cartridges, etc. Union Metallic Cartridge Co., Bridgeport, Conn.
Union Metallic Cartridge Co—10,733. November 20, 1883. Pistol and Gun Caps and Cartridges, etc. Union Metallic Cartridge Co., Bridgeport, Conn.
U N X L D.—10,814. December 25, 1883. Fire-Works. Unexcelled Fire-Works Co., New York, N. Y.
Vigorit.—3741. June 6, 1876. Explosive Compound. Charles De Lacy, San Francisco, Cal.
Victor.—15,281. March 13, 1888. Magneto Blasting-Machines, Electric Fuses, etc. James Macbeth, New York, N. Y.
Western.—4303. January 23, 1877. Gunpowder. Oriental Powder Mills, Boston, Mass.
X X.—11,248. June 10, 1884. Metallic and Paper Shells for Breech-Loading Fire-Arms. Union Metallic Cartridge Co., Bridgeport, Conn.
X L.—13,736. October 19, 1886. Shot-Guns. Hermann Boker & Co., New York, N. Y.
X L.—1323. June 17, 1873. Pistols. Merwin, Hulbert & Co., New York, N. Y.

TRADE=MARKS

FOR

FIRE=ARMS, AMMUNITION, &c.

(CLASS 24.)

Designs showing the essential feature claimed as Trade-Mark.

 885. July 9, 1872. Gunpowder. Laflin & Rand Powder Co., New York, N. Y.

 909. July 16, 1872. 2540. August 18, 1875. Gunpowder. Miami Powder Co., Xenia, Ohio.

 1103. January 21, 1873. 2465. May 11, 1875. Blasting Squibs and Fuses. Samuel Harries Daddow, St. Clair, Pa.

 1963. September 8, 1874. Guns, Sewing-Machine Tools, etc. Billings & Spencer Co., Hartford, Conn.

 4161. November 28, 1876. Drop Shot. Chicago Shot Tower Co., Chicago, Ill.

4162. November 28, 1876. Buck-Shot. Chicago Shot Tower Co., Chicago, Ill.

 6591. September 17, 1878. Cartridges and Percussion Caps. Eley Brothers, London, England.

 6708. October 8, 1878. Cartridges. Union Metallic Cartridge Co., Bridgeport, Conn.

 6824. November 26, 1878. Gun Implements. Charles D. Leet, Bridgeport, Conn.

 8602. August 30, 1881. Shot-Guns. William W. Greener, Aston, England.

 10,717. November 13, 1883. Pistol or Gun Caps and Cartridges, Primers, Shells, etc. Union Metallic Cartridge Co., Bridgeport, Conn.

 10,787. December 18, 1883. Sporting Powder. William Rudolph Burkhard, St. Paul, Minn.

 11,006. March 11, 1884. Gunpowder. Curtis's & Harvey, London, England.

 11,640. November 11, 1884. Paper Shells for Breech-Loading Fire-Arms. Union Metallic Cartridge Co., Bridgeport, Conn.

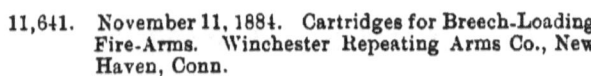

11,641. November 11, 1884. Cartridges for Breech-Loading Fire-Arms. Winchester Repeating Arms Co., New Haven, Conn.

12,270. May 26, 1885. Guns, Swords, etc. Ostheimer Bros., Philadelphia, Pa.

12,758. November 10, 1885. Caps for Blasting Purposes. Metallic Cap Manufacturing Co., Enfield, Conn.

12,779. November 17, 1885. Caps for Blasting Purposes. Metallic Cap Manufacturing Co., Enfield, Conn.

12,888. December 29, 1885. Gunpowder, Explosive Compounds, Cartridges, etc. Vereinigte Rheinisch-Westphalische Pulver-Fabriken, Cologne, Germany.

12,987. February 2, 1886. Safety-Fuse for Exploding Gunpowder, etc. Climax Fuse Co., Avon, Conn.

13,421. June 15, 1886. Sporting Goods. A. J. Reach & Co., Philadelphia, Pa.

14,159. March 8, 1886. Blasting Apparatus, High Explosives and Powders. Standard Explosives Co., New York, N. Y.

14,787. September 27, 1887. Gunpowder. Schultze Gunpowder Co., London, England.

15,727. July 31, 1888. Gunpowder. Chas. W. Curtis, London, England.

16,153. January 8, 1889. Shot-Gun Cartridges. Peters Cartridge Co., Cincinnati, Ohio.

16,190. January 15, 1889. Shot-Gun Cartridges. Peters Cartridge Co., Cincinnati, Ohio.

16,192. January 15, 1889. Shot-Gun Cartridges. Peters Cartridge Co., Cincinnati, Ohio.

16,263. February 12, 1889. Shot-Gun Cartridges. Chamberlin Cartridge Co., Cleveland, Ohio.

16,349. March 5, 1889. Explosives. Smokeless Powder Co., London, England.

16,390. March 19, 1889. Shot-Gun Cartridges. Chamberlin Cartridge Co., Cleveland, Ohio.

16,391. March 19, 1889. Shot-Gun Cartridges. Chamberlin Cartridge Co., Cleveland, Ohio.

FIRE-ARMS, ETC.   45

 17,482. February 4, 1890. Shot-guns. Hermann Boker & Co., New York, N. Y.

 17,817. April 29, 1890. Pistols, Rifles, and Shot-guns. Colt's Patent Fire-Arm Manufacturing Co., Hartford, Conn.

 18,065. June 24, 1890. Toy Torpedoes. Charles Nelson, Brooklyn, N. Y.

 18,272. August 5, 1890. Shot-gun Cartridges. Standard Cartridge Co., Chicago, Ill.

 19,223. March 24, 1891. Toy Torpedoes. Klueber Manufacturing Co., Brooklyn, N. Y.

 19,505. May 12, 1891. Gunpowder. Hazard Powder Co., New York, N. Y.

 20,107. September 8, 1891. Toy Torpedoes. Klueber Manufacturing Co., Brooklyn, N. Y.

 20,575. January 12, 1892. Shot, Shells, and Cartridge Shells. Creedmoor Cartridge Co., Barberton, Ohio.

 20,804. March 1, 1892. Fire-Arms, Ammunition, and Fishing Tackle. George Freund, Durango, Colo.

 21,252. June 7, 1892. Sporting Powder. Miami Powder Co., Xenia, Ohio.

 22,099. November 29, 1892. Explosives. Westfalisch-Anhaltische Sprengstoffact-Ges, Coswig, Germany.

COMPILED BY
WALLACE A. BARTLETT,
Patent Attorney,
WASHINGTON, D. C.

TRADE-MARKS

FOR

HOUSEHOLD ARTICLES.

(CLASS 32.)

Embracing churns, refrigerators, coolers, kitchen utensils, and the like.

Words or phrases constituting the marks arranged alphabetically.

Acme.—17,103. October 15, 1889. Basin-lifts for Wash Basins, etc. William H. Ward, Boston, Mass.
Alaska.—5826. April 2, 1878. Refrigerators. Smith Refrigerator & Manufacturing Co., Michigan City, Indiana.
Arctic.—9064. January 31, 1882. Milk Coolers. Albert R. Brown, Guilford, N. Y.
Avalanche.—9326. April 25, 1882. Flour Sifters. Brainerd T. Smith, Covington, Ky.
Blanchard Churn, The.—254. May 16, 1871. Churns. Porter Blanchard's Sons, Concord, N. H.
Centennial.—2982. September 21, 1875. Refrigerators and Ice Chests. St. Louis Wooden Gutter Manufacturing Co., St. Louis, Mo.
Challenge Iceberg.—21,810. October 4, 1892. Ice Chests, Coolers, etc. Challenge Corn Planter Co., Grand Haven, Mich.
Climax.—2469. May 11, 1875. Churn. William P. Emmert, Freeport, Illinois.
Cold Blast.—8508. July 26, 1881. Refrigerators. Andrew J. Chase, Boston, Mass.
Creamer.—7220. April 22, 1879. 9596. August 8, 1882. Vessels for Cooling milk, etc. Vermont Farm Machine Co., Bellows Falls, Vt.
Crystal.—10,149. March 27, 1883. Domestic Filters. Stoddard Lock Co., New York, N. Y.
Dover.—18,056. June 17, 1890. Household and Kitchen Articles. Dover Stamping Company, Boston, Mass.
Eclipse.—14,229. April 5, 1887. Refrigerating Machines. Frick Company, Waynesborough, Pa.
Eddy.—7102. March 11, 1879. Refrigerators. D. Eddy & Son, Boston, Mass.
Eureka.—3005. October 5, 1875. Coolers and Refrigerators. Edw. K. Howes, San Francisco, Cal.
Freezing Blast.—11,864. January 20, 1885. Refrigerators. Andrew J. Chase, Boston, Mass.
Gate City.—10,312. May 29, 1883. Water Filters. McBride & Co., Atlanta, Ga.
Glaciarium.—5392. December 4, 1877. Artificial-Ice Chambers. John Gamgee, Washington, D. C.

HOUSEHOLD ARTICLES. 47

Glacier.—20,326. November 3, 1891. Refrigerators. Chas. H. Leonard. Grand Rapids, Mich.
Globe.—9534. July 11, 1882. Refrigerators. D. Eddy & Son, Boston. Mass.
Greenland.—20,110. September 8. 1891. Refrigerators. Alaska Refrigerator Co., Michigan City, Ind.
Ice Palace (and design).—13,104. March 16, 1886. Refrigerators. Blodgett & Osgood, St. Paul, Minn.
Jack Frost.—12,321. June 16, 1885. Ice Boxes and Refrigerators. Samuel A. Suydam, New York, N. Y.
Jack Frost.—18,884. January 20, 1891. Fluid Freezers. Frederic B. Cochran. New York, N. Y.
Labrador.—16,538. April 30, 1889. Refrigerators, etc. John C. Jewett Mfg. Co., Buffalo, N. Y.
Lightning.—16,162. January 8, 1889. Ice-Cream Freezers. C. G. & W. J. Shepard, Buffalo. N. Y.
Lorillard.—12,929. January 5, 1886. Refrigerators. Geo. R. Wright, New York, N. Y.
Mountain.—16,487. April 9, 1889. Ice-Cream Freezers. White Mountain Freezer Co., Nashua, N. H.
New Era.—16,649. May 28. 1889. Water Coolers and Filters. John C. Jewett Mfg. Co., Buffalo, N. Y.
North Star.—18,534. October 14, 1890. Refrigerators and Ice Chests. Aaron N. Dukes, Peru, Ind.
Orange Co. Milk Pan.—1900. July 28, 1874. Milk Pans. Charles A. Douglas, Franklin, N. Y.
Palace.—3695. May 23, 1876. 8495. July 19, 1881. Refrigerators and Ice Chests. John C. Jewett & Sons, Buffalo, N. Y.
Perfection.—787. April 23, 1872. Refrigerating Apparatus. D. C. & G. F. Taylor, New York, N. Y.
Polar.—12,637. October 13, 1885. Refrigerators. Frederick M. Hall, Chicago, Ill.
Puritan.—15,758. August 7, 1888. Refrigerators and Water Coolers. John Wanamaker, Philadelphia, Pa.
Sitka.—20,109. September 8, 1891. Refrigerators. Alaska Refrigerator Co., Michigan City, Ind.
Union.—6451. August 6, 1878. Churns. Tiffin Union Churn Co., Tiffin, Ohio.
Uniting, Dividing, Safety.—15,396. April 24, 1888. Apparatus for Collecting and Filtering Water. Robert Cooke Sayer, Redland, Bristol, England.
Zero.—664. February 20, 1872. Refrigerators and Water Coolers. Alexander M. Lesley, New York, N. Y.

COMPILED BY
WALLACE A. BARTLETT,
Patent Attorney,
WASHINGTON, D. C.

TRADE-MARKS

FOR

HOUSEHOLD ARTICLES.

(CLASS 32.)

Designs showing the essential feature claimed as trade-mark.

 2220. February 9, 1875. 8528. August 2, 1881. Refrigerators. J. Hyde Fisher, Chicago, Ill.

 5531. January 15, 1878. Washstands. John W. Pangborn, Jersey City, N. J.

 8555. August 9, 1881. Refrigerators. Racine Refrigerator Co., Racine, Wis.

 11,581. October 21, 1884. Refrigerators. Baldwin Manufacturing Co., Burlington, Vt.

 13,104. March 16, 1886. Refrigerators. Blodgett & Osgood, St. Paul, Minn.

 16,620. May 21, 1889. Filters. Societe Anonyme du Filtre Chamberland, Systeme Pasteur, Paris, France.

 16,636. May 28, 1889. Filled Wire and wire articles. Burden Seamless Filled Wire Co., Providence, R. I.

 11,655. November 11, 1884. Refrigerators. Joel Lindsley, Burlington, Vt.

 21,117. May 17, 1892. Water Filters and Coolers. Improved Natural Stone Filter Co., Newark, N. J.

 21,274. June 7, 1892. Water Filters. C. Buhring & Co., Hamburg, Germany.

 21,301. June 14, 1892. Refrigerators and Refrigerator Cars. Joseph Francis Hanrahan, Chicago, Ill.

TRADE-MARKS

FOR

Iron, Steel, Metal Alloys, and Manufactures.

(CLASS 34.)

Comprising metal in ores, bars, rails, pigs, plates, &c., ingots, tin and terne plates, galvanized plates, &c., &c. (See also Classes 17, Cutlery; 40, Locks and Hardware; 73, Tools and Devices.)

Words or phrases constituting the marks arranged alphabetically.

A. B. M. A.—18,137. July 8, 1890. Metals for Steam Boilers. Andrew T. Douthett, Allegheny, Pa.
A. C.—19,003. February 10, 1891. Tin Plate in Sheets. Daniel Whitehouse, Abercarn, England.
A. C. C.—17,735. April 8, 1890. Refined Copper. Lewisohn Bros., New York, N. Y.
Acme.—2649. June 8, 1875. Bar Iron, Shafting, etc. Pratt & Co. Buffalo, N. Y.
Acme.—15,346. April 10, 1888. Metallic Staples and Goods United by Such Staples. Acme Staple & Machine Co., Philadelphia, Pa.
Acme.—19,570. May 26, 1891. Anti-Frictional Metal. Edward L. Hand, Philadelphia, Pa.
Acorn.—19,008. February 10, 1891. Tin Plate in Sheets. Daniel Edwards & Co., Swansea, England.
Ajax.—9035. January 17, 1882. Metals in Ingots, Castings, and Sheets. Elkins Manf. & Gas Co., Philadelphia, Pa.
Alaska.—15,504. May 22, 1888. Tin and Terne Plates. Merchant & Co., Philadelphia, Pa.
Alderly.—18,902. January 27, 1891. Tin and Terne Plates. Gummey, Spering & Co., Philadelphia, Pa.
Alpha.—18,975. February 10, 1891. Tin Plates. Webb, Shakspeare & Williams, Pontardulais, England.
A L T, J. S. T. & Son.—19,849. July 7, 1891. Sheet Iron, Tin, and Terne Plates, etc. John S. Tregoning & Son, Llanelly, England.
Aluminoid.—20,853. March 15, 1892. Aluminum and its Alloys. Geo. A. Thompkins, Cortland, N. Y.
Amman.—19,446. May 12, 1891. Tin Plates. Amman Iron Co., Swansea, England.
American Sterling.—691. March 12, 1872. Metal. American Sterling Metal Co., New York, N. Y.
Anchor.—10,181. April 10, 1883. Refined Copper Ingots, Plates, Bars, etc. Ansonia Brass & Copper Co., Ansonia, Conn.
Antifrictionate.—2930. September 14, 1875. Machinery Bearings. Lebbeus W. Lathrop, New York, N. Y.
Arcade. 1676. March 17, 1874. Malleable-Iron Castings. Arcade Malleable-Iron Co., Worcester, Mass.

Arran.—19,001. February 10, 1891. Tin Plate in Sheets. Daniel Whitehouse. Abercarn. England.
Arto.—19,015. February 10, 1891. Tin Plate in Sheets. Cwnfelin Tinplate Co., Swansea, England.
Atlas.—12,691. October 20, 1885. Bronze. Copper. Brass. etc. James R. White, Philadelphia, Pa.
A. W. (monogram).—564. November 28, 1871, and 2745. July 20, 1875. Sheet and Plate Iron. Alan Wood & Co., Philadelphia, Pa.
B. B.—14,222. March 29, 1887. Metal Alloy for Reducing Friction. Illinois Alloy Co., Chicago, Ill.
B. & C.—14,123. March 8, 1887. Ingots of Copper. Boston & Colorado Smelting Co., Boston, Mass.
Band Log Saw Mill.—14,232. April 5, 1887. Babbitt Metal. Ernst Huenefeld, Cincinnati, Ohio.
Basileus—(and design).—20,151. September 22, 1891. Metal in Ingots and Bars. Philip B. Andreae, Frankfort-on-the-Main, Germany.
Bay State.—875. July 2, 1872. And 2339. April 6, 1875. Plate Metal. Bay State Iron Co., Boston Mass.
B. B. Co.—18,843. January 13, 1891. Brass & Copper Sheets, etc. Bridgeport Brass Co., Bridgeport, Conn.
B. B. H. (and crown).—1,894. July 21, 1874. Iron and Steel. Wm. Barrows & Son, Tipton, England.
B. C. W.—16,591. May 21, 1889. Ingot Copper. Baltimore Copper Smelting and Rolling Co., Baltimore, Md.
Bedil.—19,684. June 9, 1891. Tin Plates. Cambria Tin Plate Co., Pontardulais, England.
Bessemer.—14,281. April 12, 1887. Compound to Protect Metals from Rust. John F. Nolan, San Francisco, Cal.
Best—(and design).—19,859. July 7, 1891. Tin Plates. Henry Nash & Co., Liverpool, England.
Best Charcoal Bloom, from Alan Wood & Co., XXX.—2744. July 20, 1875. Sheet or Plate Iron. Alan Wood & Co., Philadelphia, Pa.
Branch.—22,146, December 6, 1892. Tin and Terne Plates, and Sheet Metal. N. & G. Taylor Co., Philadelphia, Pa.
Brilliant.—21,876. October 18, 1892. Tin Plate, Terne Plate, etc. N. & G. Taylor Co., Philadelphia, Pa.
Bristol.—10,170. April 10, 1883. Soft-Center Steel. J. Louis Pfau, Jr., Quincy Illinois.
Bryan.—19,715. June 16, 1891. Tin Plate in Sheets. Beaufort Tin Plate Co., Morriston, England.
Burry.—19,025. February 17, 1891. Tin and Terne Plates and Tin Taggers. Old Castle Iron and Tinplate Co., Llanelly, England.
Butler.—19,089. February 24, 1891. Tin, Terne, and Black Plates. Alfred Baldwin & Co., Panteg. England.
Camaret.—19,230. March 24, 1891. Tin and Terne Plates. Joshua Williams & Co., Neath, England.
Carbon Bronze.—7074. March 4, 1879. Metals. Benjamin W. Baldwin, Pittsburg, Pennsylvania.
Castell.—19,027. February 17, 1891. Tin and Terne Plates and Tin Taggers. Old Castle Iron and Tinplate Co., Llanelly, England.
Cherry-Heat Welding Compound.—1655. March 3, 1874. Welding Compound. Hermann Schierloh, Jersey City, New Jersey.
Chetwyn (monogram.)—1118. February 4, 1873. 2423. May 4, 1875. Galvanized Sheet Iron. McCullough Iron Co., Philadelphia, Pa.
Choice XX, F. H. (and design).—6567. September 10, 1878. Cast Steel Bars, Plates. etc. Francis Hobson & Son, Sheffield, England.
Cilfrew.—18,994. February 10, 1891. Tin Plate. Richard Rosser, Son & Co., Cilfrew, England.
Codorus.—1859. June 30, 1874. Iron Ores. 1860. June 30, 1874. Wrought Iron and Steel. York County Iron Co., Codorus, Pa.

IRON, STEEL, ETC. 51

Coleman, Eagle Works.—20,628. January 19, 1892. Bolts for Carriages, Machines, etc. Upson Nut Co., Unionville, Conn.
Columbia.—20,542. January 5, 1892. Tin and Terne Plate, Sheet Metal, etc. N. & G. Taylor Co., Philadelphia, Pa.
Comet.—19,915. July 21, 1891. Tin Plates. W. Gilbertson & Co., Pontardawe, England.
Competition (and design).—21,182. May 24, 1892. Steel in Bars, Rods, etc. Francis Hobson, Seaman & Co., Sheffield, England.
Cookley K.—18.979. February 10, 1891. Tin Plates. Knight & Crowther, Cookley Works, Stafford Co., England.
Copperine.—17,662. March 11, 1890. Babbitt Metal. Alonzo W. Spooner, Port Hope, Ontario, Canada.
Coral.—19,834. June 30, 1891. Tin Plates. Edmund Boughton & Co., Pontardulais, England.
Coronet.—21,449. July 12, 1892. Steel Ingots, Slabs, Billets, etc. Albert C. Isaacs, Baltimore, Md.
Creamery.—15,208. February 21, 1888. Tin Plates. Merchant & Co., Philadelphia, Pa.
Credenda.—1377. July 22, 1873. 1482. October 7, 1873. Steel and Iron. Leng & Ogden, New York, N. Y.
Crescent.—3283. December 28, 1875. Steel Bars, Steel Plates, etc. Miller, Metcalf & Parkin, Pittsburg, Pa.
Crescent.—20,476. December 22, 1891. Phosphor Tin, Phosphor Bronze, etc. Mons R. Isaacs, Philadelphia, Pa.
Crown and Alyn.—19,248. March 31, 1891. Tin and Terne Plates. Pontypool Iron and Tinplate Co., Pontypool, England.
C. R. S.—9745. October 24, 1882. Pig Iron. R. W. Coleman's Heirs, Cornwall, Pa.
Crucible Iron.—3517. March 21, 1876. Iron. Burgess Steel and Iron Works, Portsmouth, Ohio.
Crynant.—18,995. February 10, 1891. Tin Plates in Sheets. Richard Rosser, Son & Co., Cilfrew, England.
Crystal.—19,832. June 30, 1891. Tin Plates. Edmund Boughton & Co., Pontardulais, England.
Cymro.—19,618. June 2, 1891. Tin Plates. Leach, Flower & Co., Melincrythan, England.
Cynthia.—19,831. June 30, 1891. Tin Plates. Edmund Boughton & Co., Pontardulais, England.
D ——.—19,520. May 19, 1891. Railway Rails, Fish Plates, Bolts, Spikes, etc. Plimmon H. Dudley, New York, N. Y.
Danbert.—19,005. February 19, 1891. Tin Plate in Sheets. Daniel Edwards & Co., Swansea, England.
Danube.—19,614. June 2, 1891. Tin Plates. Grovesend Tin Plate Co., Gorseinon, England.
Delta.—10,602. September 25, 1883. Alloy of Metal. Geo. Alexander Dick, Southwark, Surrey Co., England.
Deri.—19,006. February 10, 1891. Tin Plate in Sheets. Daniel Edwards & Co., Swansea, England.
Diamond.—2668. June 15, 1875. Anti-Friction Metal. George S. Hunt, Sacramento, Cal.
Diamond.—3197. December 7, 1875. Anti-Friction Metal. George S. & Benjamin E. Hunt, St. Louis, Mo.
Diamond.—5463. January 1, 1878. Rivets and Bars. Blake & Johnson, Waterbury, Conn.
Diamond.—8170. July 19, 1881. Anti-Friction Metal. Diamond Anti-Friction Metal Co., St. Louis, Mo.
Diamond.—9545. July 11, 1882. Cast Steel. Walter Spencer & Co., Rotherham, England.
Diamond, Juniata.—8984. January 3, 1882. Galvanized Sheet Iron. St. Louis Stamping Co., St. Louis, Mo.

D R D.—19,057. February 17, 1891. Tin Plate in Sheets. Port Talbot Tin-plate Co., Port Talbot, England.

Drive Your Nails Where You Please.—14,163. March 15, 1887. Corrugated Steel Box Bands. Joseph K Barton, New York, N. Y.

Duke.—19,716. June 16, 1891. Tin Plate in Sheets. Beaufort Tin Plate Co., Morriston, England.

Dyfed.—19,683. June 9, 1891. Tin Plates. Cambria Tin Plate Co., Pontardulais, England.

Earl.—22,144. December 6, 1892. Tin Plates. Asburnham Tin Plate Co., Burry Port, England.

Edgware.—15,207. February 21, 1888. Tin and Terne Plates. Merchant & Co., Philadelphia, Pa.

E. D. S.—19,298. April 7, 1891. Bessemer Steel Plates. E. Davies & Sons, Port Talbot, England.

Electricon.—21,708. August 30, 1892. Anti-Frictional Metal. Electricon Metal Co., Newark, N. J.

Elephant.—4262. January 9, 1877. Aluminous Compounds. C. N. Rogers & Co., Philadelphia, Pa.

Elgin.—19,458. May 12, 1891. Tin Plates. Phillips, Nunes & Co., Llanelly, England.

Elon.—21,507. July 19, 1892. Tin and Terne Plates, etc. C. S. Mersick & Co., New Haven, Conn.

Elyn.—18,818. January 6, 1891. Sheet Iron, Tin Plate, and Terne Plates. Mellingriffith Co., County of Glamorgan, England.

Emlyn.—18,972. February 10, 1891. Tin and Terne Plates. Birchgrove Steel Co., Swansea, England.

Eton.—19,616. June 2, 1891. Tin Plates. Grovesend Tin Plate Co., Gorseinon, England.

Fairwood.—19,920. July 21, 1891. Tin Plates. Fairwood Tin Plate Co., Gowerton, England.

Falcon.—18,991. February 10, 1891. Tin Plates. Webb, Shakspeare & Williams, Pontardulais, England.

Florence.—20,376. November 17, 1891. Tin and Terne Plates. Merchant Co., Philadelphia, Pa.

Frictionless.—20,952. April 5, 1892. Alloy. Frictionless Metal Co., Chattanooga, Tenn.

Giant.—6739. October 22, 1878. Alloy of Metal. Smith & Egge Manuf. Co., Bridgeport, Conn.

Gilbertson's Old Method.—13,631. August 31, 1886. Tin Plates, etc. W. Gilbertson & Co., near Swansea, England.

Gledwyn.—19,302. April 7, 1891. Tin, Terne, and Black Plates, etc. Gwendraeth Tin Plate Co., Kidwelly, England.

Glendale.—13,874. December 14, 1886. Tin Plates, Terne Plates, and Black Plates. W. Gilbertson & Co., near Swansea, England.

Globe.—22,238. December 27, 1892. Tin and Terne Plates and Sheet Metal. N. & G. Taylor Co., Philadelphia, Pa.

G. L. S. (monogram.)—73. November 22, 1870. 2723. July 6, 1875. Metal. Patent Metal Co., The, Philadelphia, Pa.

Glyn.—19,300. April 7, 1891. Tin and Terne Plates, etc. Gwendraeth Tin Plate Co., Kidwelly, England.

Goat.—18,999.—February 10, 1891. Tin Plate in Sheets. Port Talbot Tin-plate Co., Port Talbot, England.

Golden City (and circles).—3055. October 19, 1875. Sheet Iron. J. Wood & Bros., Philadelphia, Pa.

Golden Gate.—2101. December 1, 1874. Sheet and Plate Iron. Brittan, Holbrook & Co., San Francisco, Cal.

Gold Leaf.—21,709. August 30, 1892. Babbitt Metal. Asa W. Day, St. Louis, Mo.

Gorwydd.—19,917. July 21, 1891. Tin Plates. Fairwood Tin-Plate Co., Gowerton, England.

IRON, STEEL, ETC. 53

Granite Iron.—1829. June 9, 1874. Iron Ware. St. Louis Stamping Co., St. Louis, Mo.
Grasmere.—19,457. May 12, 1891. Tin Plates. Phillips, Nunes & Co., Llanelly, England.
Gwen.—19,299. April 7, 1891. Tin and Terne Plates, etc. Gwendraeth Tin Plate Co., Kidwelly, England.
Gwendraeth.—19,301. April 7, 1891. Tin and Terne Plates. Gwendraeth Tin Plate Co., Kidwelly, England.
Hendy.—19,833. June 30, 1891. Tin Plates. Edmund Boughton & Co., Pontardulais, England.
Howard Non-Corrosive (and design).—19,636. June 2, 1891. Metal in Bars, etc. Pope's Island Manufacturing Co., New Bedford, Mass.
Iros.—19,805. June 30, 1891. Tin Plates. Teilo Tin Plate Co., Pontardulais, England.
Iwen.—19,004. February 10, 1891. Tin Plate in Sheets. Daniel Edwards & Co., Swansea, England.
J. G.—14,955. November 22, 1887. Wrought Iron. John Groves, Denver, Colo.
Jubilee.—18,966. February 10, 1891. Tin, Terne, and Steel Plates. Alfred Baldwin & Co., Panteg, England.
Kalamein.—10,767. December 4, 1883. Sheet Metal. Republic Iron Works, Pittsburg, Pa.
K C B.—19,617. June 2, 1891. Tin Plates. Leach, Flower & Co., Melincrythan, England.
Kendal.—19,837. July 7, 1891. Tin Plates. Grovesend Tin Plate Co., Gorseinon, England.
Khartoum.—19,806. June 30, 1891. Tin Plates. Teilo Tin Plate Co., Pontardulais, England.
Killey.—19,026. February 17, 1891. Tin and Terne Plates and Tin Taggers. Old Castle Iron and Tin Plate Co., Llanelly, England.
Knoxall.—21,285. June 14, 1892. Tin and Terne Plate, etc. N. & G. Taylor Co., Philadelphia, Pa.
Kosmos.—19,447. May 12, 1891. Tin Plates. Amman Iron Co., Swansea, England.
L. E. C.—20,230. October 20, 1891. Refined Copper. Lewisohn Bros., New York, N. Y.
Lenox.—21,999. November 15, 1892. Tin and Terne Plates. Chas. A. Conklin Manufacturing Co., Atlanta, Ga.
Lily.—19,014. February 10, 1891. Tin Plates. Cwmfelin Tin-Plate Co., Cwmfelin and Swansea, England.
Lily.—20,639. January 26, 1892. Anti-Friction Metal. James Ward & Son, St. Louis, Mo.
Lincoln.—19,914. July 21, 1891. Tin Plates. W. Gilbertson & Co., Pontardawe, England.
Lion.—12,625. October 6, 1885. Galvanized Sheet Iron. John Merry, New York, N. Y.
Llan.—19,456. May 12, 1891. Tin Plate. Phillips, Nunes & Co., Llanelly, England.
Low Moor.—16,711. June 11, 1889. Metals and Manufactures Therefrom. Low Moor Co., Low Moor, York Co., England.
L. P. L., J. S. T. & Son.—19,818. July 7, 1891. Sheet Iron, Tin, Terne, and Black Plates. John S. Tregoning & Son, Llanelly, England.
L. R. B.—19,303. April 7, 1891. Tin, Terne, Zinc, and Black Plates. Redbrook Tin-Plate Co., London, England.
Luctor.—12,035. March 24, 1885. Sheet Metal for Packing, etc. D. P. Dieterich, Philadelphia, Pa.
M M M.—3534. March 28, 1876. Lead Ores and Pig Lead. Mechernicher Bergwerks-Actien-Verein, Mechernich, Prussia.
M. A.—13,976. January 11, 1887. Copper Ingots. Lewisohn Brothers, New York, N. Y.

Manor.—20,293. November 3, 1891. Tin, Terne, and Black Sheets. Stephen Thompson & Co., near Wolverhampton, England.
Mansel.—19,775. June 30, 1891. Tin and Terne Plates. Mansel Tin Plate Co., Port Talbot, England.
Maple.—22,145. December 6, 1892. Tin and Terne Plates, and Sheet Metal. N. & G. Taylor Co., Philadelphia, Pa.
Marine Flange, T. S.—6336. July 9, 1878. Boiler Iron. Joseph T. Ryerson, Chicago, Ill.
Melyn.—19,928. July 28, 1891. Tin Plates. Leach, Flower & Co., Melincrythan, Neath, England.
Mense.—18,987. February 10, 1891. Tin Plates. Webb, Shakspeare & Williams, Pontardulais, England.
Merchant's Old Method.—21,705. August 30, 1892. Tin and Terne Plates. Merchant & Co., Philadelphia, Pa.
M. F.—19,767. June 30, 1891. Tin and Terne Plates. Robert B. Byass & Co., Port Talbot, England.
Model.—22,140. December 6, 1892. Sheet Metal and Solder. E. L. Parker & Co., Baltimore, Md.
Morton.—20,651. January 26, 1892. Tin and Terne Plates. C. S. Mersick & Co., New Haven, Conn.
Moselle.—18,990. February 10, 1891. Tin Plate. Webb, Shakspeare & Williams, Pontardulais, England.
Motor.—19,773. June 30, 1891. Babbitt Metal. Ezra L. Post, New York, N. Y.
O. A.—15,511. May 22, 1888. Refined Copper. Oxford Copper Co., New York, N. Y.
O. E. W.—15,284. March 13, 1888. Pig Iron and Bituminous Coal. Ohio and Western Coal & Iron Co., Boston, Mass.
O. C.—15,617. June 19, 1888. Refined Copper. Oxford Copper Co., New York, N. Y.
O. C.—19,029. February 17, 1891. Tin and Terne Plates and Tin Taggers. Old Castle Iron and Tin-Plate Co., Llanelly, England.
Occidental.—11,857. January 13, 1885. Dental Alloy. Keller Medicine Co., Fort Wayne, Ind.
O. E. C.—15,618. June 19, 1888. Refined Copper. Oxford Copper Co., New York, N. Y.
Old Castle.—19,247. March 31, 1891. Tin and Terne Plates and Tin Taggers. Old Castle Iron and Tinplate Co., Llanelly, England.
Old Ell (and design).—19,896. July 21, 1891. Steel Castings, etc. John F. Hall, Sheffield, England.
Old Style (and design).—19,245. March 31, 1891. Tin and Terne Plates. Copper Miners Tin-Plate Co., Cwmavon, England.
Onen.—19,007. February 10, 1891. Tin Plate in Sheets. Daniel Edwards & Co., Swansea, England.
Oriole.—22,143. December 6, 1892. Sheet Metal. E. L. Parker & Co., Baltimore, Md.
P. & A.—8980. January 3, 1882. Metal Ware. Plume & Atwood Manuf. Co., Waterbury, Conn.
Palma.—20,287. November 3, 1891. Tin and Terne Plates. Merchant & Co., Philadelphia, Pa.
Palmetto.—3422. February 15, 1876. Steel and Iron. Burgess Steel & Iron Works, Portsmouth, Ohio.
Panteg.—19,175. March 17, 1891. Tin Plates, Terne Plates, etc. Alfred Baldwin & Co., Panteg, England.
Parker's.—22,141. December 6, 1892. Sheet Metal and Solder. E. L. Parker & Co., Baltimore, Md.
P. B. C.—698. March 12, 1872. Bronze Alloys. Phosphor-Bronze Co., Pittsburg, Pa.
P'Dulais.—18,989. February 10, 1891. Tin Plates. Webb, Shakspeare & Williams, Pontardulais, England.

Peerless.—14,963. November 22, 1887. White Metal. Thomas E. Purchase, Newark, N. J.
Pen.—18,817. January 6, 1891. Sheet Iron, Tin Plates, and Terne Plates. Mellingriffith Co., County of Glamorgan, England.
Penalt.—19,304. April 7, 1891. Tin, Terne, Zinc, and Black Plates. Redbrook Tin-Plate Co., London, England.
Penmar.—22,142. December 6, 1892. Sheet Metal and Solder. E. L. Parker & Co., Baltimore, Md.
Penn Old Method.—18,864. January 20, 1891. Tin and Terne Plates. Gummey, Spering & Co., Philadelphia, Pa.
Perfection.—16,793. July 9, 1889. Bronze, Copper, and Babbitt Ingots. Eastwood Wire Manufacturing Co., Belleville, N. J.
Perth.—19,661. June 2, 1891. Tin Plates. Phillips, Nunes & Co., Llanelly, England.
Phelps.—20,956. April 12, 1892. Tin and other Metal Plates. Phelps, Dodge & Co., New York, N. Y.
Phœnix (and design).—12,657. October 13, 1885. Galvanized Iron. John Merry, New York, N. Y.
Phosphor-Babbitt.—5688. February 26, 1878. Anti-Friction Metal. George K. Tryon, Son & Co., Philadelphia, Pa.
Phosphor Bronze.—2777. July 20, 1875. Bronze Alloy and Articles Made Therefrom. Charles J. A. Dick, Pittsburg, Pa.
Phosphor Bronze.—15,225. February 21, 1888. Metallic Alloys. Phosphor Bronze Smelting Co., Philadelphia, Pa.
Polar.—15,289. March 20, 1888. Babbitt Metal. James Bostwick, Detroit, Mich.
Pont-ar-tawe.—20,201. October 6, 1891. Tin Plates and Roofing Tin. W. Gilberston & Co., Pontardawe, England.
Port Henry (and design of pig).—874. July 2, 1872. Pig Iron. Bay State Iron Co., Boston, Mass.
Port Henry.—2338. April 6, 1875. Pig Iron. Bay State Iron Co., Boston, Mass.
R. B. Siberian Iron.—595. December 19, 1871. Sheet Iron. Rogers & Burchfield, Pittsburg, Pa.
Redbrook.—19,305. April 7, 1891. Tin, Terne, Zinc, and Black Plates. Redbrook Tin-Plate Co., London, England.
R. G.—18,794. January 6, 1891. Sheet Iron, Tin Plates, and Terne Plates. Mellingriffith Co., Mellingriffith Works, Glamorgan Co., England.
Rhine.—18,988. February 10, 1891. Tin Plates. Webb, Shakspeare & Williams, Pontardulais, England.
R. J. Roberts Razor Steel.—368. July 4, 1871. Razor Steel. Robert J. Roberts, New York, N. Y.
R. Mushet's Special.—10,460. July 24, 1883. Various Kinds of Steel. Samuel Osborn & Co., Sheffield, England.
R. Mushet's Titanic.—13,469. July 6, 1886. Steel. Samuel Osborn & Co., Sheffield, England.
Royal.—21,877. October 18, 1892. Tin and Terne Plates and Sheet Metal. N. & G. Taylor Co., Philadelphia, Pa.
Rydal.—19,455. May 12, 1891. Tin Plates. Phillips, Nunes & Co., Llanelly, England.
Sandvik.—16,720. June 11, 1889. Articles of Iron and Steel. Sandvikens Jernverks Aktie Bolag, Sandviken, Sweden.
Sardis.—19,801. June 30, 1891. Tin Plates. Teilo Tin-Plate Co., Pontardulais, England.
Seine.—19,193. March 17, 1891. Tin Plates. Webb, Shakspeare & Williams, Pontardulais, England.
S. F. B., T. S.—6401. July 23, 1878. Boiler Iron. Charles L. Bailey & Co., Harrisburg, Pa.
Silveroid. 6535. September 3, 1878. Metallic Alloy. Brown & Brothers, Waterbury, Conn.

Silvertin.—11,965. February 24, 1885. Alloys for Coating Metals. E. C. Converse, Pittsburg, Pa.
Sligo.—699. March 12, 1872. Bearings of Bronze Alloy for Axles. Phosphor-Bronze Co., Pittsburg, Pa.
Sligo.—3732. May 30, 1876. Wrought Iron. Phillips, Nimick & Co., Pittsburg, Pa.
Slippery Jack.—17,815. April 29, 1890. Anti-Friction Metals. George F. Bard, Norwich, Conn.
Spa.—20,288. November 3, 1891. Tin and Terne Plate. Merchant & Co., Philadelphia, Pa.
S. S.—3734. May 30, 1876. Wrought Iron. Phillips, Nimick & Co., Pittsburg, Pa.
Star.—10,180. April 10, 1883. Refined Copper Ingots, Plates, Cakes, etc. Ansonia Brass and Copper Co., Ansonia, Conn.
Star Cast Steel.—487. October 17, 1871. Cast Steel. Singer, Nimick & Co., Pittsburg, Pa.
Sterline.—7510. July 15, 1879. Compound for Refining Steel. R. A. Goodchild, New York, N. Y.
Stour.—18,967. February 10, 1891. Tin, Terne, and Steel Plates. E. P. & W. Baldwin, Wilden, England.
Stradey.—19,028. February 17, 1891. Tin and Terne Plates, Tin Taggers. Old Castle Iron and Tinplate Co., Llanelly, England.
Strick.—19,448. May 12, 1891. Tin Plates. Amman Iron Co., Swansea, England.
Syenite Iron.—10,322. May 29, 1883. Enamelled Sheet-metal Utensils. Lalance & Grosjean Manufacturing Co., New York, N. Y.
Taylor's Arctic.—13,026. February 9, 1886. Metal for Boxes and Journal Bearings. Richard Taylor, Detroit, Mich.
Taylor, The.—20,563. January 5, 1892. Roofing Tin. N. & G. Taylor Co., Philadelphia, Pa.
Teru Teru.—14,981. November 29, 1887. Bar, Plate, and other Iron. Thomas Drysdale & Co., New York, N. Y.
Thowless.—20,329. November 3, 1891. Valuable Metals. Thowless Aluminum Syndicate, Newark, N. J.
Tiber.—19,615. June 2, 1891. Tin Plate. Grovesend Tinplate Co., Gorseinon, England.
Titanic.—13,470. July 6, 1886. Steel. Samuel Osborn & Co., Sheffield, England.
Trefula, J. S. T. & Son.—19,850. July 7, 1891. Sheet Iron, Tin and Terne Plates, etc. John S. Tregoning & Son, Llanelly, England.
Tregoning, J. S. T. & Son.—19,845. July 7, 1891. Sheet Iron, Tin Plates, etc. John S. Tregoning & Son, Llanelly, England.
Trevarth, J. S. T. & Son.—19,847. July 7, 1891. Sheet Iron, Tin, Terne and Black Plates. John S. Tregoning & Son, Llanelly, England.
Triple-Planished.—9514. July 4, 1882. Tinned Sheet Copper and Brass. Andrew O'Neill, New Haven, Conn.
Tynant.—18,819. January 6, 1891. Sheet Iron, Tin Plates and Terne Plates. Mellingriffith Co., County of Glamorgan, England.
Tyrone.—3733. May 30, 1876. Wrought Iron. Phillips, Nimick & Co., Pittsburg, Pa.
U. S. (and design).—20,495. December 22, 1891. Tin and Terne Plate. U. S. Iron & Tin Plate Manufacturing Co., McKeesport, Pa.
U. S. N.—2005. October 6, 1874. Iron. Burgess Steel & Iron Works, Portsmouth, Ohio.
Victor.—10,264. May 15, 1883. Alloys of Copper in Sheets, Tubing, etc. Brown & Brothers, Waterbury, Conn.
Vivi-Flux.—12,608. September 29, 1885. Flux for Metals. B. F. Ruth & Co., Reading, Pa.
Vulcan.—20,289. November 3, 1891. Tin and Terne Plates. C. S. Mersick & Co., New Haven, Conn.

W.—13,767. October 26, 1886. Steel and Iron Tubes. Weldless Steel Tube Co., Birmingham, England.

Wer.—18,834. January 13, 1891. Tin and Terne Plates. Robert Crooks & Co., Liverpool, England.

Wilden.—19,096. February 24, 1891. Sheet Iron and Steel, etc. E. P. & W. Baldwin, Wilden, England.

W. L.—18,833. January 13, 1891. Tin and Terne Plates. Robert Crooks & Co., Liverpool, England.

Worcester.—20,571. January 5, 1892. Tin and Terne Plates, etc. Llansamlet Tin Plate Co., Morristown, England.

XXX.—505. October 24, 1871. Sheet or Plate Iron. Alan Wood & Co., Philadelphia, Pa.

XXX Best Charcoal Bloom.—2744. July 30, 1875. Iron. Alan Wood & Co., Philadelphia, Pa.

Yaddo.—19,451. May 12, 1891. Tin and Terne Plates. T. B. Coddington & Co., New York, N. Y.

Z.—11,201. May 27, 1884. Alloy Having the Appearance of Nickel. John B. Fitch, New Haven, Conn.

Zenith.—11,202. May 27, 1884. Alloy Having the Appearance of Nickel. John B. Fitch, New Haven, Conn.

Zero.—14,031. February 1, 1887. Anti-Friction Metal. Ezra L. Post, New York, N. Y.

COMPILED BY
WALLACE A. BARTLETT,
Patent Attorney,
WASHINGTON, D. C.

TRADE-MARKS
FOR
Iron, Steel, Metal Alloys, and Manufactures.
(CLASS 34.)

Designs showing essential feature claimed as trade-mark.

73. November 22, 1870. 2723. July 6, 1875. Metal. Patent Metal Co., The, Philadelphia, Pa.

564. November 28, 1871. Sheet and Plate Iron. Wood, Alan & Co., Philadelphia, Pa.

573. December 12, 1871. Cast Steel and Castings. Wm. Butcher & Co., Lewistown, Pa.

619. January 2, 1872. Wrought Iron Goods. J. Rogers, Black Brook, N. Y., and Au Sable Forks, N. Y.

874. July 2, 1872. Pig Iron. Bay State Iron Co., Boston, Mass.

1117. February 4, 1873. 2533. May 18, 1875. Galvanized Sheet Iron. McCullough Iron Co., Philadelphia, Pa.

1118. February 4, 1873. 2423. May 4, 1875. Galvanized and Sheet Iron. McCullough Iron Co., Philadelphia, Pa.

1274. May 20, 1873. Black and Galvanized Sheet Iron. Marshall Bros. & Co., Philadelphia, Pa.

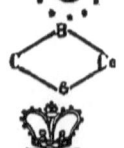
1380. July 22, 1873. 2803. August 3, 1875. Steel and Iron Ware. Sweet, Barnes & Co., Syracuse, N. Y.

1894. July 21, 1874. 7198. April 15, 1879. 9308. April 25, 1882. Iron and Steel. William Barrows & Sons, Tipton, England.

2421. May 4, 1875. Lead. Forest River Lead Co., Salem, Mass.

2838. August 24, 1874. Wrought Iron Pipe and Tools. Evans, Clow, Dalzell & Co., Pittsburg, Pa.

IRON, STEEL, ETC. 59

2888. August 31, 1875. Tin Plate. N. & G. Taylor Co., Philadelphia, Pa.

2889. August 31, 1875. Tin Plate. N. &. G. Taylor Co., Philadelphia, Pa.

2890. August 31, 1875. Tin Plate. N. &. G. Taylor Co., Philadelphia, Pa.

3002. October 5, 1875. Metallic Alloys, etc. Charles J. A. Dick, Philadelphia, Pa. 15,068. December 27, 1887. Metallic Alloys and Articles, Phosphor-Bronze Smelting Co., Philadelphia, Pa.

3055. October 19, 1875. Sheet Iron. J. Wood & Brothers, Philadelphia, Pa.

3198. December 7, 1875. Anti-Friction Metal. George S. Hunt & Benjamin E. Hunt, St. Louis, Mo.

3284. December 28, 1875. Steel-Bar, Steel-Plate, etc. Miller, Metcalf & Parkin, Pittsburg, Pa.

4072. October 24, 1876. Leaded Sheet-Iron. Marshall Brothers & Co., Philadelphia, Pa.

4144. November 21, 1876. Steel and Iron. Fried Krupp, Essen, Germany.

6223. June 11, 1878. Anti-Friction Metal. Theodore Thurber, Auburn, N. Y.

6393. July 23, 1878. Clay for Crucibles. Emil Theile, Stapleton, N. Y.

6567. September 10, 1878. 8550. August 9, 1881. Cast-Steel Bars, Plates, Rods, and Wire. Francis Hobson & Son, Sheffield, England.

8950. December 27, 1881. Certain Metal Goods. Ansonia Brass and Copper Co., Ansonia, Conn.

9540. July 11, 1882. Metals of various Kinds. P. R. Jackson & Co., Manchester, England.

9545. July 11, 1882. Cast Steel. Walter Spencer & Co., Rotherham, England.

9587. August 1, 1882. Steel. Walter Spencer & Co., Rotherham, England.

10,180. April 10, 1883. Refined Copper Ingots, Plates, Cakes, etc. Ansonia Brass and Copper Co., Ansonia, Conn.

TRADE-MARKS.

10,181. April 10, 1883. Refined Copper Ingots, Plates, Bars, etc. Ansonia Brass & Copper Co., Ansonia, Conn.

10,235. May 1, 1883. Drop Forgings and Articles Made Therefrom. Williams & Diamond, Flushing, N. Y.

10,614. October 2, 1883. Pigs of Babbit Metal. Granular Metal Co., Boston, Mass.

10,790. December 18, 1883. Sheet Iron and Steel. Republic Iron Works, Pittsburg, Pa.

10,815. December 25, 1883. Articles of Tinware. Geo. D. Winchell Manufacturing Co., Cincinnati, Ohio.

10,993. March 11, 1884. Embossed Metal Articles. A. Masse & Anglade, Paris, France.

11,037. March 25, 1884. Steel and Implements made therefrom. Wm. K. & H. K. Peace, Sheffield, England.

11,154. May 6, 1884. Steel Bars and Plates. Detroit Steel and Spring Works, Detroit, Mich.

11,181. May 13, 1884. Wire Rods, Flat Steel Strips, Hoop Iron, etc. E. Boecking & Co., Mülheim-on-the-Rhine, Germany.

11,801. December 16, 1884. Alloy Resembling Silver. Silver Metal Manufacturing Co., Cleveland, Ohio.

11,905. February 3, 1885. Metal Forgings. J. H. Williams & Co., Flushing, N. Y.

11,917. February 10, 1885. Bronze Powders, Liquid, and Metal Leaves. J. Marsching & Co., New York, N. Y.

12,625. October 6, 1885. Galvanized Sheet Iron. John Merry, New York, N. Y.

12,657. October 13, 1885. Galvanized Sheet Iron. John Merry, New York, N. Y.

12,685. October 20, 1885. Manufactures of Iron and Steel. Seebohm & Dieckstahl, Sheffield, England.

13,337. May 25, 1886. Phosphor-Bronze in Ingots and Wire and Castings. Phosphor-Bronze Co., London, England.

13,388. June 15, 1886. Metalic Alloys and Metals used for Anti-Friction Purposes. Edmond A. C. Du Plaine, Chicago, Ill.

IRON, STEEL, ETC. 61

15,226. February 21, 1888. Alloys and Articles made therefrom. Phosphor-Bronze Smelting Co., Philadelphia, Pa.

15,339. May 1, 1888. Anti-Friction Metal. American Improved Anti-Friction Metal Co., Mobile, Ala.

16,719. June 11, 1889. Manufactures of Iron and Steel. Sandvikens Jernverks Aktie Bolag, Sandviken, Sweden.

16,745. June 25, 1889. Galvanized Iron. Morewood & Co.'s Successors, Birmingham, England.

17,171. November 5, 1889. Steel in Ingots, Billets and Bars. Societe Anonyme des Acieries d'Angleur, Liege, Belgium.

17,702. March 25, 1890. Tinware. Clifton Springs Manufacturing Co., Clifton Springs, N. Y.

18,659. December 2, 1890. Tempered Steel Manufactures. J. B. Armstrong Manufacturing Co., Flint, Mich.

18,816. January 6, 1891. Sheet Iron, Tin Plates and Terne Plates. Mellingriffith Co., County of Glamorgan, England.

18,824. January 13, 1891. Manganese Bronze. B. H. Cramp & Co., Philadelphia, Pa.

18,981. February 10, 1891. Tin Plates. Phillips, Nunes & Co., Dafen, Llanelly, England.

18,986. February 10, 1891. Tin and Terne Plates. Birchgrove Steel Co., Swansea, England.

18,992. February 10, 1891. Tin Plates in Sheets. Daniel Edwards & Co., Swansea, England.

19,000. February 10, 1891. Tin Plate in Sheets. Port Talbot Tin-Plate Co., Port Talbot, England.

19,002. February, 10, 1891. Tin Plate in Sheets. Daniel Whitehouse, Abercarn, England.

19,049. February 17, 1891. Iron and Steel and Manufactures thereof. Carpenter Steel Co., New York, N.Y.

19,245. March 31, 1891. Tin and Terne Plates. Copper Miners Tin-Plate Co., Caernarvon, England.

19,246. March 31, 1891. Tin Plates. Copper Miners Tin-Plate Co., Cwmavon, England.

19,248. March 31, 1891. Tin Plates and Terne Plates. Pontypool Iron and Tin-Plate Co., Pontypool, Eng.

19,249. March 31, 1891. Tin and Terne Plates. Pontypool Iron and Tin-Plate Co., Pontypool, England.

19,250. March 31, 1891. Tin Plates. Pontypool Iron and Tin-Plate Co., Pontypool, England.

TRADE-MARKS.

19,251. March 31, 1891. Tin Plates. Pontypool Iron & Tinplate Co., Pontypool, England.

19,450. May 12, 1891. Tin Plates. F. B. Coddington & Co., New York, N. Y.

19,636. June 2, 1891. Metal in Bars and Harness Trimmings. Pope's Island Manufacturing Corporation, New Bedford, Mass.

19,846. July 7, 1891. Sheet Iron, Tin, Terne, and Black Plates. John S. Tregoning & Son, Llanelly, England.

19,859. July 7, 1891. Tin Plates. Henry Nash & Co., Liverpool, England.

19,896. July 21, 1891. Steel Castings, etc. John F. Hall, Sheffield, England.

19,909. July 21, 1891. Tin and Terne Plates. Jenkin D. Thomas & Co., Gstalyford, England.

20,151. September 22, 1891. New Metal in Ingots and Bars. Philip B. Andreae, Frankfort-on-the-Main, Germany.

20,284. November 3, 1891. Manufactures of Iron and Steel. Diamond State Iron Co., Wilmington, Del.

20,495. December 22, 1891. Tin and Terne Plate. U. S. Iron & Tin Plate Manufacturing Co., McKeesport, Pa.

20,564. January 5, 1892. Tin and Terne Plate, Sheet Metal, etc. N. & G. Taylor Co., Philadelphia, Pa.

20,701. February 9, 1892. Terne Plates. Morriston Tin-Plate Co., Morriston, England.

20,877. March 22, 1892. Tin and Terne Plates. James B. Scott & Co., Pittsburg, Pa.

20,929. April 5, 1892. Aluminium Solder. Chas. Gerard & Joseph S. Letord, Kansas City, Mo.

21,059. April 26, 1892. Malleable Castings. Eberhard Manufacturing Co., Cleveland, Ohio.

21,182. May 24, 1892. Steel in Bars, Rods, and Sheets, etc. Francis Hobson, Seaman & Co., Sheffield, England.

21,313. June 21, 1892. Iron and Steel. Dunham, Carrigan & Hayden Co., San Francisco, Cal.

21,374. June 28, 1892. Tin and Terne Plates. C. S. Mersick & Co., New Haven, Conn.

21,382. June 28, 1892. Tin and Terne Plates. American Tin Plate Machine & Manufacturing Co., Philadelphia, Pa.

21,656. August 23, 1892. Tin and Roofing Plates. Cleveland Tin-Plate Co., Cleveland, Ohio.

EXPONENT OF THE STOVE, HARDWARE, AND HOUSE-FURNISHING GOODS TRADES.

To Manufacturers of Stove, Hardware, and House-Furnishing Goods:

Unproved assertions of bombastic advertising solicitors avail not. If any journal has as many paid subscribers as the *American Artisan*, why not furnish the proofs? Our books are open for inspection, and prove that the *American Artisan* has a larger *bona-fide* circulation among paid subscribers than any other journal representing similar trade interests.

CIRCULATION GUARANTEED OR NO PAY.

DANIEL STERN, Pres., AMERICAN ARTISAN PRESS,
69 DEARBORN ST. CHICAGO, ILL.

WALLACE A. BARTLETT........

Solicitor of Patents,

WASHINGTON, D. C.

TRANSACTS ALL BUSINESS.........
..........RELATING TO

Patents,
    Designs,
        Trade-Marks,
            Copyrights,
                Caveats, &c.

IN THE......

United States or
            ——————— Foreign Offices.

Ten Years' experience as principal examiner in the Patent Office.
.........Ten Years' practice before the Office and Courts..........

TERMS REASONABLE FOR CAREFUL SERVICE.

ADDRESS:

WALLACE A. BARTLETT,
WASHINGTON, D. C.

TRADE-MARKS

FOR

JEWELRY AND PLATED WARE.

(CLASS 35.)

Embracing articles of personal adornment, plate and plated ware, &c. (See also Class 17, Cutlery, &c., and Class 70, Time-Keeping).

Words or phrases constituting the mark arranged alphabetically.

Agaloid.—12,951. January 19, 1886. Imitation of Agate. American Enamel Co., Providence, R. I.

A. S. Co.—4433. March 6, 1877. Silver and Plated Ware. Adams & Shaw Co., New York, N. Y.

Australian Pebbles.—16,139. January 1, 1889. Artificial Diamonds. Edward E. Kipling, New York, N. Y.

B.—18,562. October 28, 1890. Finger Rings. J. B. Bowden & Co., New York, N. Y.

Bi-centennial.—13,163. April 6, 1886. Medals, Seals, Stamps, etc. Anthony M. Michael, Albany, N. Y.

Big Bonanza, B B.—11,755. December 9, 1884. Sleeve and Collar Buttons and Studs. Howard & Son, Providence, R. I.

Birmah Brilliant.—19,924. July 28, 1891. Artificial Diamonds. Geo. H. Cahoone & Co., Providence, R. I.

Black Hill.—7266. May 6, 1879. Artificial Jewels. Franklin Jewelry Co., Philadelphia, Pa.

Borneo (and design).—21,759. September 20, 1892. Artificial Gems. F. H. Sadler & Co., Attleborough, Mass.

Boston Tea Party.—20,515. December 29, 1891. Gold, Silver, and Plated Spoons. N. G. Wood & Sons, Boston, Mass.

Brazilian Roses.—12,491. August 11, 1885. Artificial Precious Stones. E. E. & A. W. Kipling, New York, N. Y.

Byzanto Jewello Decor. 12,978. February 2, 1886. Imitation Jewels. Rufus H. Bragdon, New York, N. Y.

Caspian Gem, The.—19,876. July 14, 1891. Artificial Gems. Geo. H. Cahoone & Co., Providence, R. I.

Centennial.—1271. May 20, 1873. Medal. Hartell & Letchworth, Philadelphia, Pa.

Centennial.—2937. September 14, 1875. Jewelry. Freeman S. Allen, Washington, D. C.

Centennial. -3766. June 13, 1876. Badges. William Scully and Pierre A. Dufour, St. Paul, Minn.

Champion.—10,384. July 3, 1883. Ornamental Chains. Davidson Bros., New York, N. Y.

Colon. 21,972. November 15, 1892. Finger Rings. Frank N. Osborne, New York, N. Y.

Columbus.—19,769. June 30, 1891. Gold, Silver, and Plated Articles. M. W. Galt, Bro. & Co., Washington, D. C.
C. P. F.—S. B. M. C.—6423. July 30, 1878. Jewelry and Silver and Plated Ware. John H. Johnston, New York, N. Y.
Crown.—15,658. July 3, 1888. Alloy for Jewelry. Joseph Muhr, Philadelphia, Pa.
Crown Prince.—15,211. February 21, 1888. Plated Ware. G. I. Mix & Co., Yalesville, Ct.
Cryptochylon--Pure Silver Lined.—1527. November 18, 1873. Ice Pitchers. Adams, Hallock & Co., Brooklyn, N. Y.
Cypress Gem, The.—20,473. December 22, 1891. Artificial Diamond Gems. Allen & Jonassohn, Providence, R. I.
Eagle.—10,111. March 20, 1883. Sleeve Buttons. Frederick I. Marcy, Providence, R. I.
Eurema.—10,981. February 26, 1884. Gold Leaf. Stephen Hickson, New York, N. Y.
Gilt Edge.—15,834. September 4, 1888. Jewelry. Henry C. Luther, Providence, R. I.
Globe (and design).—1184. March 25, 1873. Gold Foil. Sam'l S. White, Philadelphia, Pa.
Globe.—19,594. May 26, 1891. Chain, Bracelets, Lockets, etc. W. & S. Blackinton, Attleborough, Mass.
Golden Rule Bazaar.—18,719. December 23, 1890. Plated Ware. E. Lobe & Co., Seattle, Washington.
Gymkhana.—19,011. February 10, 1891. Vest Chains. D. C. Percival & Co., Boston, Mass.
H. & E.—12,844. December 15, 1885. Imitation Silver Ware. Holmes & Edwards Silver Co., Bridgeport, Conn.
Holmes.—19,436. May 5, 1891. Solid and Plated Spoons, Forks, etc. Rand & Crane, Boston, Mass.
Imperial Casket.—5567. February, 19, 1878. Jewelry. Steinau Jewelry Co., Cincinnati, Ohio.
Lefevre.—7811. February 3, 1880. Immitation Diamond Jewelry. Abraham Steinau, Jr., Cincinnati, Ohio.
Losaic.—2376. April 13, 1875. Jewelry. Thayer Manufacturing Jewelry Co., Astoria, N. Y.
Napoline.—4107. November 7, 1876. Jewelry. Joslin, Palmer & Williams, Leominster, Mass.
N. F. Nickel Silver.—13,820. November 23, 1886. Plated Knives, Forks, and Spoons. Oneida Community, Niagara Falls, N. Y.
Nonpareil.—21,870. October 18, 1892. Watch and Neck Chains. Oscar M. Draper, North Attleborough, Mass.
Old Reliable.—19,539. May 19, 1891. Chains, Bracelets, Lockets, etc. W. & S. Blackinton. Attleborough, Mass.
Paola.—19,284. April 7, 1891. Imitation Diamonds. D. C. Percival & Co., Boston, Mass.
Princess.—14,172. March 15, 1887. Finger Rings. Sinnock & Sherrill, New York, N. Y.
Princess.—19,870. July 14, 1891. Ear Rings, Ear Knobs, and Ear Wires. Joseph Bulova, New York, N. Y.
P. S. Co.—16,866. July 23, 1889. Pins, Bracelets, Chains, etc. Plainville Stock Co., Plainville, Mass.
Queen.—19,871. July 14, 1891. Jewelry. Joseph Bulova, New York, New York.
Real—S. A. H.—730. April 2, 1872. Jewelry. Joslin, Palmer & Williams, Leominster, Mass.
Reed & Barton.—4254. January 2, 1877. 13,021. February 9, 1886. Metal Electroplated, and Silverware. Reed & Barton, Taunton, Mass.
Rogers & Brother.—4632. May 15, 1877. Plated Ware. Rogers & Brother, Waterbury, Conn.

JEWELRY AND PLATED WARE.

Royal.—19,406. April 28, 1891. Solid, Plated, and Composition Ware. Ledig & Way, Philadelphia, Pa.
Seamless—Wm. H. R. & Co.—15,579. June 5, 1888. Filled Gold Chains. Wm. H. Robinson &. Co., Providence, R. I.
Silver Ore.—13,333. May 25, 1886. Plated Silver, and other Table Ware. Holmes & Edwards Silver Co., Bridgeport, Conn.
Silver Ring. O.—3547. April 4, 1876. Plated Ware. Meriden Britannia Co., Meriden, Ct.
Simplicity.—21,971. November 15, 1892. Collar Buttons. F. D. Williams, Providence, R. I.
Stonine.—10,959. February 26, 1884. A Kind of Jewelry. Oren C. Devereaux, Providence, R. I.
Tiffany & Co.—4638. May 15, 1877. Bronzes. Tiffany & Company, New York, N. Y.
Tiffany & Co.—4639. May 15, 1877. Silver and Plated Ware. Tiffany & Co., New York, N. Y.
Victoria Jet.—415. August 1, 1871. Jewelry. John P. Turner, Birmingham, England.
Violane Du Cap.—11,734. December 2, 1884. Precious Stones. Edward E. Kipling, Paris, France.
Voltaic.—19,200. March 24, 1891. Imitation Diamond Jewelry. Bernard E. Arons, Pittsburg, Pa.
⋚.—17,530. February 11, 1890. Solid Gold Rings. J. R. Wood & Sons, New York, N. Y.
W. & S. B.—19,538. May 19, 1891. Chains, Bracelets, Lockets, etc. W. & S. Blackinton, Attleborough, Mass.
Witch.—18,838. January 13, 1891. Silver Ware. Daniel Low, Salem, Mass.
W. L. & Co.—22,101. December 6, 1892. Finger Rings. Wm. Loeb & Co., Providence, R. I.
Wm. Rogers (and design).—7497. July 8, 1879. Electroplated Table Ware. William Rogers, Hartford, Conn.
World.—11,092. April 15, 1884. Sleeve and Collar Buttons, and Studs. Howard & Son, Providence, R. I.
World's Fair Souvenir, Chicago 1893.—18,479. September 30, 1890. Jewelry, etc. E. A. Bliss & Co., New York, N. Y.
W. P. H.—13,679. September 21, 1886. Finger Rings. Wheeler, Parsons & Hayes, New York, N. Y.
XIV.—13,334. May 25, 1886. Silver Ware or Imitation Silver. Holmes & Edwards Silver Co., Bridgeport, Conn.
Ysabel.—21,973. November 15, 1892. Finger Rings. Frank N. Osborne, New York, N. Y.

COMPILED BY

WALLACE A. BARTLETT,
Patent Attorney,
WASHINGTON, D. C.

TRADE-MARKS
FOR
JEWELRY AND PLATED WARE.
(CLASS 35.)

Designs showing essential feature claimed as Trade-Mark.

 41. November 1, 1870. Silver and Plated Ware. Lippiatt Silver Plate and Engraving Co., New York, N. Y.

 237. May 21, 1871. Jewelry. Wm. M. Elias & Bro., New York, N. Y.

 732. April 2, 1872. Badges, Medals, etc. Horace Taplin, Lowell, Mass.

 733. April 2. 1872. Badges, Medals, etc. Horace Taplin, Lowell, Mass.

 796. April 30, 1872. Silver Ware. Rogers & Brother, Waterbury, Conn.

 1062. November 19, 1872. Watch Keys. Lizzie F. English, Springfield, Mass.

 1110. January 20, 1873. Spoons, Forks, etc. Hall, Elton & Co., Wallingford, Conn.

 1184. March 25, 1873. Gold Foil. Samuel S. White, Philadelphia, Pa.

 1342. July 1, 1873. Forks, Spoons, etc. C. B. Rogers & Bros. Meriden, Ct.

 1450. September 9, 1873. 8622. September 6, 1881. Gold Rings. Dueber Watch Case Manufacturing Co., Cincinnati, O.

 1732. April 21, 1874. Shirt Studs and Sleeve Buttons. Charles L. Potter, Providence, R. I.

 2210. February 2, 1875. Silver-Plated Goods. James W. Tufts, Medford, Mass.

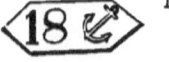 2708. July 6, 1875. Medal. John H. Hobart, Jr., Catawissa, Pa.

JEWELRY AND PLATED WARE. 69

 2950. September 21, 1875. Brass, German Silver, and Silver-Plated Goods. Brown & Brothers. Waterbury, Conn.

 3089. October 26, 1875. Finger Rings. H. Muhr's Sons, Philadelphia, Pa.

 3219. December 7, 1875. Metal and Plated Ware. Frank W. Rogers, Hartford, Conn.

 3469. February 29, 1876. Medals and Jewelry. Surville J. Delan, New York, N. Y.

 3547. April 4, 1876. Plated Ware. Meriden Britannia Co., Meriden, Conn.

 4246. December 26, 1876. Metal Badges. Joseph K. Davison, Philadelphia, Pa.

 4305. January 23, 1877. 13,022. February 9, 1886. Plated Ware. Reed & Barton, Taunton, Mass.

 5242. October 16, 1877. Jewelry. Franklin Jewelry Co., Philadelphia, Pa.

 5660. February 19, 1878. Wire and Coral Jewelry. William C. Greene & Co., New York, N. Y.

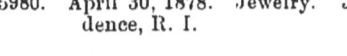 5980. April 30, 1878. Jewelry. John T. Mauran, Providence, R. I.

6679. October 8, 1878. Jewelry. Sturdy Brothers & Co., Attleborough, Mass., and New York, N. Y.

 7390. June 3, 1879. Silver-Plated Ware. Rogers & Bro., Waterbury, Conn.

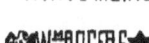 7497. July 8, 1879. Electroplated Table Ware. William Rogers, Hartford, Conn.

 7892. May 4, 1880. Britannia Silver-Plated and Solid Ware. Rogers & Brittin, West Stratford, Conn.

 8095. November 16, 1880. 8160. July 12, 1881. Lace Pins, Scarf Pins, Ear Rings, and other Jewelry. Howard Scherrieble, New York, N. Y.

 8452. July 12, 1881. Jewelry. F. G. Whitney & Co., Attleborough, Mass.

8723. October 11, 1881. Plated Silver Knives. John Russell Cutlery Co., Turner's Falls, Mass.

9464. June 12, 1882. Jet Goods of all Kinds. Veit & Nelson, New York, N. Y.

9473. June 27, 1882. Gold, Silver, and Plated Ware. Wm. N. Boynton, Manchester, Iowa.

9914. December 26, 1882. Link Cuff Buttons. Horton, Angell & Co., Attleborough, Mass.

9949. January 9, 1883. Sterling Silver Wares. Wm. Wilson & Son, Philadelphia, Pa.

9950. January 9, 1883. Electroplated Wares. Wm. Wilson & Son, Philadelphia, Pa.

10,385. July 3, 1883. Artificial Stones or Brilliants. Edward E. Kipling, New York, N. Y.

10,386. July 3, 1883. Artificial Stones or Brilliants. Edward E. Kipling, New York, N. Y.

10,418. July 10, 1883. Sleeve Buttons, Collar Buttons, and Studs. Cooke & Eddy, Providence, R. I.

10,721. November 20, 1883. Diamond Settings. Falkenau, Oppenheimer & Co., New York, N. Y.

10,770. December 11, 1883. Pins, Rings, Chains, etc. Francis S. Draper, Attleborough, Mass.

10,854. January 15, 1884. Jewelry. T. B. Hagstoz & Co., Philadelphia, Pa.

10,918. February 5, 1884. Jewelry. Fowler Bros., Providence, R. I.

11,224. June 3, 1884. Jewelry. Carter, Sloan & Co., New York, N. Y.

12,114. April 14, 1885. Watch Keys. J. S. Birch & Co., New York, N. Y.

12,128. April 14, 1885. Jewelry. Eugene Naegele, Philadelphia, Pa.

12,580. September 15, 1885. Silver-Plated Ware. Pairpoint Manufacturing Co., New Bedford, Mass.

JEWELRY AND PLATED WARE. 71

12,807. November 24, 1885. Lockets, Bracelets, etc. Waite, Mathewson, & Co., Providence, R. I.

12,846, 12,861, 12,862. December 15, 1885. Jewelry. H. Muhr's Sons, Philadelphia, Pa.

12,847. December 15, 1885. Filled Finger Rings and Thimbles. H. Muhr's Sons, Philadelphia, Pa.

12,958. January 19, 1886. Watch Cases. H. Muhr's Sons, Philadelphia, Pa.

13,117. March 16, 1886. Gold Chains. A. Wallach's Nephews, New York, N. Y.

13,232. April 27, 1886. Jewelry comprising Chains and Chain Trimmings. Hamilton & Hamilton, Jr., Providence, R. I.

13,455. June 29, 1886. Lockets, Brooches, Badges, etc. Ernest R. Shipton, London, England.

13,705. October 5, 1886. Finger Rings. Wheeler, Parsons & Hayes, New York, N. Y.

14,029. February 1, 1887. Solid Jewelry. H. Muhr's Sons, Philadelphia, Pa.

14,059. February 8, 1887. Jewelry and Silver Ware. S. F. Myers & Co., New York, N. Y.

14,083. February 5, 1886. Solid Jewelry. H. Muhr's Sons, Philadelphia, Pa.

14,298. April 19, 1887. Watch Chains. Alois Kohn & Co., New York, N. Y.

14,687. August 16, 1887. Gold and Silver Plated Ware for Household Use. Wm. Rogers Manufacturing Co., Hartford, Conn.

14,806. October 11, 1887. Silver and Plated Goods. James Dixon & Sons, Sheffield, England.

14,935. November 15, 1887. Electroplated Table Ware. Meriden Britannia Co., Meriden, Conn.

15,053. December 20, 1887. Jewelry. J. F. Hopkinson & Co., Providence, R. I.

15,658. July 3, 1888. Alloy for Jewelry. Joseph Muhr, Philadelphia, Pa.

15,715. July 24, 1888. Genuine or Imitation Jewelry. Henry E. Oppenheimer & Co., New York, N. Y.

TRADE-MARKS.

16,007. November 13, 1888. Silver or Silver-Plated Table Ware. Wm. H. Rogers, Hartford, Conn.

16,128. December 25, 1888. Gold, Silver, and Plated Household Wares. Wm. Rogers Manuf. Co., Hartford, Conn.

16,256. February 12, 1889. Ornamental Jewelry. Mosbacher & Co., New York, N. Y.

16,495. April 16, 1889. Articles of Jewelry. Hammond, Turner & Sons, Snow Hill, Birmingham, England.

16,636. May 26, 1889. Plated Seamless Filled Wire. Burdon Seamless Filled Wire Co., Providence, R. I.

16,908. August 6, 1889. Finger Rings. Sinnock & Sherrill, New York, N. Y.

18,025. June 10, 1890. Jewelry, Silver and Plated Ware, etc. C. W. Shumann & Sons, New York, N. Y.

18,081. June 24, 1890. Solid and Plated Ware. M. W. Galt, Bro. & Co., Washington, D. C.

18,232. July 29, 1890. Sterling Silver Ware. Reed & Barton Corporation, Taunton, Mass.

18,293. August 12, 1890. Jewelry and Watches. Rube R. Fogel, New York, N. Y.

18,364. August 26, 1890. Plated Filled Wire. Burdon Seamless Filled Wire Co., Providence, R. I.

18,438. September 16, 1890. Jewelry. Rube R. Fogel, New York, N. Y.

19,012. February 10, 1891. Vest Chains. D. C. Percival & Co., Boston, Mass.

19,099. February 24, 1891. Silver Ware. Daniel Low, Salem, Mass.

19,283. April 7, 1891. Vest Chains. D. C. Percival & Co., Boston, Mass.

19,495. May 12, 1891. Finger Rings. Palmer & Capron, Providence, R. I.

19,460. May 12, 1891. Plated Finger Rings. Palmer & Capron, Providence, R. I.

19,537. May 19, 1892. Chains, Bracelets, Charms, etc. W. & S. Blackinton, Attleborough, Mass.

19,593. May 26, 1891. Chains, Bracelets, Charms, etc. W. & S. Blackinton, Attleborough, Mass.

JEWELRY AND PLATED WARE. 73

19,780. June 30, 1891. Gold, Silver, and Plated Flat Ware. E. A. Whitney & Co., Boston, Mass.

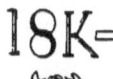
19,827. June 30, 1891. Finger Rings. Palmer & Capron, Providence, R. I.

19,828. June 30, 1891. Finger Rings. Palmer & Capron, Providence, R. I.

19,905. July 21, 1891. Silver, Flat, and Table Ware. Thomas V. Dickinson, Buffalo, N. Y.

19,995. August 11, 1891. Plated Flat and Table Ware. Harris & Shafer, Washington, D. C.

20,250. October 20, 1891. Society Emblems. Sinnock & Sherril, New York, N. Y.

20,312. November 3, 1891. Jewelry, Table and Flat Ware. Curtis & Wilkinson, North Attleborough, Mass.

20,375. November 17, 1891. Gold and Silver Table Ware. Millie B. Logan, Rochester, N. Y.

20,640. January 26, 1892. Flat Ware and Jewelry. Albert Feldenheimer, Portland, Oregon.

20,820. March 8, 1892. Plated Ware, etc. Harris & Shafer, Washington, D. C.

20,912. March 29, 1892. Flat and Table Ware and Jewelry. Wm. B. Kerr & Co., New York, N. Y.

21,423. July 5, 1892. Solid Table and Other Silverware. Ludwig, Redlitch & Co., New York, N. Y.

21,469. July 19, 1892. Jewelry. United Society of Christian Endeavor, Boston, Mass.

21,725. September 6, 1892. Watches and Jewelry. Hayden W. Wheeler & Co., New York, N. Y.

21,759. September 20, 1892. Artificial Gems. F. H. Sadler & Co., Attleborough, Mass.

21,885. October 18, 1892. Finger Rings. Frank N. Osborne, New York, N. Y.

TRADE-MARKS

FOR

LAMPS AND LANTERNS.

(CLASS 36.)

Embracing Lanterns, Burners, Gas Fixtures, &c., but not generally glassware in this art.

WORDS OR PHRASES CONSTITUTING THE MARKS ALPHABETICALLY ARRANGED.

Baby Cleveland.—20,497. December 22, 1891. Glass Lamps. Dithridge & Co., Pittsburg, Pa.
Beacon Light.—14,020. February 1, 1887. Superheating Gas Fixtures. E. P. Gleason Manufacturing Co., New York, N. Y.
Boulevard.—2132. December 22, 1874. Street Lamps. Joseph W. Bartlett, New York, N. Y.
Buckeye.—7097. March 11, 1879. Lanterns. Buckeye Lantern Co., Bellaire, Ohio.
Burglar's Horror.—11,827. December 30, 1884. Night Lights and Night Lamps. Samuel Clarke, London, England.
Canary.—17,216. November 26, 1889. Oil Cans for Filling Lamps. George H. Coursen, Baltimore, Md.
Carcel.—3363. January 18, 1876. Gas Burners and Shades. George B. Foster, Boston, Mass.
Chicago Electric.—12,361. June 30, 1885. Kerosene Lamps. Adolph Geiss and Leonard L. Kleine, Chicago, Ill.
Chirry.—16,417. March 26, 1889. Miners' Lamps. Demmler Brothers, Pittsburg, Pa.
Convex.—14,898. November 8, 1887. No Chimney Burners for Lamps, etc. Robert E. Dietz, New York, N. Y.
Crystal.—1091. September 24, 1872. Lamp Burners. Bristol Brass and Clock Co., Bristol, Conn.
Day Light.—16,975. September 3, 1889. Lamps. Kate E. Jacobson and E. H. Fessenden, Brooklyn, N. Y.
Dietz.—12,448. July 28, 1885. 14,794. October 4, 1887. Lamps and Lanterns and Burners. Robert E. Dietz, New York, N. Y.
Drummond.—4289. January 23, 1877. Lamp Burners. F. H. Lovell & Co., New York, N. Y.
Dup.ex.—12,851. December 15, 1885. Magic Lanterns. John Scheidig & Co., New York, N. Y.
Electric.—22,208. December 20, 1892. Fire Lighters. Herbert Hickman, Jersey City, N. J.
Electrophote.—22,049. November 22, 1892. Lamps and Burners. Wm. B. Robins, Cincinnati, Ohio.
Electroshade.—20,366. November 10, 1891. Incandescent Lamp Shades. James E. Treat, Boston, Mass.

Erdite.—12,539. September 1, 1885. Substitute for Carbon in Incandescent Lamps. Clinton M. Ball, Boston, Mass.
Evening Star.—5176. September 25, 1877. Night Lamps. Edward Rorke & Co., New York, N. Y.
Fairy.—13,031. Lamps, etc. Samuel Clarke, London, England.

Fairy Pyramid.—14,996. December 6, 1887. Lamps, Candle Holders, etc. Samuel Clarke, Childs Hill, London, England.
Gem Canopy.—17,431. January 28, 1890. Lamp Shades. Walter S. Berg, Philadelphia, Pa.
Guard.—4360. February 13, 1877. Lamps. Geo. H. Lomax, Somerville, N. H.
Globe Incandescent.—17,152. October 29, 1889. Lamps, Lanterns, etc. Standard Lighting Co., Cleveland, Ohio.
Hurricane.—3931. August 15, 1876. Lanterns. Hurricane Patent Lantern Co., New York, N. Y.
Illuminator.—4826. July 3, 1877. Lamp-Shade Holders. Richard Douglas & Co., New York, N. Y.
Jewel.—20,646. January 26, 1892. Incandescent Electric Lamps. William Hood, Chicago, Ill.
Jr. Rochester, The.—19,479. May 12, 1891. Lamp Burners. Rochester Lamp Co., New York, N. Y.
King of the Road.—12,730. November 3, 1885. Bicycle Lamps and Lanterns. Joseph Lucas & Son, Birmingham, England.
Kleeman.—3533. March 28, 1876. Lamps. Charles F. A. Hinrichs, Brooklyn, N. Y.
Leader.—6526. September 3, 1878. Lamp Burners. Bridgeport Brass Co., Bridgeport, Conn.
Little Harry's Night.—4560. April 17, 1877. Lamps. Leverett H. Olmsted, Brooklyn, N. Y.
Lumenoid.—12,538. September 1, 1885. Incandescent Lamps. Clinton M. Ball, Boston, Mass.
Magic.—18,135. July 8, 1890. Pocket Cigar Lighters. Magic Introduction Co., Rutherford, N. J.
Matchless.—13,921. December 28, 1886. Gas Burners. G. K. Cooke, New York, N. Y.
Mother Hubbard.—11,954. February 17, 1885. Reflector Lamps. Daniel R. Williams, Dallas, Texas.
National.—18,645. November 18, 1890. Incandescent Lighting Machinery. National Electric Manufacturing Co., Eau Claire, Wis.
Nelly Bly.—17,863. May 6, 1890. Lamps. Dithridge & Company, Pittsburg, Pa.
Niagara.—15,967. October 23, 1888. Gas Burners. Chas. Stanford Upton, New York, N. Y.
Owl (and design).—11,530. September 30, 1884. Campaign Light. Masten & Wells, Boston, Mass.
Pintsch.—20,678. February 2, 1892. Lamps. Safety Car Heating and Lighting Co., New York, N. Y.
Pyramid.—11,267. June 17, 1884. Night Lamps. Samuel Clarke, South Hampstead, London, England.
Saint Germain.—8313. May 31, 1881. 3111. November 2, 1875. Lamps. C. F. A. Hinrichs, Brooklyn, N. Y.
Security. 12,980. February 2, 1886. Lamps. J. Payson Bradley, Boston, Massachusetts.
Square Lift.—15,062. December 27, 1887. Tubular Lamps and Lanterns. R. E. Deitz Co., New York, N. Y.
Steel Check (and design). 1243. April 29, 1873. Gas Burners. Mrs. Alonzo H. Wood, Boston, Mass.
Sunbeam. 18,931. February 3, 1891. Incandescent Electric Lamps. Sunbeam Incandescent Lamp Co., Chicago, Ill.

TRADE-MARKS.

Tempest. 4058. October 17, 1876. Lanterns. Edward Miller & Co., Meriden, Conn.
Teru-Teru.—14,980. November 29, 1887. Lamps, Lanterns, and Articles for Household Use. Thos. Drysdale & Co., New York, N. Y.
Triumph.—5395. December 4, 1877. Lamp Burners. Wilmot Manufacturing Co., Bridgeport, Conn.
Tubular.—722. April 2, 1872. Lanterns. Chicago Manufacturing Co., Chicago, Ill.
Ultimatum.—3850. July 18, 1876. Lamp Burners. Henry A. Chapin, New York, N. Y.
U-Trenton-S.—21,648. August 16, 1892. Lamps, etc. Clark Bros. Lamp, Brass & Copper Co., New York, N. Y.
Victor.—20,190. October 6, 1891. Lamp Shades, etc. Wm. Foerster & Co., New York, N. Y.
Wells Light.—16,965. August 27, 1889. Lamps and Stoves. R. Wallwork and A. C. Wells, Manchester, England.

The Wheel

DEVOTED TO CYCLING.

$2.00 per Year.   Published every Friday.

A paper devoted to the sport and trade of cycling.

Since its foundation the authority on cycling.

F. P. PRIAL,

PROPRIETOR,

21 Park Row,   New York.

TRADE-MARKS

FOR

LAMPS AND LANTERNS.

(CLASS 36.)

Designs showing essential feature claimed as Trade-Mark.

706. March 19, 1872. Gas-Light Burners. Michael B. Dyott, Philadelphia, Pa.

1243. April 29, 1873. Gas Burners. Mrs. Alonzo H. Wood, Boston, Mass.

8557. August 9, 1881. Lava Gas Tips. J. Von Schwarz, Nuremberg, Germany.

9659. September 12, 1882. Lamps. Joseph J. Kittel, Brooklyn, N. Y.

11,530. September 30, 1884. Campaign Light. Masten & Wells, Boston, Mass.

12,874. December 22, 1885. Lamps. Charles S. Upton, New York, N. Y.

13,775. November 2, 1886. Lamps, Lamp Burners, and Lamp Chimneys. Charles Stanford Upton, New York, N. Y.

14,517. June 14, 1887. Gas Fixtures. United States Wonham Patent Gas Lamp Co., New York, N. Y.

14,569. July 5, 1887. Tubular Lanterns or Lamps and Stoves. R. E. Dietz Co., New York, N. Y.

16,382. March 12, 1889. Gas Burner Tips. Draper Manufacturing Co., North Attleborough, Mass.

TRADE-MARKS

FOR

LAUNDRY ARTICLES.

(Class 38.)

Embracing Washing Machines, Wringers, &c., but excluding Chemical Compounds, &c.

Words or Phrases Constituting the Marks Alphabetically Arranged.

Banner.—21,593. August 9, 1892. Wringers. American Wringer Co., Providence, R. I.

Boss.—21,651. August 23, 1892. Washing Machines. Boss Washing Machine Co., Cincinnati, Ohio.

Cataract.—15,643. June 26, 1888. Washing Machines. Recknagel & Co., New York, N. Y.

Celery City Protector, The.—15,394. March 19, 1889. Wash Boards. Charles D. and Frank D. Fuller, Kalamazoo, Mich.

Champion.—2954. September 21, 1875. Fluting Machines. Charles Felder, Newark, N. J.

Chief.—19,550. May 19, 1891. Washing Machines. Bowman & Turner, Toledo, Ohio.

Climax.—3933. August 15, 1876. Clothes Wringers. Metropolitan Washing Machine Co., New York, N. Y.

Colby.—16,909. August 6, 1889. Clothes Wringers. Colby Wringer Co., Montpelier, Vt.

Columbia.—22,224. December 20, 1892. Wringers. American Wringer Co., Providence, R. I.

Crown.—6844. November 26, 1878. Wringing, Fluting, and Plaiting Machines, etc. American Machine Co., Philadelphia, Pa.

Daisy.—22,225. December 20, 1892. Wringers. American Wringer Co., Providence, R. I.

Empire.—1800. May 26, 1874. 14,351. May 3, 1887. Clothes Wringers. Empire Wringer Co., Auburn. N. Y.

Eureka.—6923. January 7, 1879. Clothes Wringers. Eureka Clothes Wringing Machine Co., Boston, Mass.

Excelsior.—1130. February 18, 1873. 2575. May 25, 1875. Clothes Wringers. Bailey Washing and Wringing Machine Co., Woonsocket, R. I.

Favorite.—6516. August 27, 1878. Clothes Wringers. Peerless Wringer Co., Cincinnati, Ohio.

Household.—22,226. December 20, 1892. Wringers. American Wringer Co., Providence, R. I.

LAUNDRY ARTICLES. 79

Ideal.—21,592. August 9, 1892. Wringers. American Wringer Co., Providence, R. I.
I X L.—20,514. December 29, 1891. Washing Machines. J. J. & R. H. Vail, Green Valley, Ill.
Liberty.—13,997. January 18, 1887. Washboards. Union Manufacturing Co., Toledo, Ohio.
Mammoth.—3183. November 30, 1875. Clothes-Pins. R. Warner & Co., Boston, Mass.
Mascotte.—21,590. August 9, 1892. Wringers. American Wringer Co., Providence, R. I.
Moscow (with design).—2850. August 24, 1875. Clothes-Pins. Staples & Brown, Moscow, Pa.
"National."—1608. January 27, 1874. Clothes Wringers. Metropolitan Washing Machine Co., Middlefield, Conn.
Nonpareil.—6017. May 7, 1878. Washing Machines. Oakley & Keating, New York, N. Y.
Northern Queen.—17,797. April 22, 1890. Washboards. Fuller Bros. Manufacturing Co., Kalamazoo, Mich.
Novelty.—1131. February 18, 1873. 2576. May 25, 1875. Clothes Wringers. Bailey Wringing Machine Co., Woonsocket, R. I.
Novelty.—1523. November 11, 1873. Clothes Wringers. Haley, Morse & Co., Boston, Mass.
Pan American.—22,053. November 22, 1892. Washing Machines. Vandergrift Manufacturing Co., Jamestown, N.Y.
Paragon.—8609. August 30, 1881. Clothes Wringers. John Arnett and Louis K. McClymonds, Cleveland, Ohio.
Peerless.—1494. October 14, 1873. Clothes Wringers. Queen City Wringer Company, Cincinnati, Ohio.
Reliance.—326. May 23, 1871. Clothes Wringers. Albert H. Spencer, Providence, R. I.
Relief.—21,591. August 9, 1892. Wringers. American Wringer Company, Providence, R. I.
Round American (and design).—22,006. November 15, 1892. Washing Machine. Bluffton Manufacturing Co., Bluffton, Ind.
Sugar Plum (and design).—20,708. February 9, 1892. Washing Machines. Louis H. Hespos, St. Louis, Mo.
Tip Top.—1992. September 22, 1874. Washing Machines. J. and H. Campbell and W. H. Coffman, West Alexandria, Ohio.
Universal.—1609. January 27, 1874. Clothes Wringer. Metropolitan Washing Machine Co., Middlefield, Conn.
Universal Protector, The.—16,395. March 19, 1889. Washboards. Chas. D. and Frank D. Fuller, Kalamazoo, Mich.
Washboard Must Go, The. 12,553. September 8, 1885. Washing Machines. Chas. A. Beutzen, New York, N. Y.
World's.—15,236. February 28, 1888. Washing Machines. Chas. E. Ross, Lincoln, Ill.

— — —

COMPILED BY
WALLACE A. BARTLETT,
Patent Attorney,
WASHINGTON, D. C.

TRADE-MARKS

FOR

LAUNDRY ARTICLES.

(CLASS 38.)

Designs showing essential feature claimed as Trade-Mark.

   2850. August 24, 1875. Clothes-Pins. Staples & Brown, Moscow, Pa.

    3592. April 18, 1876. Washboards. Union Mfg. Co., Toledo, Ohio.

   4359. February 13, 1877. Fluting Machines. Susan R. Knox, New York, N. Y.

    16,279. February 19, 1889. Laundry Articles, Clothes Wringers, etc. Empire Wringer Co., Auburn, N. Y.

   18,667. December 2, 1890. Washboards. Lapham Dodge Co., Cleveland, O.

   20,708. February 9, 1892. Washing Machines. Louis H. Hespos, St. Louis, Mo.

    21,185. May 24, 1892. Clothes Sprinklers. Berry, Goss & Co., Boston, Mass.

   22,006. November 15, 1892. Washing Machines. Bluffton Manuf. Co., Bluffton, Ind.

   22,054. November 22, 1892. Washing Machines. Vandergrift Manuf. Co., Jamestown, N. Y.

TRADE-MARKS

FOR

LOCKS AND HARDWARE.

(CLASS 40.)

Embracing Locks, Latches, Hinges, Nails, Screws, Bale-Ties, Builders' Hardware, Wire Goods, Metal Tubes, Plumbers' Supplies, Skates, Traps, Buckles, Corset Steels, Umbrella Frames, &c., &c.

(See also Class 17, Cutlery ; 34, Iron and Steel ; 35, Jewelry ; 73, Tools, &c.)

WORDS OR PHRASES CONSTITUTING THE MARKS ALPHABETICALLY ARRANGED.

A.—8340. June 14, 1881. Horseshoe Nails. Ausable Horse Nail Co., Keesville and New York, N. Y.
A.—8841. November 15, 1881. Quicksilver Flasks. Quicksilver Mining Co., New Almaden, Cal.
Acme (monogram).—2624. June 1, 1875. Steam Fittings. Pancoast & Maule, Philadelphia, Pa.
Acme.—3221. December 7, 1875. Skates. Star Manufacturing Co., Dartmouth, Canada.
Acme.—14,578. July 12, 1887. Sight Feed Lubricators. Acme Lubricator Co., Detroit, Mich.
Acme.—16,130.—December 25, 1888. Metallic Staples, etc. Acme Staple & Machine Co., Philadelphia, Pa.
Adamant.—22,221. December 20, 1892. Enameled Hollow Ware. Bons Bros., New York, N. Y.
Albion.—12,762. November 10, 1885. Hardware Supplies. Reading Hardware Co., Reading, Pa.
Alpha Selected (and design).—1413. August 19, 1873. Nails. John Coyne, Pittsburg, Pa.
Anchor.—15,343. April 3, 1888. Wire Bale-Ties. Trenton Iron Co., Trenton, N. J.
Anchor.—15,502. May 22, 1888. Horse Nails. Livingston Nail Co., New York, N. Y.
Anchor.—18,149. July 8, 1890. Laundry Tubs, Sinks, Troughs, etc. Thomas G. Knight, Brooklyn, N. Y.
Antler.—17,872. May 6, 1890. Buckles. Jacob Gump, Baltimore, Md.
Arcus (and design).—8932. December 20, 1881. Umbrella Frames. Samuel Fox & Co., Stockbridge Works, York, England.
Arrow Tie.—314. June 6, 1871. Cotton Bale Ties. James J. McComb, Liverpool, England.

Atlas.—21,726. September 6, 1892. Metallic Bedsteads and Wire Matresses. Stephen Wilkes, Bilston, England.
Augite, The Woman's Friend.—22,002. November 15, 1892. Stove Mats. J. L. Brown Co., Pittsburg, Pa.
Au Soleil (and design).—12,969. January 26, 1886. Furniture Nails. A. Gallais & Co., Paris, France.
Automatic.—10,183. April 10, 1883. Blind Awnings. F. O. North & Co., Boston, Mass.
B (and design).—2488. May 11, 1875. Iron Pipe, etc. National Tube Works Co., Boston, Mass., and McKeesport, Pa.
Banner.—3073. October 19, 1875. Billiard-Cue Racks. J. M. Brunswick & Balke Co., Chicago, Ill.
Bay State.—7189. April 15, 1879. 8802. November 1, 1881. Horse Nails. Putnam Nail Co., Boston, Mass.
Bernstein Commonsense.—20,577. January 12, 1892. Locking Devices. Benny Bernstein, New York, N. Y.
Blymyer.—14,380. May 17, 1887. Bells for Churches, Fire Alarms, etc. John B. Dodds, Cincinnati, Ohio.
Bonanza.—9366. May 16, 1882. Saddlery Hardware, etc. William F. Ford, Newark, N. J.
Boss.—13,308. May 18, 1886. Stop Cocks for Water and Gas Pipes. Fred Adee & Co., New York, N. Y.
Boss.—21,566. October 18, 1892. Animal Shoes. Dryden Horseshoe Co., Catasauqua, Pa.
Boss, The.—6705. October 8, 1878. 8688. September 27, 1881. Well Bucket. Prewitt, Spur & Co., Nashville, Tenn.
Bridgewater (and anchor).—2637. June 8, 1875. Drawn Tubes. Bridgewater Iron Co., Bridgewater, Mass.
Brighton.—10,904. January 29, 1884. Water Closets. Meyer Sniffen Co., New York, N. Y.
Buck-Thorn.—11,350. July 22, 1884. Barbed Fencing. Buck-Thorn Fence Co., Trenton, N. J.
Cantbreakem.—1491. October 14, 1873. Corset Steel Springs. Frances Lee Egbert, New York, N. Y.
Can't-break-ems'.—1567. December 9, 1873. Steel Corset Springs. Frances Lee Egbert, Waterbury, Conn., and New York, N. Y.
Cat.—4684. May 22, 1877. Fence Strips and Caps. Cyrus L. Topliff, Brooklyn, N. Y.
Catch Em Alive.—5984. April 30, 1872. Animal Traps. Robert E. Dietz, New York, N. Y.
C. & W's. 3000 (or other figures).—978. September 3, 1872. Saddlery Hardware. Coleman, Walker & Co., Elizabethport, N. J.
C. B. K.—8934. December 20, 1881. Horseshoe Nails. W. M. Mooney & Co., Au Sable Chasm, N. Y.
Centennial.—3006. October 5, 1875. Coffee and Tea Utensils. N. S. McFarland, New York, N. Y.
Centennial.—3137. November 16, 1875. Door Locks and Latches. Mallory, Wheeler & Co., New Haven, Conn.
Centennial.—2345. April 6, 1875. Spring Beds. William Lathers, New York, N. Y.
Champion (and design).—3123. November 2, 1875. Buelde. H. S. Woodruff & Co., Janesville, Wis.
Champion.—6432. July 30, 1878. Corset Clasps. James G. Fitzpatrick, New York, N. Y.
Champion.—10,246. May 1, 1883. Sash Balances. Thomas Morton, New York, N. Y.
Clark's Gravity Locking Blind Hinge.—2894. August 31, 1875. Blind Hinge. Clark & Co., Buffalo, N. Y.
Clark's Pattern.—2365. April 13, 1875. Builders' Hardware. Clark & Co., Buffalo, N. Y.

LOCKS AND HARDWARE. 83

Climax.—4182. December 5, 1876. Barn-Door Hangers. S. H. & E. Y. Moore, Chicago, Ill.
C. M. M. P. A.—11,175. May 13, 1884. Hand-Made Tin Cans. Can Makers' Mutual Protective Association, Baltimore, Md.
Columbia.—18,052. June 17, 1890. Locks and Latches. Hopkins & Dickinson Manufacturing Co., Brooklyn, N. Y.
Columbian.—19,658. June 2, 1891. Builders' Hardware. Reading Hardware Co., Reading, Pa.
Contentment-Lock.—3591. April 18, 1876. Locks and Fittings. Isaac P. Turner, Albany, N. Y.
Coraline.—8545. August 2, 1881. Corset Ribs. Warner Brothers, New York, N. Y.
Cottage (and design).—2652. June 8, 1875. Spring Beds. Tucker Manufacturing Co., Boston, Mass.
Cottage.—16,281. February 19, 1889. Wire Fencing. Gilbert & Bennett Manufacturing Co., Georgetown, Conn.
Cranberry Pattern.—15,463. May 15, 1888. Horse and Mule Shoes. Greenwood Horse Shoe Co., Philadelphia, Pa.
Crown.—13,325. May 18, 1886. Bath Tubs and Sinks. Standard Manufacturing Co., Allegheny, Pa.
Crown.—13,503. July 13, 1886. Transom Lifters. John F. Wollensak, Chicago, Ill.
Crown.—15,664. July 3, 1888. Electrical Bells. John F. Wollensak, Chicago, Ill.
Daisy.—14,776. September 27, 1887. Nuts. Bennett, Day & Co., New York, N. Y.
Daisy.—15,814. August 28, 1888. Metallic Stove Boards. A. Irving Griggs, New York, N. Y.
Daniel.—946. August 13, 1872. Bridle-Bits and Stirrups. Kelita Brodhurst, Bloxwich, England.
Daniel.—13,920. December 28, 1886. Stirrups and Bridle-Bits. Vincent Brodhurst, Bloxwich, England.
De Witt.—12,836. December 8, 1885. Wire Cloth. De Witt Wire Cloth Co., New York, N. Y.
Dighton Rock.—9618. August 22, 1882. Baked Clay Goods. Gideon C. Francis, South Dighton, Mass.
Doherty.—10,906. January 29, 1884. Faucets, etc. Meyer Sniffen Co., New York, N. Y.
Donoghue, The.—20,660. January 26, 1892. Ice and Roller Skates. Union Hardware Co., Torrington, Conn.
Drive Well, D. W.—15,620. June 19, 1888. Horseshoe Nails. Simmons Hardware Co., St. Louis, Mo.
Eagle.—7061. March 4, 1879. Rivets, Washers, Burrs, etc. Plume & Atwood Manufacturing Co., Waterbury, Conn.
Eagle.—15,665. July 3, 1888. Transom Lifters. John F. Wollensak, Chicago, Ill.
Empire.—7188. April 15, 1879. 8801. November 1, 1881. Horse Nails. Putnam Nail Co., Boston, Mass.
Em Ess.—10,905. January 29, 1884. Water-Closet Cistern, etc. Meyer Sniffen Co., New York, N. Y.
Enterprise.—21,552. August 2, 1892. Hardware. Enterprise Mfg. Co. of Pennsylvania, Philadelphia, Pa.
Era.—9015. January 10, 1882. Water-Closet Bowls, etc. Alfred E. Jennings, New York, N. Y.
Excelsior.—9102. May 23, 1882. Measuring Tapes. Keuffel & Esser, New York, N. Y.
Excelsior.—15,033. December 20, 1887. Plumbers' Stench Traps. M. M. C. Brandeis & H. G. Dougherty, Brooklyn, N. Y.
Expert. 13,597. August 24, 1886. Roller and Ice Skates. Everett H. Barney, Springfield, Mass.

Ezekiel Page Brand.—10,467. July 24, 1883. Oars, Sweeps, Hand-Spikes, etc. New York Boat-Oar Co., New York, N. Y.
F. A. (monogram).—2857. August 31, 1875. Hardware. Frank Armstrong, Bridgeport, Ct.
Franklin Lightning Rod Factory.—354. June 27, 1871. Lightning Rods. Samuel J. Mitchell, St. Louis, Mo.
Fuller.—14,643. July 26, 1887. Bibbs, Cocks, and Faucets. Meyer Sniffen Co., New York, N. Y.
Geneva.—12,643. October 13, 1885. Hardware. Reading Hardware Co., Reading, Pa.
Giant.—5835. April 9, 1878. Locks and Keys. Smith & Egge Manufacturing Co., Bridgeport, Conn.
Giant.—5890. April 16, 1878. Chains. Smith & Egge Manufacturing Co., Bridgeport, Conn.
Globe.—4937. July 24, 1877. Horse and Animal Shoe Nails. Globe Nail Co., Boston Mass.
Globe.—7585. August 12, 1879. Rivets, Burrs, and Chains. Holmes, Booth & Haydens, Waterbury, Conn.
Globe.—15,411. May 1, 1888. Ventilators. John H. Reynolds, Troy, N. Y.
Golden Rod (and design).—21,302. June 14, 1892. Nuts. Hall & Hayward, Louisville, Ky.
Goodenough.—888. July 9, 1872. Oil Cans. Irving C. Smith, New York, N. Y.
Good Luck.—11,802. December 16, 1884. Padlocks. Horace F. Sise, New York, N. Y.
Hall's.—10,907. January 29, 1884. Gas Cocks. Meyer Sniffen Co., New York, N. Y.
Harness Menders.—17,536. February 11, 1890. Double-Pointed Tacks, Staples, etc. Buffalo Specialty Manufacturing Co., Buffalo, N. Y.
Harvard.—11,774. December 16, 1884. Roller Skates. Samuel W. Alward, Boston, Mass.
H. B.—13,167. April 6, 1886. Hames and Saddlery Hardware. P. Hayden Saddlery Hardware Co., Columbus, Ohio.
Hellyer.—14,640. July 26, 1887. Water Closets. Meyer Sniffen Co., New York, N. Y.
Helmet.—17,859. May 6, 1890. Hardware. Charles H. Besly & Co., Chicago, Ill.
Hercules.—15,889. September 25, 1888. Wire Rope. A. Leschen & Sons Rope Co., St. Louis, Mo.
Hercules.—1683. March 24, 1874. Umbrella Stretchers. Dawes & Fanning, New York, N. Y.
Hercules.—17,832. April 29, 1890. Pipe Couplings. Isaac B. Potts Pipe Fittings Co., Columbus, Ohio.
Honest Count.—13,280. May 11, 1886. Carpet Tacks. S. H. Benedict & Co., Cleveland, Ohio.
Ice King.—4331. February 6, 1877. Skates. Everett H. Barney, Springfield, Mass.
Ice Queen.—4330. February 6, 1877. Skates. Everett H. Barney, Springfield, Mass.
Ideal.—13,254. April 27, 1886. Water Closets. Richard H. Watson, Philadelphia, Pa.
Imperial.—17,104. October 15, 1889. Valves for Water-Closets, etc. William H. Ward, Boston, Mass.
Imperial.—19,578. May 26, 1891. Enameled Ware. St. Louis Stamping Co., St. Louis, Mo.
Invigorator.—7972. July 13, 1880. Spring Bed-Bottoms. George Heyman, New York, N. Y.
Iron Clad.—13,233. April 27, 1886. Coal-Hods, Cans, etc. Iron Clad Manufacturing Co., New York, N. Y.

LOCKS AND HARDWARE. 85

Iron Clad Can Co., The.—343. June 20, 1871. Sheet Metal Ware, etc. H. W. Shepard & Robt. Seaman, New York, N. Y.
Kalamein.—10,759. December 4, 1883. Metal Tubing. Edmund C. Converse, Pittsburg, Pa.
Knockdown.—6261. June 18, 1878. Metallic Cans. Geo. H. Perkins, Philadelphia, Pa.
Ku Klux.—2702. July 6, 1875. Fly Catcher. Chas. F. Burks, Fresno, Cal.
Latrine.—4630. May 15, 1877. Water-Closets. Andrew G. Myers, New York, N. Y.
Laurus.—20,632. January 26, 1892. Umbrellas, Umbrella Ribs, etc. Samuel Fox & Co., Stockbridge Works, near Sheffield, England.
Link Belt.—13,805. November 16, 1886. Drive Chains. Link Belt Machinery Co., Chicago, Ill.
Little Throttler.—10,947. February 19, 1884. Animal Traps. Elijah P. Peacock, Chicago, Ill.
Lustral.—2732. July 6, 1875. Wire Goods. Woods, Sherwood & Co., Lowell, Mass.
Magic.—5960. April 30, 1878. Hoze Nozzles. Everette B. Preston, Chicago, Ill.
Magic Disk.—566. December 5, 1871. Oil Cans. John P. Haines, Irvington, N. Y.
Magic Disk Oil Cans.—2527. May 18, 1875. Oil Cans. John P. Haines, Irvington, N. Y.
Manifold.—5696. May 7, 1878. Apparatus for Curling Hair. Ehrich & Co., New York, N. Y.
Meneely Bell Foundry, The.—335. June 20, 1871. 2717. July 6, 1875. Bells. E. A. & G. R. Meneely, West Troy, N. Y.
Mercury.—15,659. July 3, 1888. Skates. Charles L. Peirce, Milwaukee, Wis.
Merito.—18,615. November 11, 1890. Roofing Plates. Jacob Leu & Sons, Atchison, Kansas
Metalin.—13,784. November 2, 1886. Thread Composed Partly of Metal Wire. William Bennett Arnold, North Abington, Mass.
Model.—14,645. July 26, 1887. Slop Sinks. Meyer Sniffen Co., New York, N. Y.
Monarch.—16,135. January 1, 1889. Chains Formed From Sheet Metal. Bridgeport Chain Co., West Stratford, Conn.
Murdock.—14,639. July 26, 1887. Hydrants. Meyer Sniffen Co., New York, N. Y.
Musical Dum Bell.—19,688. June 9, 1891. Dumb-Bells. Narragansett Machine Co., Pawtucket, R. I.
Nail for Nail (nail design).—13,180. April 13, 1886. Nails. Hartman Steel Co., Beaver Falls, and Pittsburg, Pa.
National.—6697. October 8, 1878. Wire Cloth. David R. Morse, Brooklyn, N. Y.
Neptune (and design).—14,250. April 5, 1887. Wire Rope, etc. F. C. Guilleaume, Mulheim, Cologne, Germany.
Never Break.—17,154. October 29, 1889. Kitchen Utensils. Bronson Supply Co., Cleveland, Ohio.
New Departure.—17,455. January 28, 1890. Call Bells, Alarm Bells, and Door Bells. New Departure Bell Co., Bristol, Conn.
Nickoline. 14,257. April 12, 1887. Saddlery Hardware. Chas. C. Brown, Birmingham, England.
Nonesuch.—11,271. June 17, 1884. Furniture Caster. S. M. Michelson & Co., Milwaukee, Wis.
Norton.—12,903. December 29, 1885. Door Checks and Springs. Norton Door Check and Spring Co., New York, N. Y.
Occidental. 14,642. July 26, 1887. Water Closets. Meyer Sniffen Co., New York, N. Y.

Onyx.—21,624. August 16, 1892. Sheet Metal Ware. Herman Aich, New York, N. Y.
Onyx.—21,490. July 19, 1892. Culinary Vessels. Herman Aich, New York, N. Y.
Opal.—18,039. June 17, 1890. Enameled Sheet Metal Utensils. Lalance & Grosjean Manufacturing Co., New York, N. Y.
Pacific.—5316. November 13, 1877. Manufactured Wire in Coils. Andrew S. Hallidie, San Francisco, Cal.
Pacific Barb.—13,847. December 7, 1886. Barbed Wire. California Wire Works, San Francisco, Cal.
Painesville Metallic Binding Co.—15,878. September 18, 1888. Metallic Binding for Oil Cloths, etc. O. Tuttle and Chas. Finneran, Painesville, Ohio.
Paragon.—6168. June 4, 1878. Stench Traps. Ludwig Brandeis, Brooklyn, N. Y.
Paragon.—15,827. September 24, 1888. Umbrella Frames and Parts Thereof. Samuel Fox & Co., Deepcar, York Co., England.
Paragon (and design).—8933. December 20, 1881. Umbrella Frames. Samuel Fox & Co., Stockbridge Works, York, England.
Pargetized.—4284. January 16, 1887. Tanks, Cans, etc., for Oil. Pargetized Can Co., Keene, N. H.
Parsons.—14,641. July 26, 1887. Water-Closet Troughs. Meyer Sniffen Co., New York, N. Y.
Pearl.—11,858. January 13, 1885. Enamelled Sheet Metal Utensils, etc. Lalance & Grosjean Manufacturing Co., New York, N. Y.
Pearl.—16,282. February 19, 1889. Window-Screen Wire Cloth. Gilbert & Bennett Manufacturing Co., Georgetown, Conn.
Peeping Roofers.—16,580. May 14, 1889. Sheet Metal Roofing. Caldwell & Peterson Manufacturing Co., Wheeling, W. Va.
Peerless.—17,831. April 29, 1890. Pipe Couplings. Isaac B. Potts Pipe Fittings Co., Columbus, Ohio.
Pemberton.—14,646. July 26, 1887. Bath-Tubs, Basins and Water Closets. Meyer Sniffen Co., New York, N. Y.
Perfection (and design).—2111. December 8, 1874. Safes and Locks. John Winslow Norris, Canton, Ohio.
Phœnix.—5003. August 7, 1877. Molasses Gates. George S. Lincoln & Co., Hartford, Conn.
Plymouth Rock.—16,090. December 11, 1888. Carpet Tacks. John H. Parks, Plymouth, Mass.
Porcupine.—12,408. July 14, 1885. Barbed-Wire Fencing. Johnson & Johnson, Bradford Iron Works, Manchester, England.
P. Putnam Hot-Forged and Hammer-Pointed.—8803. November 1, 1888. Horseshoe Nails. Putnam Nail Co., Boston, Mass.
Purple-Blue.—21,389. June 28, 1892. Wire Nails. Baackes Wire Nail Co., Cleveland, Ohio.
Queene-Anne.—17,254. December 10, 1889. Metallic Shingles. National Sheet Metal Roofing Co., New York, N. Y.
R. R.—6321. July 2, 1878. Boiler Tubes. Joseph T. Ryerson, Chicago, Ill.
Racer.—13,596. August 24, 1886. Roller and Ice Skates. Everett H. Barney, Springfield, Mass.
Rapid Transit.—14,647. July 26, 1887. Bath Tubs and Basin Wastes. Meyer Sniffen Co., New York, N. Y.
Red Metal.—15,554. May 29, 1888. Window-Sash Chains. Smith & Egge Manufacturing Co., Bridgeport, Conn.
Regester.—10,251. May 1, 1883. Gage Locks. J. Regester & Sons, Baltimore, Md.
R. H. Co.—22,000. November 15, 1892. Builders' Hardware. Reading Hardware Co., Reading, Pa.
Rising Sun.—14,995. December 6, 1887. Nuts. Bennett, Day & Co., New York, N. Y.

LOCKS AND HARDWARE. 87

Round Heads.—5321. November 13, 1877. Metallic Fasteners. George W. McGill, New York, N. Y.
Royal.—7099. March 11, 1879. Horseshoe Nails. Anvil Nail Company, New York, N. Y.
Royal.—14,644. July 26, 1887. Bath-Tubs. Meyer Sniffen Co., New York, N. Y.
Royal.—22,051. November 22, 1892. Baking and Roasting Pans. John W. Oblinger, Troy, Ohio.
S.—22,177. December 13, 1892. Bolts, Nuts, Rivets, etc. J. H. Sternbergh & Son, Reading, Pa.
Safety.—11,779. December 16, 1884. Culinary Pots, Kettles, etc. Capital City Malleable Iron Co., Albany, N. Y.
Saltant.—18,643. November 18, 1890. Water Closets. Thomas G. Knight, Brooklyn, N. Y.
Serpentine Wire Corset Clasps.—3194. December 7, 1875. Corset Clasps. Cooley, Biglow & Nichols, New York, N. Y.
Shoo Fly.—5942. April 23, 1878. Door Springs. Van Wagoner & Williams, New York, N. Y.
Silverbone.—14,885. November 1, 1887. Steel Springs, etc., for Dresses and Corsets. Chas. K. Pevey, Worcester, Mass.
Silver Brown.—11,543. October 7, 1884. Butler's Sinks. Alfred W. Allen, Philadelphia, Pa.
Solid Ingot.—14,942. November 15, 1887. Bars, Tools, and Rails. Solid Ingot Co., Jersey City, N. J.
Spiral Weld.—15,171. February 7, 1888. Metallic Pipe and Couplings for Same. Spiral Weld Tube Co., East Orange, N. J.
Standard.—3708. May 23, 1876. Locks. Yale Lock Manufacturing Co., Stamford, Conn.
Standard (and design).—4401. February 27, 1877. Horseshoes. Harvey K. Flagler, Boston Mass.
Stanley.—17,737. April 8, 1890. Metal Roofing Plate. Merchant & Co., Philadelphia, Pa.
Star (design).—2040. October 27, 1874. Nails, Rivets, and Chains. Wallace & Sons, Ansonia, Conn., and New York, N. Y.
Star.—2064. November 10, 1874. Cotton Bale Ties, Charles G. Johnsen, New Orleans, La.
Star.—10,589. September 18, 1883. Pneumatic Door Check. Morton Door Check and Spring Co., Boston, Mass.
Star (and design).—4450. March 13, 1887. Door and Gate Springs. Van Wagoner & Williams, New York, N. Y.
Star.—13,501. July 13, 1886. Ventilators. Warren Webster, Philadelphia, Pa.
Star.—13,502. July 13, 1886. Transom Lifters. John F. Wollensak, Chicago, Ill.
Star Brand.—2187. January 26, 1875. Carpet Tacks. Frank F. McNair, Nunda, N. Y.
Steel Clad.—21,806. October 4, 1892. Bath Tubs. George Booth, Detroit, Mich.
Success.—20,753. February 23, 1892. Water-Closet Tanks, etc. Buick & Sherwood, Detroit, Mich.
S. X.—4258. January 9, 1877. Bale Ties and Materials. Laughland & Co., New York, N. Y.
Sypho.—20,070. August 25, 1890. Porcelain Water-Closets, etc. McCambridge & Co., Philadelphia, Pa.
Thickset.—9689. September 19, 1882. Barbed Wire. Washburn & Moen Manufacturing Co., Worcester, Mass.
Toilet Jewel.—18,700. December 16, 1890. Cases for Packing Toilet Outfits. London Toilet Bazar Co., New York, N. Y.
Triumph. 16,134. January 1, 1889. Wire Chains for Pictures, Halters, etc. Bridgeport Chain Co., West Stratford, Conn.

88 TRADE-MARKS.

Tudor.—10,079. March 6, 1883. Railway Rails and Railway Fastenings. St. Louis Bolt and Iron Co., St. Louis, Mo.

Tuxedo.—18,043. June 17, 1890. Wire Mattresses. Frederick A. Palmer, New York, N. Y.

Victor.—12,196. April 28, 1885. Roller Skates, Mops, etc. Victor Roller Skate Co., Muncie, Ind.

Vineyard.—9498. June 27, 1882. Roller Skates. Samuel Winslow, Worcester, Mass.

Vulcan.—2370. April 13, 1875. Corset Steels. Lessey & Young, Philadelphia, Pa.

Vulcan.—8265. May 24, 1881. Horseshoe Nails. Fowler Nail Co., Seymour, Ct.

Welcome.—5486. January 8, 1878. Corset Clasps. Nathan Hyman, New York, N. Y.

Weldless.—16,956. August 20, 1889. Metallic Tubes. Weldless Steel Tube Co., Birmingham, England.

Wedgeway.—17,652. March 11, 1890. Hardware. Morley Bros., East Saginaw, Mich.

Western Horse Nail.—277. May 23, 1871. 2490. May 11, 1875. Horse Nails. Northwestern Horse Nail Co., Chicago, Ill.

White Wire.—1689. March 24, 1874. Wire Cloth. Woods, Sherwood & Co., Lowell, Mass.

William Penn.—15,031. December 13, 1887. Bolts and Rivets. Welsh & Lea, Philadelphia, Pa.

World's.—16,280. February 19, 1889. Wire Fencing. Gilbert & Bennett, Manufacturing Co., Georgetown, Conn.

World's Champion.—20,654. January 26, 1892. Ice and Roller Skates. Union Hardware Co., Torrington, Conn.

World's Columbian Exposition.—20,868. March 22, 1892. Key Rings. Frederick J. Tahl, Chicago, Ill.

XX.—12,051. March 24, 1885. Sad-Irons. John Sabold, Jr., Oolebrookdale, Pa.

Yale.—3709. May 25, 1876. Time Locks. Yale Lock Manufacturing Co., Stamford, Ct.

999.—18,355. August 26, 1890. Locks. Miller Lock Company. Philadelphia, Pa.

COMPILED BY

WALLACE A. BARTLETT,

Patent Attorney,

WASHINGTON, D. C.

TRADE-MARKS

FOR

LOCKS AND HARDWARE.

(CLASS 40.)

Designs showing essential feature claimed as Trade-Mark.

T. W. (monogram). 6. October 25, 1870. Iron Pipe. Evans, Clow, Dalzell & Co., Pittsburg, Pa.

17. November 1, 1870. 2275. July 20, 1875. Metal Tube. American Tube Works, Boston, Mass.

146. January 31, 1871. Molassess Gate. Geo. S. Lincoln & Co., Hartford, Conn.

178. February 28, 1871. 2707. July 6, 1875. Locks and Hardware. Hillebrand & Wolf, Philadelphia, Pa.

219. April 11, 1871. Stationers' Hardware. Thos. S. Hudson, East Cambridge, Mass.

521. November 7, 1871. Carriage Hardware. H. D. Smith & Co., Plantsville, Conn.

608. January 3, 1872. Coffee Pot. John Ashcroft, Brooklyn, N. Y.

687. June 18, 1872. Tin-Lined Lead Pipe. Colwells, Shaw & Willard Manufacturing Co., New York, N. Y.

992. September 10, 1872. Saddler's Hardware, etc. Van Wart, Son & Co., Birmingham, England.

1357. July 8, 1873. Oil Cans or Packages. Meissner, Ackermann & Co., New York, N. Y.

1413. August 19, 1873. Nails. John Coyne, Pittsburg, Pa.

1510. October 21, 1873. Snap-Hooks. New York Wire Snap Company, New York, N. Y.

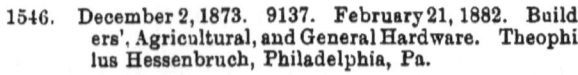

 1546. December 2, 1873. 9137. February 21, 1882. Builders', Agricultural, and General Hardware. Theophilus Hessenbruch, Philadelphia, Pa.

2040. October 27, 1874. Nails, Rivets, and Chains. Wallace & Sons, Ansonia, Conn., and New York, N. Y.

2111. December 8, 1874. Safes, Vaults, and Lock-Work. John Winslow Norris, Canton, Ohio.

 2195. January 26, 1875. Spring Beds. Tucker Manufacturing Co., The, Boston, Mass.

 2211. February 2, 1875. Wire Goods. J. H. & N. A. Williams, Utica, N. Y.

2383. April 20, 1875. Sheet-Metal Cans and Boxes. Theodore W. Burger, Plainfield, N. J.

 2488. May 11, 1875. Iron Pipe. National Tube Works Co., Boston, Mass., and McKeesport, Pa.

 2637. June 8, 1875. Seamless Drawn Tubes. Bridgewater Iron Co., Bridgewater, Mass.

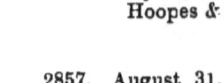 2652. June 8, 1875. Spring Beds. The Tucker Manufacturing Co., Boston, Mass.

 2761. July 20, 1875. 8435. July 5, 1881. Boiler Rivets. Hoopes & Townsend, Philadelphia, Pa.

 2857. August 31, 1875. Hardware. Frank Armstrong, Bridgeport, Conn.

 3123. November 2, 1875. Trace-Buckles. H. S. Woodruff & Co., Janesville, Wis.

 3362. January 18, 1876. 8279. May 31, 1881. Oars, Handspikes, and Capstan Bars. Degramo, Aymar & Co., Brooklyn, N. Y.

3754. June 6, 1876. 20,253. October 27, 1891. Wood Screws. American Screw Co., Providence, R. I.

 3812. June 27, 1876. Chains, Rings, Clips, etc. Krein & Oliver, St. Louis, Mo.

 4272. January 16, 1877. Bird Cages. Hendryx & Bartholomew, Ansonia, Conn.

LOCKS AND HARDWARE.

4378. February 20, 1877. Rivets and Rivet Bars. Brown Brothers, Waterbury, Conn.

4401. February 27, 1877. Horseshoes. Harvey K. Flagler, Boston, Mass.

4450. March 13, 1877. Door and Gate Springs. Van Wagoner & Williams, New York, N. Y.

4596. May 1, 1877. 8565. August 16, 1881. Railroad Spikes, Fish-Plates, etc. St. Louis Bolt & Iron Co., St. Louis, Mo.

4597. May 1, 1877. Fence Strips and Caps. Cyrus L. Topliff, Brooklyn, N. Y.

5280. October 30, 1877. Horseshoe Nails. W. M. Mooney & Co., Au Sable Chasm, N. Y.

5463. January 1, 1878. Rivets and Bars. Blake & Johnson, Waterbury, Ct.

5485. January 8, 1878. Oil-Well Supplies. Gillespie Bros. & Co., Pittsburg, Pa.

5699. March 5, 1878. Water-Closets. Bartholomew & C New York, N. Y.

5829. April 9, 1878. Horseshoe Nails. Ausable Horse Nail Co., Keeseville and New York, N. Y.

5866. April 16, 1878. Builders' Hardware. Russell & Erwin Manufacturing Co., New Britain, Conn.

5982. April 30, 1878. Horseshoe Nails. Putnam Nail Co., Boston Mass.

6266. June 18, 1878. Locks and Builders' Hardware. Mallory, Wheeler & Co., New Haven, Conn.

6471. August 13, 1878. Water Closets. Zane & Roach, Boston, Mass.

6532. September 3, 1878. Carriage and Saddlery Hardware and Trimmings. O. B. North & Co., New Haven, Conn.

6697. October 8, 1878. Wire Cloth of All Kinds. David R. Morse, Brooklyn, N. Y.

7185. April 15, 1879. Barb Fence Wire. Ohio Steel Barb Fence Co., Cleveland, Ohio.

7201. April 15, 1879. 10,762. December 4, 1883. Saddlery Hardware. North & Judd Manufacturing Co., New Britain, Conn.

92 TRADE-MARKS.

7524. July 22, 1879. Blind Awning Fixtures. Charles P. Dearborn, Boston, Mass.

7582. August 12, 1879. Spurs. August Buermann, Newark, N. J.

7635. September 2, 1889. Locks. Western Lock Co., Geneva, Ohio.

7838. February 24, 1880. Chains, Bracelets, Jewelry, etc. F. G. Whitney & Co., Attleborough, Mass.

7939. June 8, 1880. 8756. October 25, 1881. Metal Tubing. National Tube Works Co., Boston, Mass.

8537. August 2, 1881. Horseshoe Nails. W. M. Mooney & Co., Au Sable Chasm, N. Y.

8596. August 23, 1881. Wire Brooms. Marcus C. Isaacs, Chicago, Ill.

8932. December 20, 1881. Steel Umbrella Frames. Samuel Fox & Co., Stockbridge Works, York Co., England.

8933. December 20, 1881. Umbrella Frames. Samuel Fox & Co., Stockbridge Works, York Co., England.

9191. March 14, 1882. Tanks, Cans, etc. John A. Wright, Keene, N. H.

9217. March 21, 1882. Boxed Cans. George W. Banker, Brooklyn, N. Y.

9356. May 16, 1882. Spurs. August Buermann, Newark, N. J.

9440. June 6, 1882. Crucibles and other Chemical Ware. Morgan Crucible Co., Battersea, England.

9441. June 6, 1882. Crucibles. Morgan Crucible Co., Battersea, England.

9442. June 6, 1882. Crucibles. Morgan Crucible Co., Battersea, England.

9566. July 25, 1882. Oil Cups, Valves, etc. Cooper, Jones & Cadbury, Philadelphia, Pa.

10,135. March 27, 1883. Fish-Hooks. Richard Harrison, Bartleet & Co., Redditch, England.

10,189. April 17, 1883. Fish-Hooks and Fishing Tackle. Richard Harrison, Bartleet & Co., Redditch, England.

LOCKS AND HARDWARE. 93

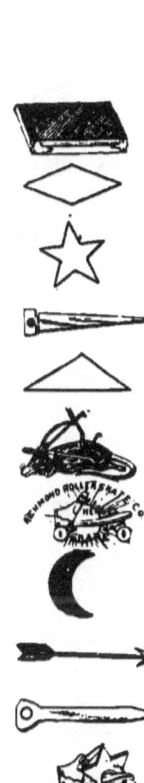

10,217. April 24, 1883. Woven Wire Fabrics. Hartford Woven Wire Matress Co., Hartford, Conn.

10,233. May 1, 1883. Barbed Wire Fencing. Thorn Wire Hedge Co., Chicago, Ill.

10,589. September 18, 1883. Pneumatic Door Checks. Norton Door Check and Spring Co., Boston, Mass.

10,676. October 30, 1883. Horseshoe Nails. Ausable Horse Nail Co., New York, N. Y.

10,781. December 18, 1883. Metal Tubing. Edmund C. Converse, Pittsburg, Pa.

10,965. February 26, 1884. Rat Traps. Elijah P. Peacock, Chicago, Ill.

11,074. April 8, 1884. Roller Skates. Micajah C. Henley, Richmond, Indiana.

11,184. May 13, 1884. Pipes, Fittings, and Plumbers' Supplies. Reuter & Mallory, Baltimore, Md.

11,261. June 17, 1884. Harness, Saddlery, and Carriage Hardware. O. B. North & Co., New Haven, Conn.

11,485. September 16, 1884. Horseshoe Nails. Essex Horse Nail Co., Essex, N. Y.

11,515. September 23, 1884. Roller Skates. Jacob V. Rowlett, Richmond, Ind.

11,521. September 30, 1884. Round Head Screws. P. & F. Corbin, New Britain, Conn.

11,838. December 30, 1884. Staples. Self-Clinching Barbed Staple Co., Boston, Mass.

12,075. April 7, 1885. Roller Skates. Diamond Roller Skate Co., Richmond, Ind.

12,129. April 14, 1885. Oars, Sweeps, and Sculls. New York Boat Oar Co., New York, N. Y.

12,171. April 21, 1885. Oars and Sculls. New York Boat Co., New York, N. Y.

12,201. May 5, 1885. Wire Netting for Fencing, etc. Washington Brockner & Lemuel E. Evans, New York, N. Y.

12,219. May 5, 1885. Nails. Plume & Atwood Manufacturing Co., Waterbury, Conn.

12,367. June 30, 1885. Tacks. Pennsylvania Tack Works, Philadelphia, Pa.

94   TRADE-MARKS.

12,609. September 29, 1885. Dust Pans. Steel Edge Dust Pan Co., Boston, Mass.

12,829. December 1, 1885. Wire Nails, etc. Wire Goods Co., Worcester, Mass.

12,969. January 26, 1886. Furniture Nails. A. Gallais & Co., Paris, France.

13,060. March 2, 1886. Wire Nails. Albert Nail Co., New York, N. Y.

13,180. April 13, 1886. Wire Nails. Hartman Steel Co., Beaver Falls, Pa.

13,261. May 4, 1886. Buckles. Geoffroy Frères, Paris, France.

13,497. July 13, 1886. Sash Balances. Wm. F. Lennon, New York, N. Y.

13,502. July 13, 1886. Transom Lifters. John F. Wollensak, Chicago, Ill.

13,503. July 13, 1886. Transom Lifters. John F. Wollensak, Chicago, Ill.

13,731. October 12, 1886. 14,666. August 9, 1887. Bale Ties. etc. Kilmer Manufacturing Co., Schenectady, N. Y.

13,733. October 19, 1886. Call Bells and Alarms for House Doors. Nathum Judson Busby, Maplewood, Mass.

13,902. December 21, 1886. Hydrants. John C. Kupferle, St. Louis, Mo.

13,979. January 11, 1887. Horseshoe Nails. Simmons Hardware Co., St. Louis, Mo.

14,167. March 15, 1887. Saddlery Hardware, etc. R. S. Luqueer & Co., New York, N. Y.

14,234. April 5, 1887. Embossed Metal Goods. Osborn & Peck, New York, N. Y.

14,250. April 5, 1887. Wire, Wire Rope, Wire Works, etc. Franz Carl Guilleaume, Mülheim, Cologne, Germany.

14,768. September 13, 1887. Metal Tubes. Warren Tube Co., Warren, Ohio.

15,073. January 3, 1888. Picture Supports or Hangers. Brinkerhoff Co., Auburn, N. Y.

LOCKS AND HARDWARE.   95

 15,361. April 17, 1888. Barbed Fence-Cable. Baker Wire Co., Des Moines, Iowa.

 15,372. April 17, 1888. Wire Nails. Pittsburg Wire Nail Co., Pittsburg, Pa.

 15,473. May 15, 1888. Screws, Bolts, Rivets. etc. Shelton Co., Birmingham, Conn.

 15,502. May 22, 1888. Horse Nails. Livingston Nail Co., New York, N. Y.

 15,664. July 3, 1888. Electrical Bells. John F. Wollensak, Chicago, Ill.

 15,665. July 3, 1888. Transom Lifters. John F. Wollensak, Chicago, Ill.

 15,826. September 4, 1888. Umbrella Frames and Parts Thereof. Samuel Fox & Co., Deepcar, York County, England.

 16,025. November 20, 1888. Horseshoe Nails. Samuel G. Winternitz & Bro., Baltimore, Md.

 16,049. November 27, 1888. Galvanized Wire Netting, Wire Cloth, etc., New Jersey Wire Cloth Co., Trenton, N. J.

 16,097. December 11, 1888. Transom Lifters. John F. Wollensak, Chicago, Ill.

 16,137. January 1, 1889. Oars, Handspikes, and Capstan Bars. De Grauw, Aymar & Co., New York, N. Y.

 16,220. January 29, 1889. Safes and Locks. Thomas Barnes, Pittsburg, Pa.

16,333. March 5, 1889. Metal Roofing. Canton Steel Roofing Co., Canton, Ohio.

16,412. March 19, 1889. Horseshoe Nails. Samuel G. Winternitz & Bro., Baltimore, Md.

16,415. March 26, 1889. Oil-Can Spouts. Geo. W. Banker, New York, N. Y.

16,428. April 2, 1889. Oars, Handspikes, and Capstan Bars. De Grauw, Aymar & Co., New York, N. Y.

16,889. July 30, 1889. Bells. Henry McShane & Co., Baltimore, Md.

16,890. July 30, 1889. Bells. Henry McShane & Co., Baltimore, Md.

17,360. January 7, 1890. Locks. Beasley Supply Co., Philadelphia, Pa.

TRADE-MARKS.

17,370. January 7, 1890. Barbed Wire. Freeman Wire and Iron Co., St. Louis, Mo.

17,385. January 7, 1890. Wire for Pictures, Bonnets and Flowers, etc. Tate & Co., Malden, Mass.

17,814. April 22, 1890. Hardware. Warner Manuf. Co., Freeport, Ill.

17,859. May 6, 1890. Hardware. Chas. H. Besly & Co., Chicago, Ill.

17,957. June 3, 1890. Umbrella and Cane Heads, Thimbles, etc. Simons, Bro. & Co., Philadelphia, Pa.

18,203. July 22, 1890. Household Sheet-Metal Wares. Stransky & Co., New York, N. Y. 19,095. February 24, 1891. Johann Baumann, Amberg, Germany.

19,315. April 14, 1891. Shoe Tacks. Dunbar, Hobart & Co., Whitman, Mass.

20,077. August 25, 1891. Kitchen Ware. Haberman Manuf. Co., Berlin and New York, N. Y.

20,128. September 15, 1891. Bird Cages. O. Lindemann & Co., New York, N. Y.

20,716. February 16, 1892. Barbed Wire. Washburn & Moen Manuf. Co., Worcester, Mass.

20,741. February 23, 1892. Metal Fence Pickets. James E. Emerson, Beaver Falls, Pa.

21,019. April 26, 1892. Saddlery Hardware. Eberhard Manuf. Co., Cleveland, Ohio.

21,036. April 26, 1892. Tea Trays. Estate of Walter M. Conger, Jr., Newark, N. J.

21,081. May 10, 1892. Oars, Handspikes, and Capstan Bars. De Grauw, Aymar & Co., New York, N. Y.

21,405. July 5, 1892. Thimbles. Stern Bros. & Co., New York, N. Y.

21,496. July 19, 1892. Chains, Rings, Clips, etc., for Carriages. Baker Chain & Wagon Iron Manuf. Co., Allegheny, Pa.

21,513. July 26, 1892. Hardware. Cash Buyers' Union, Chicago, Ill.

21,840. October 4, 1892. Sash Locks and Fasteners. Wm. A. Bomar, Metropolis, Ill.

22,072. November 28, 1892. Horseshoe Nails. New Process Nail Co., Torrington, Conn.

22,139. December 6, 1892. Sad-Irons. Colebrookdale Iron Co., Pottstown, Pa.

TRADE-MARKS

FOR

MACHINES.

(CLASS 41.)

Embracing Engines, Paper and Printing Machinery, Leather, Textile and Wood-working Machines, and generally all machines not otherwise specially classified.

(See also Classes 1, 12, 17, 34, 40, 50, 58, 66, 68, 70, 73, 76.)

Words or phrases constituting the marks arranged alphabetically.

A.—9101. February 7, 1882. Quicksilver Flasks. Quicksilver Mining Co., New Almaden, Cal.

Adder, The.—16,322. February 26, 1889. Adding Machines. Charles Henry Webb, New York, N. Y.

Admiralty.—17,909. May 13, 1890. Steam Condensers, etc. Fred. M. Wheeler, New York, N. Y.

Advance.—16,854. July 23, 1889. Paper-Cutting Machines. Schniedewend & Lee Co., Chicago, Ill.

Ajax.—13,229. April 27, 1886. Boring Machines. Thomas B. A. David, Pittsburg, Pa.

Aldine.—1766. May 5, 1874. Printing Presses. B. F. Renick & Co., Canton, Ohio.

Alpha.—20,967. April 12, 1892. Centrifugal Creamers. Aktiebolaget Separator, Stockholm, Sweden.

Alpine.—15,190. February 21, 1888. Safe. Alpine Safe Co., Cincinnati, Ohio.

American Turbine Water Wheel.—3465. February 29, 1876. Turbine Water Wheels. Stout, Mills & Temple, Dayton, Ohio.

Americus.—2336. March 30, 1875. Cider Mills. Whitman Agricultural Works, St. Louis, Mo.

Arctic.—8806. November 1, 1881. Soda-Water Apparatus. James W. Tufts, Medford, Mass.

Arctic Soda Apparatus.—678. February 27, 1872. 2431. May 4, 1875. Soda-Water Apparatus, James W. Tufts, Medford, Mass.

Artifex.—13,201. April 20, 1886. Printing Presses. Babcock Printing Press Manufacturing Co , New London, Conn.

Aquarius.—2176. January 19, 1875. Pumps. W. & B. Douglas, Middletown, Conn.

Aquometer.—2998. October 5, 1875. Steam Pumps, Steam and Hydraulic Apparatus. Aquometer Steam Pump Co., Philadelphia, Pa.

Auto.—6453. August 13, 1878. Printing Plates. Louis Brown & Co., Philadelphia, Pa.
Babcock Fire Extinguisher, The.—356. June 27, 1871. Fire Extinguisher. Northwestern Fire Extinguisher Co., Chicago, Ill.
Baby.—20,968. April 12, 1892. Centrifugal Creamers. Aktiebolaget Separator, Stockholm, Sweden.
Ball.—19,019. February 17, 1891. Automatic Cut-Off Engines. Ball Engine Co., Erie, Pa.
Battlefield.—17,352. December 31, 1889. Hydraulic Pumps. John A. Livers, Gettysburg, Pa.
Birch (and design).—13,386. June 15, 1886. Printing Machines. Wm. Birch, Broughton, Salford, England.
Blakeslee.—13,752. October 26, 1886. Steam Siphon Pumps, Injecting Pumps, etc. Blakeslee Manufacturing Co., Du Quoin, Ill.
Boss.—4581. April 24, 1877. Sickle-Grinders. Powell & Stevens, Waukegan, Ill.
Boston.—5042. August 14, 1877. Plaiting Machines. David Miller, New York, N. Y.
Buckeye.—7496. July 8, 1879. Pumps. Mast, Foos & Co., Springfield, Ohio.
Buffalo.—7022. February 11, 1879. Scales. Buffalo Scale Co., Buffalo, N. Y.
Bundy.—17,822. April 29, 1890. Valves for Stoves and Heaters. A. A. Griffing Iron Co., Jersey City, N. J.
Caligraph.—12,168. April 21, 1885. Writing Machines. American Writing Machine Co., New York, N. Y.
Calculagraph.—21,747. September 13, 1892. Calculating Machines. Calculagraph Co., East Orange, N. J.
Cashier.—18,289. August 12, 1890. Cash Indicators, Registers, etc. American Cash Register Co., Charlevoix, Mich.
Caxton (monogram).—3134. November 16, 1875. Printing Press. Griffith & Byrne, New York, N. Y.
Centennial.—9266. April 4, 1882. Atomizers. Young, Ladd & Coffin, New York, N. Y.
Centennial.—20,085. August 25, 1891. Rotary Windmills. Pech Manufacturing Co., Storm Lake, Iowa.
Chace.—6556. September 10, 1878. Oilers for Machines. Consol Fruit Jar Co., New Brunswick, N. J., and New York city.
C. F. S.—13,057. February 23, 1886. Type Writers. Charles Spiro, New York, N. Y.
Challenge.—7827. February 17, 1880. Stone Crushers. Blake Crusher Co., New Haven, Conn.
Challenge.—12,896. December 29, 1885. Spice Mills. Jabez Burns & Sons, New York, N. Y.
Challenge.—16,855. July 23, 1889. 16,856. July 23, 1889. Printing Presses and Paper-Cutting Machines. Shniedewend & Lee Co., Chicago, Ill.
Champion.—740. April 9, 1872. Muley-Saw Hangings. William S. Colwell, Allegheny, Pa.
Champion.—12,249. May 19, 1885. Incubators. Maurice H. Strong, Cincinnati, Ohio.
Champion.—21,165. May 24, 1892. Coffee Hullers. Marcus Mason & Co., New York, N. Y.
Cherub.—14,421. May 17, 1887. Ship Logs and Sounding Machines. Thos. Walker & Son, Birmingham, England.
Chicago Iron Clad Dry Kiln.—16,150. January 1, 1889. Drying Houses or Kilns. I. & M. Wolff & Coleman, Chicago, Ill.
Cleveland Scale Works (and design).—2738. July 13, 1875. Platform Scales. Jones & Lyman, Cleveland, Ohio.
Coll.—15,146. January 31, 1888. Steam Water Ejectors. William J. Sheriff, Pittsburg, Pa.

MACHINES. 99

Columbia.—13,058. February 23, 1886. Type-Writers. Charles Spiro, New York, N. Y.
Columbia.—21,717. September 6, 1892. Cash-Registering Machines. Columbia Cash Register Co., Miamisburg, Ohio.
Columbian.—22,149. December 6, 1892. Centrifugal Creamers. Philip M. Sharples, West Chester, Pa.
Comptometer.—18,154. July 8, 1890. Computing and Transcribing Machines. Felt & Tarrant Manufacturing Co., Chicago, Ill.
Cooper's Engine and Mill Works.—269. May 23, 1871. Machinery. John Cooper, Mount Vernon, Ohio.
Comet.—18,508. October 7, 1890. Oilers. William Vogel & Bros., Brooklyn, N. Y.
D (and lozenge).—2320. March 30, 1875. Loom Temple. Dutcher Temple Co., Hopedale, Mass.
D.—19,433. May 5, 1891. Car Couplings. Standard Car Coupling Co., Troy, N. Y.
Dead Lock.—14,511. June 14, 1887. Hay Elevators, Carriers, and Forks. Janesville Hay Tool Co., Janesville, Wis.
Defiance.—15,043. December 20, 1887. Steam Jet Pumps. William J. Sheriff, Pittsburg, Pa.
Delamater.—17,520. February 11, 1890. Propeller Wheels. Samuel L. Moore & Sons Co., Elizabeth, N. J.
Diamond.—19,133. March 3, 1891. Type-Writer Ribbons. John Underwood & Co., New York, N. Y.
Disc Fan.—14,824. October 11, 1887. Exhaust or Fan Wheels. Levi J. Wing, New York, N. Y.
Dooley.—5327. November 20, 1877. Paper-Cutting Machines. Dooley Manufacturing Co., Boston, Mass.
Double Grip.—19,326. April 14, 1891. Chucks. Westcott Chuck Co., Oneida, N. Y.
Dunning Boiler (and design). 14,769. September 20, 1887. Steam Boilers. William B. Dunning, Geneva, N. Y.
Dynamograph.—14,784. September 27, 1887. Electrical Type-Writers. James F. McLaughlin, Philadelphia, Pa.
Eclipse.—7790. January 6, 1880. Portable Engines. Frick & Co., Waynesborough, Pa.
Eclipse.—19,468. May 12, 1891. Filter Press. Niles Tool Works, Hamilton, Ohio.
Economist.—2678. June 15, 1875. Planing and Matching Machines. Frank & Co., Buffalo, N. Y.
Economize.—3441. February 22, 1876. Steam Boilers and Engines. Porter & Co., Syracuse, N. Y.
Edland.—21,998. November 15, 1892. Type-Writers. Liberty Manufacturing Co., New York, N. Y.
Electro Tint.—16,619. May 21, 1889. Engraved Relief Plates. Purton, Stearns & McIntyre, Philadelphia, Pa.
Empire.—21,322. June 21, 1892. Valves. Dunham, Carrigan & Hayden Co., San Francisco, Cal.
Endurance.—435. August 22, 1871. Pump Barrels. Woodbury, Booth & Co., Rochester, N. Y.
Eureka.—8614. August 30, 1881. Watchman's Time Detectors. Elise Imhauser, Brooklyn, N. Y.
Excelsior.—1473. September 30, 1873. Windmills. Atwood & Bodwell, San Francisco, Cal.
Excelsior.—6352. July 9, 1878. Paper-Cutting Machines. Standard Machine Co., Mystic River, Conn.
Fairbanks.—6131. May 28, 1878. Weighing Scales. E. & F. Fairbanks & Co., St. Johnsbury, Vt.
Fairbanks Infallible. 13,440. June 22, 1886. Coin Scales. Walter H. Harrison, Baltimore, Md.

Farmer's Favorite.—2274. March 2, 1875. Grinding Mills for Fruit, etc. Higganum Manufacturing Co., Higganum, Conn.
Favorite.—5023. August 14, 1877. Scales. John Chatillon & Sons, New York, N. Y.
Favorite.—16,794. July 9, 1889. Dental Instruments and Machinery. George W. Fels, Cincinnati, Ohio.
Fearless.—10,225. May 1, 1883. Horse Powers. Minard Harder. Cobleskill, N. Y.
Florida.—15,410. May 1, 1888. Steam and Hot-Water Boilers. Pierce, Butler & Pierce Manufacturing Co., Syracuse, N. Y.
Fountain Pump (and design).—1339. June 24, 1873. Pumps. Josiah A. Whitman, Cranston, R. I.
Gem.—6198. June 11, 1878. Paper-Cutting Machines. Rufus L. Howard, Buffalo, N. Y.
Gem.—6239. June 18, 1878. Paper-Cutting Machines. Geo. H. Sanborn, Brooklyn, N. Y.
Globe.—1935. August 18, 1874. Gas Regulator. Ward, Ellet & Co., St. Louis, Mo.
Globe.—18,380. September 2, 1890. Blowpipes. Globe Light and Heat Co., Chicago, Ill.
Gravity.—10,035. February 13, 1883. Scales. Fulton Gravity Scale Co., Cincinnati, Ohio.
Great American.—13,944. January 4, 1887. Meat-Mincing Machines. Lloyd & Supplee Hardware Co., Philadelphia, Pa.
Harpoon.—14,450. May 24, 1887. Ship Logs and Sounding Machines. Thomas Walker & Son, Birmingham, England.
Hazelton.—17,121. October 22, 1889. Boilers. Hazelton Boiler Co., New York, N. Y.
He Pays The Freight.—19,572. May 26, 1891. Weighing Scales. Jones of Binghamton, Binghamton, N. Y.
Hercules.—12,186. April 28, 1885. 16,691. June 4, 1889. Wheat Scourers, Separators, Smutters, and Coffee Scourers. Hercules Manufacturing Co., Cardington, Ohio.
Hercules.—17,874. May 6, 1890. Turbine Water Wheels. Holyoke Machine Co., Holyoke, Mass.
Hercules.—20,679. February 2, 1892. Chucks. Oneida Manufacturing Chuck Co., Oneida, N. Y.
Hercules.—21,836. October 4, 1892. Engines. Palmer & Rey, San Francisco, Cal.
Hero.—13,988. January 18, 1887. Grinding Mills. Peter Hobler, Chicago, Ill.
Hero.—14,417. May 17, 1887. Cane and Sorgo Mills. L. M. Rumsey Manufacturing Co., St. Louis, Mo.
H. K.—3585. April 18, 1876. Loom Pickers and Machine Belting. A. & C. W. Holbrook, Providence, R. I.
Hoosier.—16,172. January 15, 1889. Iron and Wood Pumps. Flint & Walling Manufacturing Co., Kendallville, Ind.
Horton Lathe Chuck, The.—518. November 7, 1871. Lathe Chucks. E. Horton & Son, Windsor Locks, Conn.
Huntoon Governor.—334. June 30, 1871. Steam-Engine Governor. J. A. Lynch & E. B. Buckingham, Boston, Mass.
Hydro-Steam.—22,001. November 15, 1892. Machinery for Elevators. Cahill & Hall Elevator Co., San Francisco, Cal.
Ideal.—19,501. May 12, 1891. Steam Engines. A. L. Ide & Son, Springfield, Ill.
Icy.—8436. July 5, 1881. Soda-Water Fountains. John C. Johnson, Philadelphia, Pa.
Improved Fairhaven.—1106. January 21, 1873. Printing Presses. Boston & Fairhaven Iron Works, Fairhaven, Mass.
Improved Fairhaven.—2506. May 11, 1875. Printing Presses. Job C. Tripp, Fairhaven, Mass.

MACHINES. 101

Improved Hercules.—21,834. October 4, 1892. Engines. Palmer & Rey, San Francisco, Cal.
Independence.—13,779. November 2, 1886. 19.665. June 9, 1891. Belt Pulleys. Dodge Manufacturing Co., Mishawaka, Ind.
Intelligent.—19,818. June 30, 1891. Oil Cans. Harry Dutton, Boston, Mass,
I X L.—9305. April 18, 1882. Pipe Cutting and Threading Machines. D. Saunders' Sons, Yonkers, N. Y.
Jenkins.—15,321. March 27, 1888. Valves, and Packing for Valves, Cocks, etc. Jenkins Bros. New York, N. Y.
Keystone.—1849. June 23, 1874. Middlings, Separators, or Purifiers. Brennan & Tucker, Paris, Ill.
Keystone.—16,269. February 12, 1889. Type, Printers' Rules, etc. Mather Manufacturing Co., Philadelphia, Pa.
Keystone Safety (and design). 1928. August 11, 1874. Gas Machine. Keystone Safety Gas Machine Co., Philadelphia, Pa.
Leader.—22,074. November 29, 1892. Machinery for Making Paper Boxes, etc. Lester & Wasley, Norwich Conn.
Leviathan.—12,316. June 16, 1885. Turbine Water Wheels. Henry Reese Mathias, Athens, Ohio.
Liberty.—6608. September 24, 1878. Printing Presses. Francis M. Weiler, New York, N. Y.
Lightning.—8653. September 20, 1881. Wood-Working Machinery. J. A. Fay & Co., Cincinnati, Ohio.
Lightning.—16,269. February 19, 1889. Bank-Check Punches. Frederick J. Lockwood, Bridgeport, Conn.
Linotype.—18,297. August 12, 1890. Machines for Producing Type-Bars. Mergenthaler Printing Co., New York, N. Y.
Little Detective.—7654. September 2, 1879. Scales or Weighing Instruments. Chicago Scale Co., Chicago, Ill.
Little Giant.—1851. June 23, 1874. Injectors for Steam Boilers. Rue Manufacturing Co., Philadelphia, Pa.
Little Giant.—6394. Paper-Cutting Machine. Standard Machinery Co., Mystic River, Conn.
Little Giant.—16,546. April 30, 1889. Chucks. Westcott Chuck Co., Oneida, N. Y.
Lyman.—16,366. March 12, 1889. Steam Exhaust Heads. Wilfred C. Lyman, Chicago, Ill.
Manhattan.—7949. June 22, 1880. Electrotype Plates. Frederick A. Ringler, New York, N. Y.
Merritt.—17,677. March 18, 1890. Type-Writers. Merritt Manufacturing Co., Springfield, Mass.
Milliograph.—18,751. December 30, 1890. Reproducing Drawings and Writings. Milliograph Co., Washington, D. C.
Mineral Arc. -7881. April 20, 1880. Soda Fountains. Alvin D. Puffer & Sons, Boston, Mass.
Model.—5839. April 9, 1878. Printing Presses. J. N. Daughaday & Co., Philadelphia, Pa.
Mohawk Dutchman.—17,975. June 3, 1890. Band-Saw Guides. Goodell & Waters, Philadelphia, Pa.
Monarch.—9618. September 5, 1882. Baling Presses. Wrenn. Whitehurst & Co., Norfolk, Va.
Monitor. 22,056. November 22, 1892. Windmills. Baker Manufacturing Co., Evansville, Wis.
Mouse Hole Forge (and design).—19,862. July 7, 1891. Machinery, Iron, and Steel. Brookes & Cooper, Sheffield, England.
National. 7116. June 17, 1879. 18,911. February 3, 1891. Steam and Vacuum Pumps and Steam Boilers. William E. Kelly, New Brunswick, N. J.
National. 14,656. August 2, 1887. Heel-Nailing Machines. National Heeling Machine Co., Portland, Me.

New England.—19,916. July 21, 1891. Pulp Grinders. Scott & Roberts Co., Bennington, Vt.
New Hercules.—21,835. October 4, 1892. Engines. Palmer & Rey, San Francisco, Cal.
Niagara.—4445. March 13, 1577. Pumps. J. Ryer, A. H. Van Holsen & S. Hardick. Exnrs.. Brooklyn, N. Y.
Ocean Pump.—3193. December 7, 1875. Pumps. Coffin & Woodward. Boston, Mass.
Oneida.—17,719. March 25, 1890. Lathe Chucks. Wescott Chuck Co., Oneida, N. Y.
One Metal.—17,637. March 11, 1890. Digesters for Paper Pulp. De-Oxidized Metal Co., Bridgeport, Conn.
Optimus.—12,552. September 8, 1885. Printing Presses. Babcock Printing Press Manufacturing Co., New London, Conn.
Papyrograph.—4495. March 27, 1877. Apparatus for Multiplying Copies of Writings. W. H. W. Campbell, Norwich, Conn.
Paragon.—19,462. May 12, 1891. 21,819. October 4, 1892. Type-Writing Machines and Attachments. Wyckoff, Seamans & Benedict. New York, N. Y.
Paris.—5533. January 22, 1878. Plaiting Machines. Frank Calvert, Lowell, Mass.
Peerless.—12,106. April 7, 1885. Lubricators, Ejectors, and Cups. Peerless Oil Ejector Co., Quincy, Ill.
Pelton.—17,270. December 10, 1889. Water Wheels and Water Motors. Pelton Water Wheel Co., San Francisco, Cal.
Pendulum.—2177. January 19, 1875. Pumps. W. & B. Douglas, Middleton, Conn.
Peninsular.—20,553. January 5, 1892. Machine for Attaching Buttons to Boots and Shoes. Heaton Peninsular Button Fastener Co., Providence, R. I.
Perfection.—19,124. March 3, 1891. 19,125. March 3, 1891. Wire-Stitching Machines and Wire for same. James L. Morrison, New York, N. Y.
Phœnix.—8510. July 26, 1881. Weighing Scales. Phœnix Scale Co., Milwaukee, Wis.
Porcupine.—17,120. October 22, 1889. Boilers. Hazelton Boiler Co., New York, N. Y.
Pressure Extract.—5336. November 20, 1877. Apparatus for Making Extracts. Pressure Extract Co., Trenton, N. J.
Printers.—6616. September 24, 1878. Paper-Cutting Machines. Standard Machinery Co., Mystic River, Conn.
Pulsometer.—6605. September 24, 1878. Steam Pumps. Pulsometer Steam Pump Co., New York, N. Y.
Queen of the South.—1497. October 14, 1873. Grinding Mills. Isaac Straub & Co., Cincinnati, Ohio.
Queen of the West.—1230. April 22, 1873. Grinding Mills. Straub Mill Co., Cincinnati, Ohio.
Queen Mill, The.—1295. June 3, 1873. Grinding Mills. Alexander W. Winall, Cincinnati, Ohio.
Real S. A. H.—731. April 2, 1872. Copying Presses. Arthur Le Clercq. New York, N. Y.
Remington.—15,375. April 17, 1888. 15,960. October 23, 1888. Type-Writing Machines. Standard Type-Writer Manufacturing Co., New York, N. Y.
Remington Standard.—14,823. October 11, 1887. 15,961. October 23, 1888. Type-Writing Machines. Standard Type-Writer Manufacturing Co., New York, N. Y.
Rensselaer.—20,672. February 2, 1892. Weighing Scales. Jones of Binghamton, Binghamton, N. Y.
Rival.—14,337. April 26, 1887. Paper-Cutting Machine. P. A. Noyes & Co., Groton, Conn.

Royal.—15,044. December 20, 1887. Carpet Beaters. Simmons & Tullidge, London, England.
Rusher.—21,991. November 15, 1892. Thrashing, Stacking, and Weighing Machines, and Steam Engines. Port Huron Engine and Thresher Co., Port Huron, Mich.
Russian.—19,757. June 23, 1891. Centrifugal Creamers. Phillip M. Sharples, West Chester, Pa.
Sensitive.—9938. January 9, 1883. Drilling Machines. Dwight Slate, Hartford, Conn.
Silence (and design).—9803. November 14, 1882. Pneumatic Door Checks. Elliot Pneumatic Door Check Co., Boston, Mass.
Skinner.—7685. September 16, 1879. Steam Engines and Boilers. Skinner & Wood, Erie, Pa.
Sleeve Roller.—10,683. October 30, 1883. Pulley Blocks. Herbert Lond. Boston, Mass.
Snow Flake.—7551. July 29, 1879. Middlings Purifiers. Straub Mill Co., Cincinnati, Ohio.
Solid Wrought.—10,968. February 26, 1884. Anvils. Peter Wright & Sons, Dudley, Worcester County, England.
Special.—4193. December 12, 1876. Steam Pumps. Adam S. Cameron, New York, N. Y.
Spiral Draft (and design).—3729. May 30, 1876. Spark Arresters. Hawkesworth & Colford, Halifax, Canada.
Standard.—10,205. April 24, 1883. Printing Presses. Babcock Printing Press Manufacturing Co., New London, Conn.
Standard.—13,018. February 9, 1886. Grinding Mills. R. L. Orr & Co., Pittsburg, Pa.
Standard.—15,357. April 10, 1888. 15,962. October 23, 1888. Type Writing Machines. Standard Type Writer Manufacturing Co., New York, N. Y.
Stanley.—18,792. January 6, 1891. Wood-Working Tools and Machines. Stanley Rule and Level Co., New Britain, Conn.
Star.—1429. August 26, 1873. Gas Machines. F. W. Ofeldt & Co., Newark, N. J.
Star.—11,701. November 25, 1884. Coffee and Spice Mills. Henri H. Coles, Philadelphia, Pa.
Star Of The West *.—432. August 22, 1871. Pump. Hiram Smith, Hillsdale, N. Y.
Steam * Pump.—1015. October 1, 1872. Steam Pumps. Norwalk Iron Works, South Norwalk, Conn.
Straight Line.—10,248. May 1, 1883. Steam Engines. Straight Line Engine Co., Syracuse, N. Y.
Sure Grip.—19,666. June 9, 1891. Tackle Blocks. Fulton Iron and Engine Works, Detroit, Mich.
Swan.—2178. January 19, 1875. Pumps. W. & B. Douglas. Middletown, N. Y.
Technicon.—12,310. June 16, 1885. Instruments for Exercising Hands, Wrist, etc. James Brotherhood, Stratford, Ontario, Canada.
Telegraph.—13,082. March 2, 1886. Hay, Fodder, and Straw Cutters. Willson Bros. & Co., Harrisburg, Pa.
Test-Tubes—Fused Ends. 1591. January 6, 1874. Test-Tubes for Water-Gages for Steam Boilers. E. H. Ashcroft, Boston, Mass.
Time Telegraph.—9977. January 23, 1883. Mechanism used as Electrical Time Indicators. Time Telegraph Co., New York, N. Y.
Trade Engine. 1837. June 16, 1874. Steam Engines. Herchelrode & Hill, Dayton, Ohio.
Triumph, The.—11,696. November 18, 1884. Steam Boilers. Rice, Whitacre & Co., Chicago, Ill.
Tucker. 10,903. January 29, 1884. Grease Traps. Meyer Sniffen & Co., New York, N. Y.

Turntable.—1385. July 29, 1873. Apple-Paring Machines. D. H. Goodell, Antrim, N. H.
Typograph.—15,959. October 23, 1888. Stereotype-Making Machines. John R. Rogers, Cleveland, Ohio.
Universal.—13,179. April 13, 1886. Printing and Embossing Presses. Merritt Gally, New York, N. Y.
Universal Wood Worker.—381. July 18, 1871. 2715. July 6, 1875. Wood-Working Machines. McBeth, Bentel & Margedant, Hamilton, Ohio.
V A C.—20,594. January 12, 1892. Electrotypes, Stereotypes, and Wood Cuts. Vilmorin, Andrieux & Co., Paris, France.
Valadium.—19,134. March 3, 1891. Type-Writer Ribbons. John Underwood & Co., New York, N. Y.
Victor.—49. November 1, 1870. Scale. Victor Scale Company, Dixon, Illinois.
Victor.—12,661. October 13, 1885. Turbine Water Wheels. Stilwell & Bierce Manufacturing Co., Dayton, Ohio.
Victor.—17,871. May 6, 1890. Telegraph Instruments, etc. E. S. Greely & Co., New Haven, Conn.
Victor.—21,164. May 24, 1892. Coffee Polishers. Marcus Mason & Co., New York, N. Y.
Vulcan.—12,036. March 24, 1885. Water, Steam, and other Valves. D. P. Dieterich, Philadelphia, Pa.
Vulcanine.—1703. March 31, 1874. Top-Rollers for Drawing Frames. Edward Page, Lawrence, Mass.
Walker's Ship Log A1.—14,420. May 17, 1887. Ship Logs and Sounding Machines. Thos. Walker & Son, Birmingham, England.
Walker's Ship Log A2.—14,422. May 17, 1887. Ship Logs. Thos. Walker & Son, Birmingham, England.
Welcome.—1883. July 21, 1874. Carpet Sweepers. Haley, Morse & Co., Boston, Mass.
Westcott.—17,068. September 24, 1889. Lathe Chucks. Westcott Chuck Co., Oneida, N. Y.
Wharfedale.—826. May 21, 1872. Printing Presses. Victor E. Mauger, New York, N. Y.
Wick-ed Oiler.—2563. May 18, 1875. Oiling Apparatus. Sam'l Hutchinson, Jr., Salem, Mass.
Wilson Belt-Hooks.—18,973. February 10, 1891. Hooks for Machine Belting. Walter O. Talcott, Providence, R. I.
Woodbury.—21,256. June 7, 1892. Steam Engines. Stearns Manufacturing Co., Erie, Pa.
X L.—6001. May 7, 1878. Printers' Galleys. R. F. Cole & Co., New York, N. Y.
Zazel.—6748. October 22, 1878. Gymnastic Apparatus, etc. William Farini, Westminster, England.
Zero.—16,994. September 10, 1889. Ice-Making Machines. Alexander Conacher, New York, N. Y.

COMPILED BY

WALLACE A. BARTLETT,

Patent Attorney,

WASHINGTON, D. C.

TRADE-MARKS

FOR

MACHINES.

(CLASS 41.)

Designs showing essential feature claimed as trade-mark.

68. November 22, 1870. Steam Governor. John Augustus Lynch & Co., Boston, Mass.

133. January 10, 1871. Steam Engine. Joel Sharp, Salem, O.

198. March 21, 1871. 3129. November 16, 1875. Pumps. Chas. G. Blatchley, Philadelphia, Pa.

200. March 21, 1871. Scales. Edward F. Jones, Binghamton, N. Y.

243. May 2, 1871. Pumps. Rich & Burlingham, New York, N. Y.

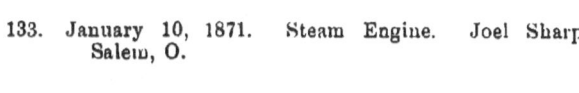
496. October 24, 1871. Loom Temples. Dutcher Temple Co., Hopedale, Mass.

886. July 9, 1872. Printing Machinery and Materials. Victor E. Mauger, New York, N. Y.

995. September 17, 1872. Cloth-Cutting Machines. Isaac Fenno & Co., Boston, Mass.

1339. June 24, 1873. Pumps. Josiah A. Whitman, Cranston, R. I.

1359. July 8, 1873. Water Gage for Steam Boilers. Tomey and Sons, Perth, Scotland.

1591. January 6, 1874. Test Tubes for Water Gages. E. H. Ashcroft, Boston, Mass.

1628. February 10, 1874. Pumps and Pumping Machines. John A. Rumsey, Seneca Falls, N. Y.

1805. May 26, 1874. Grinding Mills. Straub Mill Co., Cincinnati, Ohio.

 1928. August 11, 1874. Gas Machines. Keystone Safety Gas Machine Co., Philadelphia, Pa.

 1989. September 15, 1874. Injectors for Steam Generators. Rue Manufacturing Co., Philadelphia, Pa.

2259. February 23, 1875. Steam Engines and Paper Machinery. Victor E. Mauger, New York, N. Y.

 2320. March 30, 1875. Loom Temples. Dutcher Temple Co., Hopedale, Mass.

 824. May 11, 1872. 2563. May 18, 1875. Oiling Apparatus. Samuel Hutchinson, Jr., Salem, Mass.

 2738. July 13, 1875. Platform Scales. Jones & Lyman, Cleveland, Ohio.

2897. August 31, 1875. Force Pumps. William J. Johnson, Newton, Mass.

 2963. September 21, 1875. Nautical Instruments. Robert Merrill & Sons, New York, N. Y.

 3134. November 16, 1875. Printing Presses. Griffith & Byrne, New York, N. Y.

 3729. May 30, 1876. Spark-Arresters, etc. Daniel Hawkesworth & Henry Colford, Halifax, Canada.

3825. June 27, 1876. Horse Power. Aultman & Taylor Co., Mansfield, Ohio.

 3993. September 19, 1876. Steam Gages. Edward H. Ashcroft, Boston, Mass.

4486. March 27, 1877. Chilled Rolls, etc. J. Morton Poole & Co., Wilmington, Delaware.

4696. June 5, 1877. Fire Escapes, etc. Herbert R. Houghton, New York, N. Y.

 5126. September 4, 1877. Locomotive Boiler Tubes. National Tube Works Co., Boston, Mass.

 5762. March 19, 1878. Gas and Water Registering Apparatus. American Meter Co., New York, N. Y.

5763. March 19, 1878. Gas and Water Registering Apparatus. American Meter Co., New York, N. Y.

MACHINES. 107

5764.   March 19, 1878. Gas and Water Registering Apparatus. American Meter Co., New York, N. Y.

5916.   April 23, 1878. Steam Engines. Armington & Sims, Lawrence, Mass.

6636.   October 1, 1878. Weighing Scales. E. & T. Fairbanks & Co., St. Johnsbury, Vt.

7144.   April 1, 1879. Standard Weights and Measures. College of Pharmacy of the City of New York, New York, N. Y.

7792.   January 6, 1880. Beating and Mixing Machines. Chas. Lehmann, Brooklyn, N. Y.

8486.   July 19, 1881. Horse Powers. Aultman & Taylor Co., Mansfield, Ohio.

9042.   January 24, 1882. Tackle Blocks. Penfield Block Co., Lockport, N. Y.

9281.   April 11, 1882. Watchman's Time Detectors. Elise Imhauser, New York, N. Y.

9423.   May 30, 1882. Ring Travellers. Nathan P. Hicks, Pawtucket, R. I.

9454.   June 13, 1882. Millstones. North Carolina Millstone Co., Westminster, Md.

9566.   July 25, 1882. Oil-Cups, Valves, Cocks, etc. Cooper, Jones & Cadbury, Philadelphia, Pa.

9572.   July 25, 1882. Machinery of Various Kinds. P. R. Jackson & Co., Manchester, England.

9690.   September 19, 1882. Type-Writing Machines. H. H. Unz, Chicago, Ill.

9803.   November 14, 1882. Pneumatic Door Checks. Elliot Pneumatic Door Check Co., Boston, Mass.

9925.   January 2, 1883. Cards for Carding Cotton. L. S. Watson & Co., Leicester, Mass.

10,517. August 28, 1883. Resaws, Molding Machines, Planes, etc. James S. Graham & Co., Rochester, N. Y.

10,611. October 2, 1883. Roller Mills, Centrifugal Reels, etc. Louis B. Fiechter Manufacturing Co., Minneapolis, Minn.

10,648. October 23, 1883. Tackle and Pulley Blocks Bagnall & Loud, Boston, Mass.

TRADE-MARKS.

11,011. March 18, 1884. Telegraphic Call Boxes. Augustus G. Davis, Baltimore, Md.

11,284. June 24, 1884. Float Logs. J. Spencer & Co., Baltimore, Md.

11,501. September 23, 1884. Smutters, Separators, and BrushMachines. Martin Deal & Co., Bucyrus, Ohio.

11,701. November 25, 1884. Coffee and Spice Mills. Henri H. Coles, Philadelphia, Pa.

12,029. March 17, 1885. Valves and Hydrants. Chapman Valve Manufacturing Co., Boston, Mass.

12,098. April 7, 1885. Top Rolls for Cotton, Silk, etc. Frank L. Huston, Providence, R. I.

12,147. April 21. 1885. Writing Machines. American Writing Machine Co., New York, N. Y.

12,370. June 30, 1885. Mathematical Instruments. Conrad Proebster, Jr., Nuremberg, Germany.

12,476. August 4, 1885. Valves, Lubricators, Plugs, etc. Wm. Powell & Co., Cincinnati, Ohio.

12,811. December 1, 1885. Self-Spacing Type. Henry Bledsoe, Fort Worth, Texas.

13,072. March 2, 1886. Printing Type. MacKellar, Smiths & Jordan Co., Philadelphia, Pa.

13,097. March 9, 1886. Windmills and Tanks. O. G. Stowell, Delavan, Wis.

13,380. June 8, 1886. Weighing Scales having Torsion Pivots. United States Torsion Balance and Scale Co., New York, N. Y.

13,386. June 15, 1886. Machines for Printing and Finishing Textile Fabrics. Wm. Birch, Broughton, Lancaster Co., England.

13,619. August 31, 1886. Steam Boilers. Buerkel & Co., Boston, Mass.

13,823. November 23, 1886. Springs and Balances. Geo. Salter & Co., West Bromwich, Stafford, England.

14,071. February 15, 1887. Spool Holders. Solomon Danelius & Co., Philadelphia, Pa.

14,258. April 12, 1887. Rock-Drilling Machines. M. C. Bullock Manufacturing Co., Chicago, Ill.

MACHINES. 109

14,423. May 24, 1887. Mills, Machinery, Steam Engines, etc. Edward P. Allis & Co., Milwaukee, Wis.

14,769. September 28, 1887. Steam Boilers. Wm. B. Dunning, Geneva, N. Y.

14,945. November 15, 1887. Centrifugal Pumps. William O. Webber, Lawrence and Boston, Mass.

15,099. January 10, 1888. Steam Gages. Star Brass Manufacturing Co., Boston, Mass.

15,234. February 28, 1888. Gage-Pins, Feed-Guides, Tools, and Machinery for Printing. Edward L. Megill, New York, N. Y.

15,376. April 17, 1888. Type-Writing Machines. Standard Type-Writer Manufacturing Co., New York, N. Y.

15,453. May 15, 1888. Gate Valves. Arthur Co., New York, N. Y.

15,623. June 19, 1888. Safety Fusible Plugs for Boilers. Geo. Van Wagener, New York, N. Y.

15,861. September 11, 1888. Printing Presses, Types, and Printers' Tools, etc. Union Type Foundry, Chicago, Ill.

16,108. December 18, 1888. Ribbons for Type-Writing Machines. J. Underwood & Co., New York, N. Y.

16,269. February 12, 1889. Printers' Furniture. Mather Manufacturing Co., Philadelphia, Pa.

16,287. February 19, 1889. Churns. John C. Kearns, Maitland, Pa.

16,402. March 19, 1889. Stitching Horses. Randall & Co., Cincinnati, Ohio.

16,787. July 9, 1889. Display Frames. Wm. A. Aiken, Norwich, Conn.

16,807. July 9, 1889. Chemical Fire Extinguishing Apparatus. Worcester Fire Appliance Co., Worcester, Mass.

16,898. Steam and Water Valves. Fairbanks & Co., New York, N. Y.

16,899. August 6, 1889. Steam and Water Valves. Fairbanks & Co., New York, N. Y.

17,122. October 22, 1889. Boilers. Hazelton Boiler Co., New York, N. Y.

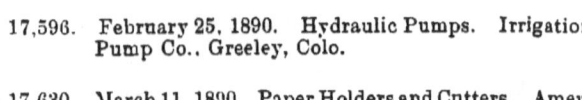

17,596. February 25, 1890. Hydraulic Pumps. Irrigation Pump Co., Greeley, Colo.

17,630. March 11, 1890. Paper Holders and Cutters. American Roll Paper Co., St. Louis, Mo.

17,636. March 11, 1890. Digesters for Paper Pulp. De-Oxidized Metal Co., Bridgeport, Conn.

17,638. March 11, 1890. Digesters for Paper Pulp. De-Oxidized Metal Co., Bridgeport, Conn.

17,639. March 11, 1890. Digesters for Paper Pulp. De-Oxidized Metal Co., Bridgeport, Conn.

17,670. March 18, 1890. Exercising Machines. Daniel L. Dowd, New York, N. Y.

17,771. April 15, 1890. Pulley Weights and similar Exercising Apparatus. John E. Dowd, Chicago, Ill.

18,156. July 8, 1890. Coin-Operated Machines. John U. O'Meara, Washington, D. C.

18,887. January 30, 1891. Card-Clothing. Mechanical Fabric Co., Providence, R. I.

19,252. March 31, 1891. Automatic Sprinklers. Robert Wood, Syracuse, N. Y.

19,682. July 7, 1891. Machinery and Manufactures of Iron and Steel. Brookes & Cooper, Sheffield, England.

20,371. November 17, 1891. Steel Stamps for Numbering, etc. E. J. Brooks & Co., New York, N. Y.

20,849. March 15, 1892. Air-Brake Apparatus. Westinghouse Air Brake Co., Wilmerding, Pa.

21,236. May 31, 1892. Cash-Registering Machines. Boston Cash Register Co., Northampton, Mass.

21,391. June 28, 1892. Woodworking Machinery. Berlin Machine Works, Beloit, Wis.

21,599. August 9, 1892. Meat Choppers and Presses. Enterprise Manufacturing Co. of Pennsylvania, Philadelphia, Pa.

22,057. November 22, 1892. Post-Office Letter Boxes. Keyless Lock Co., Indianapolis, Ind.

Established in 1857.

The Age of Steel.

ST. LOUIS.

NEW YORK.   CHATTANOOGA.

WM. E. BARNS, Editor.   JOURNAL OF COMMERCE CO., Publishers.

THE AGE OF STEEL represents the Highest Degree of Excellence, and is the Recognized Leader and Standard in the great South and West, in all matters pertaining to

APPLIED MECHANICS, STEAM AND HYDRAULIC ENGINEERING, ELECTRICITY AND HARDWARE.

Its Editorials and Market Reviews, and its treatment of all questions in Theoretical and Applied Mechanics, cover every phase of the most

ADVANCED MODERN TRADE JOURNALISM.

Eastern Branch Office:

Vanderbilt Building, 15 and 17 Beekman Street, New York.

L. S. STONE, Vice-President and Manager.

The St. Louis Lumberman,

ST. LOUIS.   NEW YORK.   CHATTANOOGA.

WM. E. BARNS, Editor.   JOURNAL OF COMMERCE CO., Publishers.

THE ST. LOUIS LUMBERMAN is the regularly adopted and official organ of the Lumber Organizations of the South and West. Its reviews of the Lumber and Allied Trades of the great South-West cover every branch of these important interests. It has no successful rival in the

GREAT LUMBER FIELDS OF THE SOUTHWEST.

Eastern Branch Office:

Vanderbilt Building, 15 and 17 Beekman Street, New York.

L. S. STONE, Vice-President and Manager.

TRADE-MARKS
FOR
NEEDLES AND PINS.
(CLASS 47.)

Embracing Knitting and Sewing Needles, Common Pins, Safety Pins, Needle-Threaders, &c. (See also Class 58, Sewing Machines and Attachments.)

Words or Phrases Constituting the Marks Alphabetically Arranged.

Aunt Mary's.—20,572. January 12, 1892. Threaded Needles. Frank W. Hall, Madison, Wis.
Calyxeyed.—15,656. July 3, 1888. Needles. Henry Milward & Sons, Redditch, England.
Cleopatra.—8099. November 23, 1880. 9260. April 4, 1882. Sewing Needles. John Thornton, Jr., Brooklyn, N. Y.
Columbia.—21,888. October 25, 1892. Straight Pins. Plume & Atwood Manufacturing Co., Waterbury, Conn.
Crown.—11,311. July 8, 1884. Safety Pins. J. G. Whitmore and New England Pin Co., Winsted, Conn.
Duplex.—18,832. January 13, 1891. Safety Pins. Consolidated Safety Pin Co., New York, N. Y.
Excelsior.—1056. November 12, 1872. 2561. May 18, 1875. Sewing-Machine Needles. Excelsior Needle Co., Wolcottville, Conn.
Family.—10,436. July 17, 1883. Pins. Plume & Atwood Manufacturing Co., Waterbury, Conn.
Fil-Tenax.—17,605. February 25, 1890. Side-Threading Needles. James Smith & Son, Astwood Bank, England.
Flexor.—9862. December 12, 1882. Hair Pins. Kirby, Beard & Co., London, England.
Flower City (and design).—6540. September 3, 1878. Pins. Judson & Fountain Pin Works, Rochester, N. Y.
Genesee (and design).—6541. September 3, 1878. Pins. Judson & Fountain Pin Works, Rochester, N. Y.
Globe (with design).—1738. April 28, 1874. Needles, etc. Cooley, Bigelow & Nichols, and Globe Manufacturing Co., New York, N. Y.
Grip (and design).—20,793. March 1, 1892. Hair Pins. Albert Angell, Orange, N. J.
H. Baylis.—6474. August 13, 1878. Sewing and Knitting Needles. Henry Baylis, New York, N. Y.
James Smith & Son.—9931. January 2, 1883. Sewing Needles. James Smith & Son, Astwood Bank, Worcester Co., England.
La Fatinitzi.—7853. March 16, 1880. Braid Pins. Aldrich Cook, Leominster, Mass.
La Perlee.—21,184. May 24, 1892. Hair Pins. S. Beaumont & Co., Roubaix, France.
Lion.—21,289. June 14, 1892. Pins. Kirby, Beard & Co., Birmingham, England.

NEEDLES, PINS, ETC. 113

Magic.—1693. March 24, 1874. Needle Threaders and Setters. Henry Weels, Woburn, Mass.

Merchant's Adamantine.—2443. May 11, 1875. Pins. Star Pin Co., Birmingham, Conn.

Ne Plus Ultra (and design).—3967. September 5, 1876. Hair Pins. Blake & Johnson, Waterbury, Conn.

O. N. T.—8976. January 3, 1882. Needles and Pins. George A. Clark & Bro., New York, N. Y.

Oriental.—2442. May 11, 1875. Pins. Star Pin Co., Birmingham, Conn.

Parabola.—358. June 27, 1871. Needles. Robert J. Roberts, New York, N. Y.

Parabola.—6047. May 14, 1878. Needles. Robert J. Roberts, West Brighton, N. Y.

Paragon.—9494. June 27, 1882. Needles for Hand and Machine Sewing. David Evans, Studley, England.

Perfection.—18,152. July 8, 1890. Needles. Blumenthal & Boas, New York, N. Y.

Phœnix.—18,036. June 17, 1890. Needles. Thos. H. Harper, Redditch, England.

Puritan.—20,816. March 8, 1892. Pins. American Pin Co., Waterbury, Conn.

Queen's Own.—11,812. December 23, 1884. Pins. Dieckerhoff, Raffloer & Co., New York, N. Y.

Standard.—6222. June 11, 1878. Needles. National Needle Co., Springfield, Mass.

Star (and design).—2444. May 11, 1875. Pins. Star Pin Co., Birmingham, Conn.

Star Pin.—2445. May 11, 1875. Pins. Star Pin Company, Birmingham, Conn.

Stewart's.—11,307. July 8, 1884. Safety Pins. J. W. Stewart, New York, N. Y.

Tourist.—21,264. June 7, 1892. Pins. American Pin Company, Waterbury, Conn.

COMPILED BY

WALLACE A. BARTLETT,

Patent Attorney,

WASHINGTON, D. C.

TRADE-MARKS
FOR
NEEDLES, PINS, ETC.
(CLASS 47.)

Designs showing essential feature claimed as Trade-Mark.

1738. April 28, 1874. Needles. Cooley, Biglow & Nichols and the Globe Manufacturing Co., New York, N. Y.

1850. June 23, 1874. Sewing-Machine Needle. Herman B. Goodrich, Chicago, Ill.

2444. May 11, 1875. Pins. Star Pin Co., Birmingham, Conn.

2446. May 11, 1875. Pins. Star Pin Co., Birmingham, Conn.

3563. April 4, 1876. 10,919. February 5, 1884. Pins. Thomas Porter, Mount Clair, N. J., and New York, N. Y.

3947. August 22, 1876. 10,948. February 19, 1884. Pins. Thomas Porter, Mount Clair, N. J.

3967. September 5, 1876. Hair Pins. Blake & Johnson Waterbury, Conn.

4259. January 9, 1877. Pins. Oakville Co., Waterbury, Conn.

4571. April 24, 1877. Safety Pins. William A. Butler, New York, N. Y.

6048. May 14, 1878. Needles. Robt. J. Roberts, West Brighton, N. Y.

6105. May 21, 1878. Needles. John Thornton & Co., New York, N. Y.

6540. September 3, 1878. Pins. Judson & Fontaine Pin Works, Rochester, N. Y.

NEEDLES, PINS, ETC. 115

6541. September 3, 1878. Pins. Judson & Fontaine Pin Works, Rochester, N. Y.

6542. September 3, 1878. Pins. Judson & Fontaine Pin Works, Rochester, N. Y.

7093. March 11, 1879. Needles. Liebenroth, Von Auw & Co., New York, N. Y.

7141. April 1, 1879. Needles. Liebenroth, Von Auw & Co., New York, N. Y.

8100. November 23, 1880. 9261. April 4, 1882. Sewing Needles. John Thornton, Jr., Brooklyn, N. Y.

9833. November 21, 1882. Needles. Wolff & Kruppenberg, Ichtershausen, Germany.

10,066. February 20, 1883. Sewing Needles. James Smith & Son, Astwood Bank, Worcester County, England.

10,166. April 10, 1883. Needles. Thos. H. Harper, Redditch, Worcester County, England.

10,437. July 17, 1883. Pins. Plume & Atwood, Manufacturing Co., Waterbury, Conn.

11,311. July 8, 1884. Safety Pins. J. G. Whetmore and New England Pin Co., Winsted, Conn.

11,416. August 12, 1884. Needles for Hand Sewing and for the Sewing Machine. Henry Milward & Sons, Redditch, Worcester County, England.

11,653. November 11, 1884. Needles for Hand and Machine Sewing. John James & Sons, Redditch, Worcester County, England.

12,011. March 10, 1885. Spiral Hair Pins. Henry G. Thompson & Sons, New Haven, Conn.

12,537. August 25, 1885. Needles. Alfred A. Wright, St. Louis, Mo.

12,584. September 22, 1885. Needles for Hand Sewing. Wm. Bartlett & Sons, Redditch, Worcester County, England.

12,585. September 22. Needles, Toilet Pins, Bodkins, etc. Wm. Bartlett & Sons, Redditch, Worcester County, England.

12,675. October 20, 1885. Safety Pins. Joel Jenkins, New York, N. Y.

116 TRADE-MARKS.

12,676. October 20, 1885. Safety Pins. Joel Jenkins, New York, N. Y.

12,989. February 2, 1886. Needles, Pins, &c. T. H. Harper, Redditch, England.

15,731. July 31, 1888. Needles. Henry Milward & Sons, Redditch, England.

15,944. October 16. 1888. Needles. Claude M. Boland, New York, N. Y.

18,321. August 19, 1890. Needles. Stephan Beissel Sel. Wove. & Sohn, Olachen, Germany.

18,530. October 14, 1890. Pins. Alfred Shrimpton & Sons, New York, N. Y.

18,574. November 4, 1890. Sewing Needles. Stephan Beissel Sel., Wove. & Sohn, Aachen, Germany.

19,062. February 24, 1891. Needles and Fish-Hooks. Wm. E. Compton, Redditch, England.

19,196. March 17, 1891. Sewing Needles. Geo. Printz & Co., Aachen, Prussia, Germany.

COMPILED BY
WALLACE A. BARTLETT,
Patent Attorney,
WASHINGTON, D. C.

TRADE-MARKS

FOR

Machine Packing, Belting, Hose, Etc.

(CLASS 50.)

Embracing Piston and other Packing, Hose, Belting, Boiler Coverings, &c. (See also Class 40, Locks and Hardware; Class 41, Machines.)

WORDS OR PHRASES CONSTITUTING THE MARKS ALPHABETICALLY ARRANGED.

Acequia.—17,604. February 24, 1890. Rubber Belting, Hose, and Packing. Revere Rubber Co., Boston, Mass.
Adriatic.—19,292. April 7, 1890. Fire Hose. Cornelius Callahan Co., Boston, Mass.
Albino (and design).—21,445. July 12, 1892. Leather and Belting. A. & C. W. Holbrook, Providence, R. I.
Arabian.—17,302. December 24, 1889. Rubber Belting, Hose, and Packing. Stephen Ballard & Co., New York, N. Y.
Asbestos Fringed Edge (and design). 5760. March 19, 1878. Boiler Covering. Henry W. Johns, Brooklyn, N. Y.
Asbesto-Sponge.—16,177. January 15, 1889. Boiler and Pipe Covering, etc. H. W. Johns Manufacturing Co., New York, N. Y.
Astafalta. 21,605. August 16, 1892. Flange Packings. Alfred W. Case, Highland Park, Conn.
Belt (and design).—20,855. March 22, 1892. Belting. Stephen Ballard Rubber Co., New York, N. Y.
Bianca.—17,303. December 24, 1889. Rubber Hose. Stephen Ballard & Co., New York, N. Y.
Black Line (and design). 17,792. April 22, 1890. Hose. Boston Woven Hose Co., Boston, Mass.
Blake's Belt Stud.—13,831. November 23, 1886. Belt Fastenings. Greene, Tweed & Co, Brooklyn, N. Y.
Blue (with blue thread in hose).—3711. May 23, 1876. Pump Hose. Wannalanset Manufacturing Co., Boston, Mass.
Boston Extra.—17,143. October 29, 1889. Belts and Hose. Boston Woven Hose Co., Boston, Mass.
Bull Dog.—21,713. August 30, 1892. Rubber Belting. Boston Woven Hose and Rubber Co., Boston, Mass.
Cable.—7761. October 28, 1879. Fire Hose. Henry F. Herkner, New York, N. Y.
Camel Hair Belting (and design). 21,346. June 21, 1892. Machine Belting. F. Reddaway & Co., Manchester, England.
Carbon. 16,065. December 4, 1888. Rubber Belting and Hose. New York Belting and Packing Co., New York, N. Y.
Chesapeake. 13,848. December 7, 1886. Belting of Canvas, Duck and Woven Cotton. Chesapeake Belting Co., Baltimore, Md.

Clinton Brand (and design).—14,487. June 7, 1887. Packing. Clinton Mfg. Co , Brooklyn, N. Y.
Compress.—17,301. December 24, 1889. Rubber Belting. Stephen Ballard & Co., New York, N. Y.
Crescent.—16,371. March 12. 1889. Hose of Rubber, Cotton or Linen. Revere Rubber Co., Boston, Mass.
Czar.—17,511. February 11. 1890. Hose, Belting, and Packing. John H. Cheever. New York, N. Y.
Diamond (and design).—15,510. May 22, 1888. Leather Belting. W. S. Nott Co., Minneapolis, Minn.
Diamond.—16,064. December 4, 1888. Rubber Belting and Hose. New York Belting and Packing Co., New York, N. Y.
Diamond (and design).—18,673. December 2, 1890. Mechanical Rubber Goods, etc. New York Belting and Packing Co., New York, N. Y.
Diamond.—18,706. December 16, 1890. Hose and Belting. New Jersey Car Spring and Rubber Co., Jersey City, N. J.
Eagle.—1436. September 2, 1873. Steam Packing, etc. James Glanding & Co., Philadelphia, Pa.
Eden.—13,300. May 11, 1886. Rubber Articles for Mechanical Purposes. Revere Rubber Co., Boston, Mass.
Elastic Waste.—1463. September 23, 1873. Packing for Journals. Patrick S. Devlan, New York, N. Y.
Electric.—12,785. November 17, 1885. Leather Belting. Chas. A. Schieren & Co., New York, N. Y.
Emerald.—16,714. June 11, 1889. Hydraulic Hose. New Jersey Car Spring and Rubber Co., Jersey City, N. J.
Empire, The.—18,379. September 2. 1890. Studs for Machine Belting. Greene, Tweed & Co., New York, N. Y.
Eureka.—5593. January 29, 1878. Hydraulic Hose. Eureka Fire Hose Co., New York, N. Y.
Eureka.—7231. April 22. 1879. Steam and Hydraulic Packing. Symonds & Co., Philadelphia, Pa.
Eureka Belt.—16,171. January 15, 1889. Fabric Machine Belting. Eureka Belting Manufacturing Co., New York, N. Y.
Eureka Dynamo (and design).—20,833. March 15, 1892. Belting, etc. Page Belting Co., Concord, N. H.
Eureka Underwriters (and design).—17,107. October 15, 1889. Hose. Eureka Fire Hose Co., New York, N. Y.
Excelsior.—16,464. April 9, 1889. Rubber Goods forming Parts of Machinery, etc. Boston Belting Co., Boston, Mass.
Excelsior Anchor Bolting Cloth.—2615. June 1, 1875. Bolting Cloth. Huntley, Holcombe & Heine. Silver Creek, N. Y.
Favorite (The) (and design).—15,169. February 7, 1888. Machine Packing. Alexander Montgomery, Boston, Mass.
Flexite.—19,607. May 26, 1891. Rubber Tubing for Electrical Purposes. Revere Rubber Co., Boston, Mass.
Four Aces (and design).—13,301. May 11, 1886. Rubber Articles for Mechanical Purposes. Revere Rubber Co., Boston, Mass.
Gandy's Belting (and design).—10,303. May 22, 1883. Cotton Belting. Maurice Gandy, Liverpool, England.
Genesee.—17,843. May 6, 1890. Rubber Belting and Rubber Hose. Stephen Ballard & Co., New York, N. Y.
Giant.—13,299. May 11, 1886. Rubber Articles for Mechanical Purposes. Revere Rubber Co., Boston, Mass.
Giant Belting, Seamless and Stitched (and design).—14,415. May 17, 1887. Rubber Belting. Revere Rubber Co., Boston, Mass.
Globe Packing, The.—18,852. January 20, 1891. Machine Packing. Jas. H. Billington, Philadelphia, Pa.
Granite.—13,384. June 8, 1886. Rubber Hose. Revere Rubber Co., Boston, Mass.

PACKING, BELTING, ETC.

Granite Hose.—1175. March 18, 1873. Rubber Hose. Boston Elastic Fabric Co., Boston, Mass.
Granite Seamless Belting.—15,042. December 20, 1887. Rubber Belting. Revere Rubber Co., Boston, Mass.
Hecla.—16,038. November 27, 1888. Piston Packings. Byron W. Goodsell, Chicago, Ill.
Helvetia.—8911. December 6, 1881. Leather Lace and Belting. A. Wetter & Co., Lancaster, Pa.
Hercules.—12,555. September 8, 1885. Rubber Hose. Commercial Rubber Co., New York, N. Y.
High Grade (and design).—18,491. October 7, 1890. Belting, Hose, Packing, etc. Cleveland Rubber Co., Cleveland, Ohio.
Imperial.—16,463. April 9, 1889. Rubber Goods forming Parts of Machinery, etc. Boston Belting Co., Boston, Mass.
Iron Clad.—16,414. March 26, 1889. Conducting Hose. Stephen Ballard & Co., New York, N. Y.
I X L.—15,496. May 22, 1888. Rubber Hose. Harper & Reynolds Co., Los Angeles, Cal.
J. B. Hoyt & Co., 28 and 30 Spruce St., N. Y.—20,441. December 8, 1891. Leather Belting. Fayerweather & Ladew, New York, N. Y.
Lion (and design).—1399. August 5, 1873. Steam Packing. Silver Lake Co., Newtonville, Mass.
Luctor.—12,035. March 24, 1885. Sheet Metal for Packing, etc. D. P. Dieterich, Philadelphia, Pa.
Magnabestos.—22,005. November 15, 1892. Covering for Pipes and Boilers. Magnesia Sectional Covering Co., Ambler, Pa.
Manhattan.—17,054. September 24, 1889. Machinery Packing. Greene, Tweed & Co., New York, N. Y.
Mastiff.—20,848. March 15, 1892. Rubber Belting, Hose, and Packing. Revere Rubber Co., Boston, Mass.
Mining Special (and design).—19,844. July 7, 1891. Rubber Belting. New York Belting and Packing Co., New York and London.
Missing Link, The (and design).—15,279. March 13, 1888. Leather Belting. Chas. L. Ireson, Boston, Mass.
Mogul.—16,06). December 4, 1888. Rubber Belting and Hose. Revere Rubber Co., Boston, Mass.
Navy.—16,372. March 12, 1889. Hose of Rubber, Cotton, or Linen. Revere Rubber Co., Boston, Mass.
Neptune.—16,426. March 26, 1889. Rubber Belting, Hose, and Packing. Revere Rubber Co., Boston, Mass.
Oak Leaf (and design).—18,807. January 6, 1891. Belting. Main Belting Co., Philadelphia, Pa.
Paragon.—5591. January 29, 1878. Hydraulic Hose. Eureka Fire Hose Co., New York, N. Y.
Perfection.—19,695. June 16, 1891. Belting. Boston Woven Hose Co., Boston, Mass.
Premier.—1704. March 31, 1874. Machine Belting. Edward Page, Lawrence, Mass.
Protective.—16,404. March 19, 1889. Rubber, Linen, or Cotton Hose. Revere Rubber Co., Boston, Mass.
Red (and design).—20,135. September 15, 1891. Packing. Revere Rubber Co., Boston, Mass.
Red Cord, The.—15,674. July 10, 1888. Flax Fibre Packing. William T. Y. Schenck, San Francisco, Cal.
Red Line.—2327. March 30, 1875. 8686. September 27, 1881. Hose. Wannalanset Manufacturing Co., Boston, Mass.
Revere.—19,558. May 19, 1891. Hose, Belting, and Packing. Revere Rubber Co., Boston, Mass.
Rob Roy.—12,845. December 15, 1885. Canvas Hose. John McGregor, Dundee, Scotland.

Rossendale Hair Belt (and design). 19,470. May 12, 1891. Belting. Rossendale Belting Co., Newark, N. J.
Salamanda.—10,345. June 12, 1883. Steam Packing. John H. Cheever, New York, N. Y.
S. A. P.—16,893. July 30, 1889. Rubber or Cotton Hose. Revere Rubber Co., Boston, Mass.
Saturn (and design).—11,897. February 3, 1885. Machine Belting. New York Belting and Packing Co., New York, N. Y.
Shawmut.—15,002. December 6, 1887. Rubber Belting, Hose, and Packing. Revere Rubber Co., Boston, Mass.
Sphincter.—19,560. May 16, 1891. Hydraulic Hose. Waterbury Rubber Co., Jersey City, N. J.
Standard.—5736. March 12, 1878. Leather Beltings and Lacings. Anton Heim, New York, N. Y.
Standard.—9435. June 6, 1882. Packing. Jenkins Bros., Boston, Massachusetts.
Staple (and design).—18,744. December 30, 1890. Hose and Belting. New Jersey Car Spring and Rubber Co., Jersey City, N. J.
Steel Armor Protected.—16,403. March 19, 1889. Rubber and Cotton Hose, Metal Covered. Revere Rubber Co., Boston, Mass.
Super Extra (and design).—15,155. January 31, 1888. Belting. H. D. Edwards & Co., Detroit, Mich.
Test.—3876. July 25, 1876. India-Rubber Hose. New York Belting and Packing Co., Newton, Conn., and New York, N. Y.
Thistle.—14,573. July 5, 1887. Linen or Fabric Fire Hose. John McGregor, Dundee, Scotland.
Thrasher.—16,211. January 22, 1889. Rubber Belting. New York Belting and Packing Co., New York, N. Y.
Tiger.—16,892. July 30, 1889. Rubber or Cotton Hose. Revere Rubber Co., Boston, Mass.
Trade Linen.—15,528. May 29, 1888. Hydraulic Hose. Eureka Fire Hose Co., New York, N. Y.
Trident.—16.370. March 12, 1889. Hose of Rubber, Cotton, or Linen. Revere Rubber Co., Boston, Mass.
Typha (and design).—6686. October 8, 1878. Boiler Felt. Squires Radcliff, Little Falls, N. J.
Union (and design).—10,115. March 13, 1883. Tubing of Rubber, etc. Union Tubing Co., New York, N. Y.
Usudurian.—4390. February 20, 1877. Steam Packing. Solomon J. Gordon, New York, N. Y.
Usudurian.—13,539. August 3, 1886. Compound for Packing Joints of Steam Engines, etc. Revere Rubber Co., Boston, Mass.
Veteran.—17,308. December 24, 1889. Fire Hose. W. C. Gleason & J. C. Ryan, Chicago, Ill.
Volt.—20,446. December 8, 1891. Leather Belting. Geo. W. Snider, Indianapolis, Ind.
Vulcanized Fibre.—1965. September 8, 1874. Washers, Bearings, etc. William Courtenay, Wilmington, Del.
Wheeler's Fibrous Metallic Packing (and design).—20,404. November 24, 1891. Packing. Topping & Fox, New York, N. Y.
While I Live I'll Crow (and design).—16,186. January 15, 1889. Packing. Moran & Saunderson, New York, N. Y.
Wine Hose.—13,318. May 18, 1886. Rubber Hose. New York Belting and Packing Co., New York, N. Y.
Woveknit.—19,167. March 10, 1891. Fire Hose. Eureka Fire Hose Co., New York, N. Y.

TRADE-MARKS

FOR

MACHINE PACKING, BELTING, ETC.

(CLASS 50.)

Designs showing essential feature claimed as Trade-Mark.

360. July 4, 1871. 4079. October 31, 1876. Steam and Hydraulic Packing. Wm. M. Canfield, Philadelphia, Pa.

1086. December 17, 1872. Boiler Covering. U. S. and Foreign Salamander Filtering Co., Troy, N. Y.

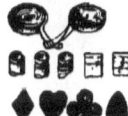
1162. March 11, 1873. Hose and Belting. National Rubber Co., Bristol, R. I.

1174. March 18, 1873. Rubber Hose. Boston Elastic Fabric Co., Boston, Mass.

1397. August 5, 1873. Steam Packing for Engines. Silver Lake Co., Newtonville, Mass.

1398. August 5, 1873. Steam Packing for Engines. Silver Lake Co., Newtonville, Mass.

1399. August 5, 1873. Steam Packing for Engines. Silver Lake Co., Newtonville, Mass.

1435. September 2, 1873. Steam Packing, etc. James Glauding & Co., Philadelphia, Pa.

2239. February 16, 1875. Packing for Stuffing Boxes, etc. William Hartley Miller, Philadelphia, Pa.

3711. May 23, 1876. Hose for Pumps, Engines, etc. Wannalauset Manufacturing Co., Boston, Mass.

3929. August 15, 1876. Hose. Combination Rubber Co., New York, N. Y.

4533. April 10, 1877. Steam and Hydraulic Packing. Adam Schwartz, New York, N. Y.

4681. May 22, 1877. Leather Belting and Lace Leather. Chas. A. Schieren, Brooklyn, N. Y.

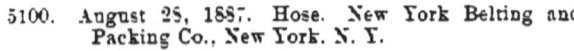

 5100. August 25, 1887. Hose. New York Belting and Packing Co., New York. N. Y.

 5592. January 29, 1878. Hydraulic Hose. Eureka Fire Hose Co., New York, N. Y.

 5760. March 18, 1878. Material for Covering Roofs, Pipes, etc., Composed of Asbestos. Henry W. Johns, Brooklyn, N. Y.

 6656. October 8, 1878. Boiler Covering. Squires Radcliff, Little Falls, N. J.

 7513. February 3, 1880. A Compound for Coating Metals to Prevent Rust. A. B. Brown & Sons, Worcester, Mass.

 9602. August 8, 1882. Hose. Geo. P. Dodge, Manhasset, N. Y.

 10,115. March 13, 1883. Tubing of Rubber or Gas-Tight Composition. Union Tubing Co., New York, N Y.

 10,303. May 22, 1883. Cotton Belting. Maurice Gandy, Liverpool, England.

 10,451. August 7, 1883. Cotton Belts or Bands. Maurice Gandy, Liverpool, Eng., and Baltimore, Md.

 11,897. February 3, 1885. Belting for Machinery. New York Belting and Packing Co., New York. N. Y.

 12,891. December 29, 1885. Non-Conducting Boiler Covering. Wm. Berkefeld, Hanover, Germany.

 13,301. May 11, 1886. Rubber Articles for Mechanical Purposes. Revere Rubber Co., Boston, Mass.

 13,426. June 15, 1886. Engine and Pump Packing. Reuben B. H. Gould, East Cambridge, Mass.

 13,604. August 24, 1886. Belting. Samuel Kidder, Boston, Mass.

 14,415. May 17, 1887. Rubber Belting. Revere Rubber Co., Boston, Mass.

 14,457. June 7, 1887. Flax Packing for Hydraulic and Steam Purposes. Clinton Mfg. Co., Brooklyn, N. Y.

 14,820. October 11, 1887. Rubber Belting. Newark Machine Co., Columbus, Ohio.

15,155. January 31, 1888. Rubber Belting. H. D. Edwards & Co., Detroit, Mich.

PACKING, BELTING, ETC. 123

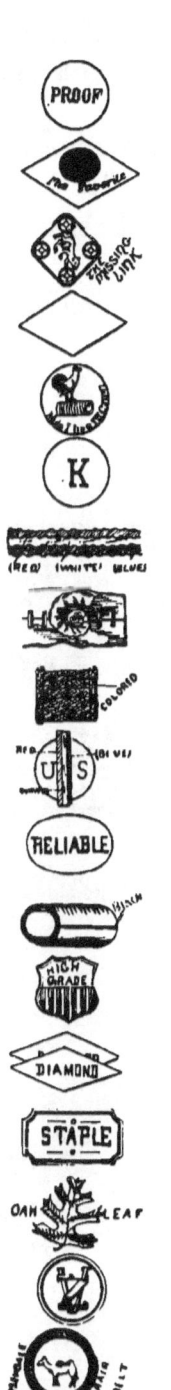

15,156. January 31, 1888. Rubber Belting. H. D. Edwards & Co., Detroit, Mich.

15,169. February 7, 1888. Packing for Machinery. Alexander Montgomery, Boston, Mass.

15,279. March 13, 1888. Self-Adjusting Leather Link Belting. Chas. L. Ireson, Boston, Mass.

15,510. May 22, 1888. Leather Belting. W. S. Nott Co., Minneapolis, Minn.

16,186. January 15, 1889. Steam and Hydraulic Piston Packing. Moran & Saunderson, New York, N. Y.

16,868. July 30, 1889. Mill or Fire Hose. Boston Woven Hose Co., Boston, Mass.

17,107. October 15, 1889. Linen Hydraulic Hose. Eureka Fire Hose Co., New York, N. Y.

17,168. November 5, 1889. Wire Lacing for Belting. Hugh Kerr, New York, N. Y.

17,220. November 26, 1889. Fire Hose. Henry F. Herkner, New York, N. Y.

17,641. March 11, 1890. Hydraulic Hose. Eureka Fire Hose Co., New York, N. Y.

17,710. March 25, 1890. Hydraulic Hose and Machine Belting. New Jersey Car and Spring Rubber Co., Jersey City, N. J.

17,791. April 22, 1890. Hose. Boston Woven Hose Co., Boston, Mass.

18,491. October 7, 1890. Rubber Belting, Hose, Packing, etc. Cleveland Rubber Co., Cleveland, Ohio.

18,673. December 2, 1890. Mechanical Rubber Goods, Belts, etc. New York Belting and Packing Co., New York, N. Y.

18,744. December 30, 1890. Hose and Belting. New Jersey Car Spring and Rubber Co., Jersey City, N. J.

18,807. January 6, 1891. Leather Belting. Main Belting Co., Philadelphia, Pa.

19,078. February 24, 1891. Hose, Belting, and Packing for Machinery. Revere Rubber Co., Boston, Mass.

19,470. May 12, 1891. Driving Belts. Rossendale Belting Co., Newark, N. J.

124   TRADE-MARKS.

 19,823. June 30, 1891. Metallic Packing. John H. Harris, New York, N. Y.

 19,844. July 7, 1891. Rubber Belting. New York Belting and Packing Co., New York and London.

 20,135. September 15, 1891. Composition Packing. Revere Rubber Co., Boston, Mass.

 20,269. October 27, 1891. Machine Belting. Jewell Belting Co., Hartford, Conn.

 20,404. November 24, 1891. Packing for Machinery. Topping & Fox, New York, N. Y.

 20,833. March 15, 1892. Leather Belting, etc. Page Belting Co., Concord, N. H.

 20,855. March 22, 1892. Rubber Belting. Stephen Ballard Rubber Co., New York, N. Y.

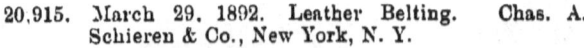 20,915. March 29, 1892. Leather Belting. Chas. A. Schieren & Co., New York, N. Y.

 21,346. June 21, 1892. Woven Machine Belting. F. Reddaway & Co., Manchester, England.

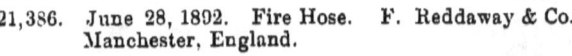 21,386. June 28, 1892. Fire Hose. F. Reddaway & Co., Manchester, England.

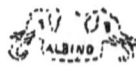 21,445. July 12, 1892. Leather, including Belting. A. & C. W. Holbrook, Providence, R. I.

 21,538. August 2, 1892. Machine Belting. F. Reddaway & Co., Manchester, England.

COMPILED BY
WALLACE A. BARTLETT,
Patent Attorney,
WASHINGTON, D. C.

TRADE-MARKS
FOR
Sewing Machines and Attachments.
(CLASS 58.)

Embracing Sewing Machines and Parts. (See also Class 47, Needles, &c.)

Words or Phrases Constituting the Marks Alphabetically Arranged.

Alliance.—19,776. June 30, 1891. Sewing Machines. Demorest Fashion and Sewing Machine Co., Williamsport, Pa.

B. Cold Swaged. N. Co.—1232. April 29, 1873. Sewing-Machine Needles. Bridgeport Cold-Swaged Needle Co., Bridgeport, Conn.

Bureau.—1081. December 10, 1872. Sewing-Machine Cases. Florence Sewing Machine Co., Florence, Mass.

Centennial.—3430. February 15, 1876. Sewing Machines. White Manufacturing Co., Cleveland Ohio.

Champion.—3607. April 25, 1876. Sewing Machines. John McCloskey, New York, N. Y.

Columbia.—16,562. May 14, 1889. Sewing Machines, etc. Demorest Fashion & Sewing Machine Co., New York, N. Y.

Companion.—8128. December 21, 1880. Sewing Machines. Thurston Manufacturing Co., Marlborough, N. H.

Companion.—11,297. July 1. 1884. Sewing Machines. Companion Sewing Machine Co., New Britain, Conn.

Crown (and design).—7570. August 5, 1879. Sewing Machines. Florence Machine Co., Florence. Mass.

Domestic.—414. August 1, 1871. Sewing Machines. Domestic Sewing Machine Co., Norwalk, Ohio.

Domestic.—530. November 14, 1871. Sewing-Machine Attachments. Domestic Sewing Machine Co., Toledo, Ohio.

Domestic.—12,254. May 19, 1885. Sewing Machines and Attachments. Domestic Sewing Machine Co., New York, N. Y.

Excelsior Wilson.—679. February 12, 1872. Sewing Machines. Wilson Sewing Machine Co., Cleveland, Ohio.

F. F.—51. November 1, 1870. Sewing Machines. Weed Sewing Machine Co., Hartford, Conn.

Family.—13,932. December 28, 1886. Button-Hole Attachments for Sewing Machines. Smith & Egge Manufacturing Co., Bridgeport, Conn.

G.—8356. June 14, 1881. Sewing Machines. Willcox & Gibbs Sewing Machine Co., New York, N. Y.

Great Western (G. W. monogram).—2931. September 14, 1875. Sewing Machines. John B. Meyers, Cleveland, Ohio.

H. B. G (and design).—1850. June 22, 1874. Sewing-Machine Needles. Herman B. Goodrich, Chicago, Ill.

Helpmate.—15,114. January 17. 1888. Sewing Machines. Williams Manufacturing Co., Plattsburg, N. Y.
Home.—20,832. March 15, 1892. Sewing Machines and Attachments. Johnson, Clark & Co., New York, N. Y.
Homestead.—21,481. July 19, 1892. Sewing Machines. Chas. G. Akam, Chicago, Ill.
Hope.—21,272. June 7. 1892. Sewing Machines and Attachments. New Home Sewing Machine Co., New York, N. Y.
Household.—5895. April 23, 1878. Sewing Machines. Providence Tool Co., Providence, R. I.
Ideal.—20,512. December 29, 1891. Sewing Machines, etc. New Home Sewing Machine Co., New York, N. Y.
Incomparable.—21,897. October 25, 1892. Sewing Machines. New York Sewing Machine and Manufacturing Co., Plattsburg, N. Y.
Interlock.—20,016. August 11. 1891. Sewing Machines. Union Special Sewing Machine Co., Chicago, Ill.
Kenwood.—21,650. August 23, 1892. Sewing Machines. Cash Buyers' Union, Chicago, Ill.
National.—4371. February 13. 1877. 8526. August 2, 1881. Wax-Thread Sewing Machines. Consolidated Wax Thread Sewing Machine Co., Boston, Mass.
New England.—8657. September 20, 1881. Wax Thread Sewing Machines. National Sewing Machine Co., Boston, Mass.
New Home.—5356. November 20, 1877. Sewing-Machine Needles, &c. Johnson, Clark & Co., New York, N. Y.
No Sewing Machine Perfect Without It (and design).—3901. August 1, 1876. Sewing-Machine Attachments. American Attachment Co., New York, N. Y.
Pan-American.—19,128. March 3, 1891. Sewing Machines. James P. Page, New York, N. Y.
Politype.—14,262. April 12, 1887. Sewing Machines for Leather. Emile James, New York, N. Y.
Remington Empire.—552. November 21, 1871. Sewing Machines. Remington Empire Sewing Machine Co., Ilion, N. Y.
Rival.—21,321. June 21, 1892. Sewing Machines. Dives, Pomeroy & Stewart, Reading, Pa.
Royal.—9667. September 12, 1882. Sewing Machines. St. John Sewing-Machine Co., Springfield, Ohio.
R, The Remington Sewing Machine.—3095. October 26, 1875. Sewing Machines. E. Remington & Sons, Ilion, N. Y.
Safe.—20,015. August 11, 1891. Sewing Machines. Union Special Sewing-Machine Co., Chicago, Ill.
Singer (and design).—2651. June 8, 1875. 12,396. July 7, 1885. Sewing Machines and Attachments. Singer Mfg. Co., New York, N. Y.
Speedwell.—20,536. December 29, 1891. Sewing Machines. Edward Ridley & Sons, New York, N. Y.
St. John.—7607. August 19, 1879. 9668. September 12, 1882. Sewing Machines. St. John Sewing-Machine Co., Springfield, Ohio.
Time Utilizer.—5397. December 4, 1877. Sewing Machines. R. M. Wanzer & Co., Hamilton, Canada, and Buffalo, N. Y.
Union.—8529. August 2, 1881. Wax-Thread Sewing Machine. National Sewing Machine Co., Boston, Mass.
Union Special.—20,014. August 11, 1891. Sewing Machines. Union Special Sewing-Machine Co., Chicago. Ill.
Victor (and design).—631. January 9, 1872. Sewing Machine. Finkle & Lyon Mfg. Co., Middletown, Conn.
W. & G.—2918. September 7, 1875. Sewing Machines, Needles and Attachments. Willcox & Gibbs Sewing-Machine Co., New York, N. Y.
W. N. Co.—5105. August 28, 1877. Sewing-Machine Needles. William Wilcox, Worcester, Mass.

TRADE-MARKS

FOR

Sewing Machines and Attachments.

(CLASS 58.)

Designs showing essential feature claimed as Trade-Mark.

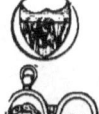
181. February 28, 1871. 2943. September 14, 1875. Sewing Machine. Wheeler & Wilson Manufacturing Co., Bridgeport, Conn.

399. July 25, 1871. Sewing Machines. James H. Whitney, Paterson, N. J.

631. January 9, 1872. 2429. May 4, 1875. Sewing Machine. Finkle & Lyon Manufacturing Co., Middletown, Conn.

1019. October 8, 1872. 2341. April 6, 1875. Sewing Machines. Grover & Baker Sewing Machine Co., Boston, Mass.

1344. July 1, 1873. Machine-Wound Sewing-Machine Bobbins. James H. Bullard, Chicopee Falls, Mass.

1708. April 7, 1874. Wound Bobbins for Sewing Machines. J. H. Bullard, Chicopee Falls, Mass.

2651. June 8, 1875. 12,396. July 7, 1885. Sewing Machines and parts. Singer Manufacturing Co., New York, N. Y.

2917. September 7, 1875. 8357. June 14, 1881. Sewing Machines. Willcox & Gibbs Sewing Machine Co., New York, N. Y.

2918. September 7, 1875. 8393. June 21, 1881. Sewing Machines. Willcox & Gibbs Sewing Machine Co., New York, N. Y.

2931. September 14, 1875. Sewing Machines. John B. Meyers, Cleveland, Ohio.

3901. August 1, 1876. Sewing-Machine Attachments. American Attachment Co., New York, N. Y.

3902. August 1, 1876. Sewing-Machine Attachments. Edwin J. Toof, New Haven, Conn.

128 TRADE-MARKS.

 4207. December 12, 1876. Sewing Machines. Goodes Ornamental, Plain and Overseaming Lock-Stitch Sewing Machine Co., Philadelphia, Pa.

 4255. January 2, 1877. Sewing Machines. Wilson Sewing Machine Co., Chicago, Ill.

 5397. December 4, 1877. Sewing Machines. R. M. Wanzer & Co., Hamilton, Canada.

 6433. July 30, 1878. Sewing Machines. Tryber & Sweetland, Chicago, Ill.

 6761. October 29, 1878. Sewing-Machine Needles. R. M. Wanzer & Co., Buffalo, N. Y.

 7570. August 5, 1879. Sewing Machines. Florence Machine Co., Florence, Mass.

 8132. December 21, 1880. Sewing-Machine Tables, Clothes Wringers, etc. Samuel C. Tantum & Co., Cincinnati, Ohio.

 11,098. April 15, 1884. White Sewing Machines. White Sewing Machine Co., Cleveland, Ohio.

12,717. October 27, 1885. Sewing Machines, Attachments and Supplies. Singer Manufacturing Co., New York, N. Y.

 17,600. February 25, 1890. Sewing Machines. Miranda McGloin, New York, N. Y.

 17,985. June 3, 1890. Sewing Machines. Singer Manufacturing Co., New York, N. Y.

COMPILED BY
WALLACE A. BARTLETT,
Patent Attorney,
WASHINGTON, D. C.

TRADE-MARKS
FOR
STOVES AND HEATERS.
(CLASS 66.)

Embracing Stoves and Parts Thereof, Ranges, Furnaces, Cookers, Grates &c. (See also Class 40, Locks and Hardware.)

WORDS OR PHRASES CONSTITUTING THE MARKS ALPHABETICALLY ARRANGED.

Abernant.—9324. April 25, 1882. Fire Bricks, etc. Henry Lamplough, London, England.
Aerated.—17,269. December 10, 1889. Stoves and Furnaces. Michigan Stove Co., Detroit, Mich.
Agate Iron.—4670. May 22, 1877. Enameled Sheet-Metal Ware. Lalance & Grosjean Manufacturing Co., New York, N. Y.
Air Blast.—21,241. May 31, 1892. Hot-Air Furnaces. May & Fieberger, Akron, Ohio.
Aldine.—3549. April 4, 1876. Stoves and Ranges. Isaac A. Sheppard, Philadelphia, Pa.
American (and design).—592. December 19, 1871. Stoves. Bridgeford & Co., Louisville, Ky.
Anti-Clinker.—1496. October 14, 1873. Stoves. James Spear & Co., Philadelphia, Pa.
Anti-Clogger.—2663. June 8, 1875. Stoves. Dennis G. Littlefield, Albany, N. Y.
Argalia.—4045. October 10, 1876. Stoves. Jewett & Root, Buffalo, New York.
Argand.—1828. June 9, 1874. Stoves and Ranges. Perry & Co., Albany, N. Y.
Avalon.—6276. June 25, 1878. Parlor Stoves. Sherman S. Jewett & Co., Buffalo, N. Y.
B. & B.—20,991. April 19, 1892. Stoves, Heaters, and Furnaces. Glazier-Strong Oil Stove Co., Chelsea, Mich.
Bakewell.—12,853. December 15, 1885. Stoves and Ranges. Western Stove Manufacturing Co., St. Louis, Mo.
Bakr.—19,829. June 30, 1891. Hot-Water Furnaces, etc. Baker Heater Co., New York, N. Y.
Baltimore.—501. October 24, 1871. Fire-Place Heaters. Richardson, Boynton & Co., New York, N. Y.
Baltimore Kitchener. 513. November 7, 1871. 2514. May 18, 1875. Kitchen Range and Stoves. Bartlett, Robbins & Co., Baltimore, Md.

Banner.—1370. July 15, 1873. Stoves. Southerd, Robinson & Co., New York, N. Y.
Beebe.—4069. October 24, 1876. 9111. February 21, 1882. 13,927. December 28, 1886. Cooking Ranges. Janes & Kirtland, New York, N. Y.
Blue Flame.—18,068. June 24, 1890. Stoves. Blue Flame Manufacturing Co., North Plainfield, N. J.
Blue Light.—18,069. June 27, 1890. Stoves. Blue Flame Manufacturing Co., North Plainfield, N. J.
Brilliant.—3786. June 20, 1876. Cook Stoves. Charles H. Buck, St. Louis, Mo.
Brilliant.—11,286. July 1, 1884. Base-Burner Stoves. Brand & Co., Milwaukee, Wisconsin.
Bundy.—15,404. May 1, 1888. Radiators. A. A. Griffing Iron Co., Jersey City, N. J.
Bundy.—17,822. April 29, 1890. Valves for Stoves and Heaters. A. A. Griffing Iron Co., Jersey City, N. J.
Centennial.—1688. March 24, 1874. Stoves, Ranges, and Hot-Air Furnaces. J. Reynolds & Son, Philadelphia, Pa.
Central.—21,703. August 30, 1892. Stoves. Central Oilgas Stove Co., Northampton, Mass.
Century.—520. November 7, 1891. Stoves. Redway & Burton, Cincinnati, O.
Charter Oak.—328. June 20, 1871. 2706. July 6, 1875. Cooking Stoves. Giles F. Filley, St. Louis, Mo.
Chester.—3435. February 22, 1876. Stoves. Greer & King, Dayton, Ohio.
Cinderella.—14,106. March 1, 1887. Stoves and Ranges. De Haven & Co., Pittsburg, Pa.
Climax.—15,278. March 13, 1888. Radiators. A. A. Griffing Iron Co., Jersey City, N. J.
Clinkerless.—9018. January 10, 1882. Fire Bricks. Newton & Co., Albany, N. Y.
Columbia.—20,297. November 3, 1891. Steam or Hot-Water Radiators. A. A. Griffing Iron Co., Jersey City, N. J.
Common Sense.—11,533. September 30, 1884. Fire-Place Fixtures. Chas. L. Page, Chicago, Ill.
Cotton Option.—18,932. February 3, 1891. Stoves and Ranges. Bowie & Terhune, Rome, Ga.
Cotton Plant.—306. June 6, 1871. Ranges and Stoves. Abendorth Bros., New York, N. Y.
Crowning Glory.—3833. July 4, 1876. Cooking Stoves. Jewett & Root, Buffalo, N. Y.
Crown of India.—6466. August 13, 1878. Stoves. Sherman S. Jewett & Co., Buffalo, N. Y.
Cyclone.—4859. July 17, 1877. Heaters, Stoves, and Heating-Pipe. Hiram Purdy, Burlington, Iowa.
Daisy.—15,814. August 28, 1888. Stove Boards. A. Irving Griggs, New York, N. Y.
Delmonico.—3494. March 7, 1876. Cooking Ranges. Rathbone, Sard & Co., Albany, N. Y.
Dighton Rock.—9618. August 22, 1882. Stoves. Gideon C. Francis, South Dighton, Mass.
Dinner Bell.—9310. April 25, 1882. Cooking Stoves. James Beakley & Co., St. Louis, Mo.
Double Crown.—19,070. February 24, 1891. Hot-Water Heaters. Gurney Hot Water Heater Co., Boston, Mass.
Double Quick.—5703. March 5, 1878. Cook Stoves. Benj. R. Hawley Hyde Park, Ill.
Dubuque.—1863. July 7, 1874. Stoves. Burdett, Smith & Co., Troy, N. Y.

STOVES AND HEATERS. 131

Duplex.—12,371. June 30, 1885. Ranges and Furnaces. Jeremiah J. Richardson, New York, N. Y.
Eclectic.—2077. November 17, 1874. Ranges and Stoves. G. G. Richmond, Providence, R. I.
Economy.—295. May 30, 1871. 2558. May 18, 1875. 8449. July 12, 1881. Stoves. Comstock, Castle & Co., Quincy, Ill.
Elite.—15,520. May 22, 1888. Radiators. Thos. H. Williams and S. D. Tompkins, Jersey City, N. J.
Excellent.—161. February 14, 1871. Stoves. I. Droege & Co., Covington, Ky.
Excelsior.—284. May 23, 1871. Frying Pan. Sam'l Smith, New York, N. Y.
Excelsior.—342. June 20, 1871. Ranges. Scranton Stove and Manufacturing Co., Scranton, Pa.
Excelsior.—5182. September 25, 1877. Hot-Air Furnaces. Isaac A. Sheppard & Co., Philadelphia, Pa.
Excelsior.—8613. August 30, 1881. Range, Bath, and Other Boilers. Joseph G. Hibbs, Jr., Philadelphia, Pa.
Excelsior Cook.—3537. March 28, 1876. Stoves and Furnaces. Isaac A. Sheppard & Co., Philadelphia, Pa.
Expert.—18,313. August 19, 1890. Heaters. Sherman S. Jewett & Co., Buffalo, N. Y.
Fashion.—1995. September 22, 1874. Stoves. Charles Noble & Co., Philadelphia, Pa.
Favorite.—2863. August 31, 1875. 6232. June 18, 1878. Stoves and Ranges. W. C. Davis & Co., Cincinnati, Ohio.
Favorite.—8081. November 2, 1890. Zinc Stove Board. A. Irving Griggs, Westford, N. Y.
Florida.—15,410. May 1, 1888. Steam and Hot-Water Boilers. Pierce, Butler and Pierce Manuf. Co., Syracuse, N. Y.
Franklin Cook.—2159. January 12, 1875. Cooking Stoves. Bonnet, Duffy & Co., Quincy, Ill.
Front Rank.—12,377. July 7, 1885. Cooking and Heating Stoves. American Vapor Stove Co., Cleveland, Ohio.
Garland.—10,007. January 30, 1883. Stoves, Ranges, and Heaters. Michigan Stove Co., Detroit, Mich.
General Lee.—4399. February 27, 1877. Stoves. Comstock, Castle & Co., Quincy, Ill.
Giant Heater.—19,115. March 3, 1891. Portable Heaters. Daniel H. Erdman, Camden, N. J.
Glad Tidings.—5258. June 18, 1878. Cooking Stoves. Sherman S. Jewett & Co., Buffalo, N. Y.
Goldemar.—6475. August 13, 1878. Cooking Stoves. Sherman S. Jewett & Co., Buffalo, N. Y.
Golden Star.—11,378. August 5, 1884. Stoves. Myers, Osborne & Co., Cleveland, Ohio.
Good Luck.—18,256. August 5, 1890. Stoves, Ranges. etc. Baldwin & Graham, Pittsburg, Pa.
Good Will.—19,238. March 31, 1891. Stoves. Frank A. Klaine, Cincinnati, Ohio.
Granger.—1715. April 7, 1874. Cooking Stoves. Western Stove Manufacturing Co., St. Louis, Mo.
Granite Iron.—1759. April 18, 1874. Iron Cooking Utensils. St. Louis Stamping Co., St. Louis, Mo.
Graphic.—3337. January 4, 1876. Heating Stoves and Ranges. Swett, Quinby & Perry, Troy, N. Y.
Griselda.—6476. August 13, 1878. Wood Heating Stoves. Sherman S. Jewett & Co., Buffalo, N. Y.
Guarantee.—3785. June 20, 1876. Cook Stoves. Charles H. Buck, St. Louis, Mo.

Gurney.—14,064. February 8, 1887. Hot-Water Heaters. Gurney Hot Water Heater Co., Boston, Mass.
Happy Home.—13,615. August 24, 1886. Cooking and Heating Stoves and Ranges. Harry D. Silsby, Springfield, Mo.
Happy Thought.—7567. August 5, 1879. 8524. August 2, 1881. Stoves and Ranges. Union Stove and Manufacturing Co., Pittston, Pa.
Harvest Home.—2505. May 11, 1875. Stoves and Ranges. Thomas, Roberts, Stevenson & Co., Philadelphia, Pa.
Health.—6847. November 26, 1878. Heaters. Gold's Heater Manufacturing Co., New York, N. Y.
Helion.—11,325. July 15, 1884. Gas Stoves With Radial Burners. Chas. Burnham & Co., Philadelphia, Pa.
Home Comfort.—9414. May 23, 1882. Stoves and Ranges. Wrought Iron Range Co., St. Louis, Mo.
Howard.—22,003. November 15, 1892. Heating Furnaces. Howard Furnace Co., Syracuse, N. Y.
Howe.—17,674. March 18, 1890. Ventilating Stoves and Ranges. Hezekiah Howe, Cortland, N. Y.
Hub.—14,744. September 6, 1887. Heating and Cooking Stoves and Furnaces. Smith & Anthony Stove Co., Boston, Mass.
Ideal.—8839. November 15, 1881. Stove. Magee Furnace Co., Boston, Massachusetts.
Ideal.—15,441. May 8, 1888. Radiators. Pierce Steam Heating Co., Buffalo, N. Y.
Iron Clad Copper Reservoir.—1182. March 25, 1873. Cooking Stoves. Bussey, McLeod & Co., Troy, N. Y.
Iron Clad Lamp Stove.—12,696. October 20, 1885. Lamp or Oil Stoves. John McConnell, Cleveland, Ohio.
Iron King.—4578. April 24, 1877. Stoves. Charles Noble & Co., Philadelphia, Pa.
Jubilee.—8121. December 21, 1880. Cook Stoves and Ranges. Bissell & Co., Pittsburg, Pa.
Jewel.—6435. August 6, 1878. Heating and Cooking Stoves. Detroit Stove Works, Detroit, Mich.
Keystone.—21,966. November 8, 1892. Steam and Hot-Water Radiators. Philadelphia Hardware & Malleable Iron Works, Philadelphia, Pa.
Kiesel.—17,876. May 6, 1890. Fire-Brick Shapes and Tiles. Kiesel Fire Brick Co., Rochester, N. H.
Ladies' Delight.—22,075. November 29, 1892. Stoves. Page Bros. & Co., Boston, Mass.
Lexington.—12,311. June 16, 1885. Cook Stoves. Cutler & Proctor Stove Co., Peoria, Ill.
Mayflower.—10,830. January 1, 1884. Cook Stoves. Miami Stove Works, Lawrenceburg, Ind.
Merry Christmas.—287. May 23, 1871. Stoves. Scranton Stove & Manufacturing Co., Scranton, Pa.
Miller.—17,828. April 29, 1890. Grates for Fire Places. Miller Grate Co., Cleveland, Ohio.
Multum In Parvo.—2531. May 18, 1875. Pocket Cook Stove. Houchin Manufacturing Co., New York, N. Y.
Never-Break.—19,706. June 16, 1891. Cooking Vessels. Bronson Supply Co., Cleveland, Ohio.
New American.—278. May 23, 1871. Cooking Stoves. Perry & Co., Albany, N. Y.
New Process.—19,638. June 2, 1891. Vapor Stoves and Burners. Standard Lighting Co., Cleveland, Ohio.
Non-Clinker.—1457. September 16, 1873. Stoves. Wm. J. Keep, Troy, N. Y.
Norman.—14,818. October 11, 1887. Stoves, Ranges, Furnaces, etc. Norman H. Galusha, Rochester, N. Y.

STOVES AND HEATERS. 133

Oilgas.—21,250. June 7, 1892. Oil and Gas Stoves. Central Oilgas Stove Co., Northampton, Mass.
Our Crown.—16,722. June 11, 1889. Portable Stoves, Ranges, Heaters, etc. Samuel A. Snydam, New York, N. Y.
Palace King.—13,099. March 9, 1886. Hot-Air Furnaces. R. and F. E. Wheeler and Francis Kernan, Jr., Utica, N. Y.
Palace Queen.—15,717 July 24, 1888. Hot-Air Furnaces. Russel Weeeler, Son & Co. Utica, N. Y.
Peerless.—2657. June 8, 1875. Grates. Frank S. Bissell, Pittsburg, Pennsylvania.
Peerless.—13,768. November 2, 1886. Furnaces, Cooking Stoves and Ranges. Highland Foundry Co., Boston, Mass.
Peninsular.—10,059. February 20, 1883. Heating and Cooking Stoves and Furnaces. Peninsular Stove Co., Detroit, Mich.
Peoria.—12.379 July 7, 1885. Stoves. Culter and Proctor Stove Co., Peoria, Ill.
Perfect.—13,124. March 23, 1886. Stoves, Ranges, etc. Richardson & Boynton Co., New York, N. Y.
Pittston Cook.—1518. November 4, 1873. Stoves. Union Stove and Manufacturing Co., The, Pittston, Pa.
Porcelain Iron.—4671. May 22, 1877. Enameled Sheet Metal Ware. Lalance and Grosjean Manufacturing Co., New York, N. Y.
Prince Royal.—20,363. November 10, 1891. Heating Furnaces. H. Gilbert Hart & Co., Utica, N. Y.
Prize Baker.—10,328. June 5, 1883. Stoves. J. E. Forbes & Co., Ottawa, Kans.
Pyro.—20,296. November 3, 1891. Steam or Hot-Water Radiators. A. A. Griffing Iron Co., Jersey City, N J.
Quick Meal.—12,047. March 24, 1885. Stoves, etc. Quick Meal Stove Co., St. Louis, Mo.
Radiant.—8563. August 16, 1881. Open Fire Places or Grates. Innes, Magill & Co.. Cincinnati, Ohio.
Red Cross.—13,792. November 9, 1886. Cooking Stoves. Co-Operative Foundry Co., Rochester, N. Y.
Reflex.—9087. February 7, 1882. Grates for Stoves and Ranges. Spicers & Peckham, Providence, R. I.
Reporter.—2168. January 12, 1875. Cooking Stoves. Fuller, Warren & Co., Troy, N. Y.
Retort.—10,764. December 4, 1883. Cooking Stoves, Ranges, Furnaces, etc. Clarence Rathbone, Albany, N. Y.
Revolution.—2566. May 18, 1875. Stoves. Mitchell, Stephenson & Co., Pittsburg, Pa.
Rochester.—19,985. August 4, 1891. Oil Stoves. Silver & Co., New York, N. Y.
Rose City.—13,377. June 8, 1886. Cooking and Heating Stoves. Fones Bros., Little Rock, Ark.
Rossmore.—13,755. October 26, 1886. Stoves, Ranges, Heaters, etc. Ely & Ramsay, New York, N. Y.
Round Oak.--1089. December 24, 1872. 2516. May 18, 1875. Stoves. Philo D. Beckwith, Dowagiac, Mich.
Royal.—14,358. May 3, 1887. Pots and Kettles. Palmer Manuf. Co., New York, N. Y.
Royal, The.—13,972. January 11, 1887. Hot-Air Furnaces. H. Gilbert Hart & Co., Utica, N. Y.
Rubicon.—3896. August 1, 1876. Cooking Stoves. William J. Keep, Troy, New York.
Russian, The.—2323. March 30, 1875. Heaters, Ranges, and Grate-Work. Daniel Mershon's Sons, Philadelphia, Pa.
Sanitary.—1381. July 22, 1873. Heaters. Gold Heating Co., New York, New York.
Sensation.—989. September 10, 1872. 2500. May 11, 1875. Cooking Stoves. Schinnick, Woodside & Gibbons, Zanesville, Ohio.

Sereno.—6259. June 18, 1878. Cooking Stoves. Sherman S. Jewett & Co., Buffalo, N. Y.
Side Burner.—624. January 2, 1872. Stoves. William J. Keep, Troy, New York.
Side Burning.—625. January 2, 1872. Stoves. William J. Keep, Troy, New York.
Spirit of '76.—2360. April 6, 1875. Cooking Stoves. Fuller, Warren & Co., Troy, N. Y.
Stag (and design).—18,891. January 20, 1891. Cooking Ranges. John Tettlebach, Cleveland, Ohio.
Stone-Iron.—4784. June 26, 1877. Enameled Sheet-Metal Ware. Metal Manuf. Co., St. Louis, Mo.
Stonewall.—3623. April 25, 1876. Cooking Stoves. Conklin, Willis & Co., Baltimore, Md.
Success.—15,531. May 29, 1888. Gas Stoves. Gem City Gas Stove Co., Dayton, Ohio.
Summer King.—2398. April 20, 1875. Stoves. Summer King Stove Co., Pittsburg, Pa.
Summer Queen.—2671. June 15, 1875. 8981. January 3, 1882. Summer Furnaces. Christopher Riessner, Washington, D. C.
Sun Dial.—Wm. W. Goodwin & Co. 7070. March 4, 1879. Gas Stoves. Wm. W. Goodwin & Co., Philadelphia, Pa.
Sunnyside.—710. March 19, 1872. 7438. June 24, 1879. Heaters, Stoves, and Ranges. Stuart, Peterson & Co., Philadelphia, Pa.
Sunny South.—307. June 6, 1871. Ranges and Stoves. Abendorth Bros., New York, N. Y.
Superb.—1303. June 10, 1873. Stoves, Heaters, and Ranges. Hicks & Wolfe, Troy, N. Y.
Superior.—3372. January 25, 1876. 3421. February 15, 1876. 9296. April 18, 1882. Cooking Stoves. Bridge, Beach & Co., St. Louis, Mo.
Superior (and leaf).—3401. February 8, 1876. Cook Stoves. Bridge, Beach & Co., St. Louis, Mo.
Sycamore (and design).—7934. June 8, 1880. Stoves. Evers & Teeme, St. Louis, Mo.
Texas Girl.—2288. March 16, 1875. Cooking Stove. Marcus L. Filley, Lansingburg, N. Y.
Torrid.—6569. September 10, 1878. Stoves and Fireplaces. Mehurin & Mehurin, Zanesville, Ohio.
Triumph.—15,414. May 1, 1888. Radiators. T. H. Williams & S. D. Tompkins, Jersey City, N. J.
Triumph.—19,127. March 3, 1891. Kitchen Stove Furniture. Alex. G. Patton, Columbus, Ohio.
Tubular.—12,089. April 7, 1885. Portable Stoves. Robert E. Dietz, New York, N. Y.
Tuscola.—3693. May 23, 1876. Stoves. Greer & King, Dayton, Ohio.

Vacuum.—15,735. July 31, 1888. Feed Water Purifiers and Heaters. Warren Webster & Co., Philadelphia, Pa.
Volunteer.—15,128. January 24, 1888. Oil Stoves. C. Reissner & Co., New York, N. Y.
Welcome.—16,234. January 29, 1889. Stoves, Ranges, and Furnaces. Syracuse Stove Works, Syracuse, N. Y.
Western.—12,976. January 26, 1886. Stoves. Western Stove Manufacturing Co., St. Louis, Mo.
Woman's Rights.—1068. November 26, 1872. 2522. May 18, 1875. Stoves and Stove Trimmings. Culter & Proctor, Peoria, Ill.
World's Best.—17,000. Heating and Cooking Stoves. Michigan Stove Co., Detroit, Mich.
Zeb Vance.—4534. April 10, 1877. Cooking Stoves and Ranges. Thomas, Roberts, Stevenson & Co., Philadelphia, Pa.
76. 2215. February 9, 1875. Stoves and Ranges. March, Brownback & Co., Limerick Station, Pa.

TRADE-MARKS

FOR

STOVES AND HEATERS.

(CLASS 66.)

Designs showing essential feature claimed as Trade-Mark.

592. December 19, 1871. Stoves. Bridgeford & Co., Louisville, Ky.

793. April 30, 1872. Baking and Roasting Apparatus. Thos. J. T. Cummings, Fort Wayne, Ind.

982. September 3, 1872. Stoves, etc. Michigan Stove Co., Detroit, Mich.

2258. February 23, 1875. Pocket Spirit Stoves. George P. Houston, Washington, D. C.

2624. June 1, 1875. Steam Heating Apparatus, Steam Fittings, etc. Pancoast & Maule, Philadelphia, Pa.

3260. December 21, 1875. Stoves. Michigan Stove Co., Detroit, Mich.

3401. February 8, 1876. 9298. April 18, 1882. Cooking Stoves. Bridge, Beach & Co., St. Louis, Mo.

4964. July 31, 1877. Stove Castings. Detroit Stove Works, Detroit, Mich.

7934. June 8, 1880. Cooking Stove and Range. Evers & Teeme, St. Louis, Mo.

7946. June 22, 1880. 9005. January 10, 1882. Slow Combustion Stoves. Chas. Portway, Halstead, England.

9297. April 18, 1882. Cooking Stoves. Bridge & Beach Manufacturing Co., St. Louis, Mo.

TRADE-MARKS.

9618. August 22, 1882. Baked Clay Goods, Stove and Range Linings, etc. Gideon C. Francis, South Dighton, Mass.

10,008. January 30, 1883. Stoves, Ranges, and Heaters. Michigan Stove Co., Detroit, Mich.

11,824. December 23, 1884. Fire-Bricks, Stove Linings, etc. Francis A. Ostrander, Troy, N. Y.

12,103. April 7, 1885. Stove-Pipe Elbows. Lock Seam Elbow Co., Indianapolis, Ind.

12,332. June 23, 1885. Stoves and Ranges for Cooking and Heating. Jacob Born, New Orleans, La.

13,003. February 9, 1886. Stoves and Ranges. Western Stove Manufacturing Co., St. Louis, Mo.

13,096. March 9, 1886. Stoves and Ranges. Union Stove and Machine Works, Leavenworth, Kansas.

13,124. March 23, 1886. Stoves, Ranges, Furnaces, etc. Richardson & Boynton Co., New York, N. Y.

13,425. June 15, 1886. Stoves, Furnaces, and Ranges. Fuller & Warren Co., Troy, N. Y.

13,791. November 9, 1886. Fireplaces and Open Grates. Wm. H. Jackson & Co., New York, N. Y.

16,272. February 12, 1889. Stoves and Stove Furniture. Quick Meal Stove Co., St. Louis, Mo.

16,380. March 12, 1889. Fire-Brick, Stove Linings, etc. Francis A. Ostrander, Troy, N. Y.

16,449. April 2, 1889. Heating Apparatus. Howard Furnace Co., Syracuse, N. Y.

16,595. May 21, 1889. Stoves and Ranges. Buck's Stove & Range Co., St. Louis, Mo.

17,190. November 12, 1889. Stoves and Ranges. Michigan Stove Co., Detroit, Mich.

17,319. December 24, 1889. Stoves, Furnaces, Ranges, etc. Peninsular Stove Co., Detroit, Mich.

18,257. August 5, 1890. Stoves, Ranges, etc. Baldwin & Graham, Pittsburg, Pa.

STOVES AND HEATERS.

   18,891. January 20, 1891. Cooking Ranges. John Tettlebach, Cleveland, Ohio.

   19,198. March 17, 1891. Heaters and Furnaces. Superior Furnace Co., Little Falls, N. Y.

   20,345. November 10, 1891. Stoves, Ranges, and Furnaces. Anshutz, Bradberry & Co., Allegheny, Pa.

   21,029. April 26, 1892. Cooking Stoves. Bridge & Beach Manufacturing Co., St. Louis, Mo.

   22,004. November 15, 1892. Heaters, Ranges, and Stoves. Majestic Manufacturing Co., St. Louis, Mo.

   22,052. November 22, 1892. Stoves, Ranges, and Furnaces. Co-operative Foundry Co., Rochester, N. Y.

The ENGINEERING AND MINING JOURNAL

27 PARK PLACE,   NEW YORK.

RICHARD P. ROTHWELL, C. E., M. E., *Editor*.
ROSSITER W. RAYMOND, PH. D., M. E., *Special Contributor*.
SOPHIA BRAEUNLICH, *Business Manager*.
THE SCIENTIFIC PUBLISHING CO., *Publishers*.

THE ENGINEERING AND MINING JOURNAL IS THE BEST, THE MOST INFLUENTIAL, AND WIDEST CIRCULATED MINING PAPER IN THE WORLD. THE TECHNICAL INFORMATION IT GIVES, ITS FINANCIAL MARKET REPORTS, AND ITS FEARLESS AND IMPARTIAL CRITICISMS OF THINGS CALCULATED TO INJURE LEGITIMATE MINING INVESTMENTS HAVE GAINED FOR IT THE ADMIRATION AND CONFIDENCE OF THE ENTIRE MINING INDUSTRY.

The Largest Circulation of any Technical Paper in America.
THE BEST ADVERTISING MEDIUM.

Subscription, including postage.—For the United States, Canada, and Mexico, $5 per annum; $2.50 for Six Months. Foreign Countries in the Postal Union and Australia, $7.

TRADE-MARKS

FOR

SURGICAL AND ELECTRICAL APPLIANCES.

(CLASS 68.)

———•———

Embracing bandages, trusses, artificial limbs, vaporizers, electrical body-wear, and electrical apparatus generally other than chemicals. (See also Class 17, Cutlery, &c.)

———•———

WORDS OR PHRASES CONSTITUTING THE MARKS ALPHABETICALLY ARRANGED.

———•———

A B C.—19,519. May 19, 1891. Electrical Instruments, etc. Alexander, Barney & Chapin, New York, N. Y.
Acme.—10,870. January 22, 1884. Conducting Wires for Electrical Purposes. Ansonia Brass & Copper Co., Ansonia, Conn.
Actina.—13,081. March 2, 1886. Pocket Battery. Wm. C. Wilson. Philadelphia, Pa.
Adenoid.—11,825. December 30, 1884. Apparatus for Increasing the Mammary Glands. Frank M. Blodgett, Boston, Mass.
Ætna.—22,148. December 6, 1892. Electric Insulators. A. and J. M. Anderson, Boston, Mass.
Ajax.—18,482. September 30, 1890. Electric Batteries. Franklin S. Terry, Chicago, Ill.
Alexandra.—1981. September 15, 1874. Breast Pumps. Orwell H. Needham, New York, N. Y.
Alexite.—19,518. May 19, 1891. Material for Insulating Electric Wire. Alexander, Barney & Chapin, New York, N. Y.
American Nebulizer.—15,232. February 28, 1888. Atomizers. August P. Lighthill, Boston, Mass.
Ammoniaphone.—11,677. November 18, 1884. Apparatus for Inhaling Vapors, etc. Cornelius B. Harness, Lavender Hill, Surrey Co., England.
Angel Girdle.—18,626. November 18, 1890. Medical Belt. Geo. W. Angell, Newark, N. J.
Arago.—10,275. May 15, 1883. Dynamo and Magneto Electric Machines. John R. Tibbits, Hoosac, N. Y.
Axion.—19,971. August 4, 1891. Trusses. Geo. V. House, Jr., New York, N. Y.
Balloon.—19,334. April 14, 1891. Surgical Appliances. Robert A. Brown, Lynden, Washington.
Belfast Linen.—14,133. March 8, 1887. Catheters. Sardy, Coles & Co., New York, N. Y.
Bi-Polar.—16,690. June 4, 1889. Electric Belts or Bands. John E. Hetherington, New York, N. Y.

SURGERY AND ELECTRICITY. 139

Brepheostoma.—1982. September 15, 1874. Breast Pumps. Orwell H. Needham, New York, N. Y.
Burgess, The.—20,667. February 2, 1892. Atomizers. John E. Shaw, Philadelphia, Pa.
Candee.—14,988. November 29, 1887. Insulated Wires or Electrical Conductors. Okonite Co., New York, N. Y.
Centennial.—2337. March 30, 1875. Atomizers and Perfumers. Young, Ladd & Coffin, New York, N. Y.
Champion.—2491. May 11, 1875. Telegraph Instruments. Patrick & Carter, Philadelphia, Pa.
Champion.—22,155. December 13, 1892. Vaporizers, Volatilizers, etc. Chas. L. Coulter, New York, N. Y.
Chickasaw.—19,590. May 26, 1891. Cases for Medical and Surgical Instruments. Samuel G. Warner, Memphis, Tenn.
Clark.—21,763. September 20, 1892. Electric Insulated Wire. Eastern Electric Cable Co., Boston, Mass.
Climax Rubber Tape.—18,402. September 9, 1890. Covering for Electric Wires. Boston Rubber Shoe Co., Boston, Mass.
Common Sense.—933. July 30, 1872. 9589. August 8, 1882. Trusses. Bartlett & Butman, Boston, Mass.
Declat.—10,424. July 17, 1883. Surgical Instruments and Appliances. Déclat Manufacturing Co., New York, N. Y.
Domestic.—3646. May 2, 1876. Syringes, Breast Pumps, etc. American Rubber Co., Boston, Mass.
Double Grip (and design).—20,438. December 1, 1891. Splicing Tape for Insulating. E. S. Greeley & Co., New York, N. Y.
Electric.—11,527. September 30, 1884. Nerve Pencils. Geo. L. Lawerence, Boston, Mass.
Electrical Supply (and design).—20,066. August 25, 1891. Electric Appliances. Electrical Supply Co., Chicago, Ill.
Electric Sand—21,611. August 16, 1892. Battery Compounds. Wright Universal Electric Co., New York, N. Y.
Electro-Massage.—17,396. January 14, 1890. Electrical Machines for Curative Purposes. John E. Hetherington, New York, N. Y.
Electropoise.—17,810. April 22, 1890. Instruments for the Cure of Diseases. Hercules Sanche, Detroit, Mich.
Electropoise.—21,892. October 25, 1892. Electro-Curative Apparatus. Electrolibration Co., Birmingham, Ala.
Electro Voltair Chain Belt, Paolis.—1990. September 22, 1874. Electro Voltair Belt. James Bryan, New York, N. Y.
E. S.—20,018. August 11, 1891. Electric Appliances. Electrical Supply Co., Chicago, Ill.
E. S. C.—20,017. August 11, 1891. Electric Appliances. Electrical Supply Co., Chicago, Ill.
Excelsior.—8502. July 19, 1881. Rubber Syringes. Rubber Comb and Jewelry Co., New York, N. Y.
Family Syringe.—3347. January 11, 1876. Syringes. Morris Mattson, New York, N. Y.
Favorite.—3775. June 13, 1876. Perfumers or Atomizers. Thomas J. Holmes, Boston, Mass.
Favorite.—4652. May 15, 1877. Syringe. Macdonald & Sulton, New York, N. Y.
Firnol.—21,628. August 16, 1892. Nose and Throat Douche. W. C. Downey & Co., Washington, D. C.
Franco-German. 17,101. October 15, 1889. Metallic Rings for Cure of Rheumatism, etc. Leonard G. Abbott, Boston, Mass.
Gonda.—12,516. August 18, 1885. Electric Batteries. Leclanche Battery Co., The, New York, N. Y.
Hard Rubber Truss. 9924. January 2, 1883. Hernial Trusses. I. B. Seeley & Co., Philadelphia, Pa.

Hercules.—19,194. March 17, 1891. Electrical Wire. Electrical Supply Co., Chicago, Ill.
High Insulation.—20,484. December 22, 1891. Brackets for Use in Electrical Works. Electrical Supply Co., Chicago, Ill.
Holmes Boston Perfumer.—480. October 17, 1871. 2710. July 6, 1875. Atomizers. Thos. J. Holmes, Boston, Mass.
Household.—10,034. February 13, 1883. Elastic Bulb Syringes. Joseph Davol, Providence, R. I.
Insulatine.—17,880. May 6, 1890. Material for Insulating against Electricity. Roessler & Hasslacher Chemical Co., New York, N. Y.
I-X-L.—11,556. October 7, 1884. Medical and Surgical Appliances. Alfred A. McLean, San Francisco, Cal.
K. K.—11,833. December 30, 1884. Insulated Electric Wires. Holmes, Booth & Hayden, Waterbury, Conn.
Lean on Me.—7923. May 25, 1880. Crutches. Joshua Whittemore, Wakefield, Mass.
Magneso.—20,058. August 18, 1891. Insulating Material. Robert M. Gilmour, New York, N. Y.
Mesco.—20,082. August 25, 1891. Galvanic Batteries. Manhattan Electrical Supply Co., New York, N. Y.
Microphone.—16,445. April 2, 1889. Galvanic Batteries. Peter C. Burns, St. Louis, Mo.
Monitor.—16,797. July 9, 1889. Electric Batteries. Geo. A. Harmount, Chicago, Ill.
Ocean Spray.—6896. December 17, 1878. Cologne Atomizers. Vogeler, Son & Co., Baltimore, Md.
O. K.—20,339. November 10, 1891. Insulated Conducting Wires. Phillips Insulated Wire Co., Pawtucket, R. I.
Okonite.—11,737. December 2, 1884. Insulated Wire. New York Insulated Wire and Vulcanite Co., New York, N. Y.
P. & B.—17,564. February 18, 1890. Wire for Electrical Purposes. Electrical Supply Co., Chicago, Ill.
Paragon.—10,720. November 20, 1883. Insulated Electric Conductors. Ansonia Brass and Copper Co., Ansonia, Conn.
Paramite.—20,916. March 29, 1892. Insulated Wires, Cables, etc. Indiana Rubber and Insulated Wire Co., Jonesborough, Ind.
Phonopore.—16,477. April 9, 1889. Electrical Instruments. Phonopore Syndicate, London, England.
Pocket Electropoise, Victory.—17,811. April 22, 1890. Instruments for Cure of Diseases. Hercules Sanche, Detroit, Mich.
Pulverflator.—21,072. May 3, 1892. Tubes, Atomizers, and Powder Distributers. McKesson & Robbins, New York, N. Y.
Roxite.—17,240. December 3, 1889. Composition for Electrical Insulators, etc. Roxite Co., New York, N. Y.
Royal.—8323. June 7, 1881. Rubber Syringes. Rubber Comb and Jewelry Co., New York, N. Y.
Sachet de Medecin.—5329. November 20, 1877. Ring Pessaries. Robert H. Kline, Philadelphia, Pa.
S. A. D.—13,210. April 20, 1886. Anatomical Health Corsets, etc. Sarah A. Drewry, New York, N. Y.
Savars.—10,393. July 3, 1883. 10,394. July 3, 1883. Articles for Nursery Use, and Surgical Instruments. Henry Sugden Evans, Montreal, Canada.
Sedox.—20,410. November 24, 1891. Bandages and Like Appliances. W. Whitaker and Rebecca S. Donisthorpe, London, England.
Semper Sersum, Indestructible.—17,448. January 28, 1890. Trusses. Daniel H. Hastings, Philadelphia, Pa.
Shield.—17,706. March 25, 1890. Wire for Electric Use. Electrical Supply Co., Ansonia, Conn.
Silver Insoles Win Golden Opinions, The (and design).—19,111. March 3, 1891. Electric Insoles. Estella Wingren & Co., Burlington, Kansas.

Simplex.—18,552. October 28, 1890. Insulated Conducting Wire. Simplex Electrical Co., Boston, Mass.
Smoke Ball.—14,720. August 30, 1887. Medical Appliances. Andrew J. Spinner, Indianapolis, Ind.
Snapper.—1792. May 12, 1874. Telegraph Instruments. Ralph W. Pope, Elizabeth, N. J.
Sun, The.—12,374. June 30, 1885. Portable Case Containing Medical Instruments, etc. Sun Chemical Co., Cincinnati, Ohio.
Thermopoise.—20,796. March 1, 1892. Electrical Appliance. Wm. I. Smith, Memphis, Tenn.
T. Z. R.—18,551. October 28, 1890. Conducting Wire. Simplex Electrical Co., Boston, Mass.
Utericon, D. R. G. D.—12,159. April 21, 1885. Uterine Supporters. Geo. Desborough, Utica, N. Y.
Vapoflator.—21,905. November 1, 1892. Boxes, Bottles, Atomizers, etc. McKeeson & Robbins, New York, N. Y.
Victory, Electrolibration Rules Life (and design).—18,024. June 10, 1890. Instruments for Cure of Diseases. Hercules Sanche, Detroit, Mich.
Volta Eclipse.—18,437. September 16, 1890. Electric Batteries. United States Volta Electric Battery Co., Portland, Maine.
Volta Magnetic (and design).—10,846. January 8, 1884. Magnetic Medical Appliances, etc. August P. Lighthill, Boston, Mass.
Vulcn.—20,344. November 10, 1891. Electrical Appliances. New York Insulated Wire Co., New York, N. Y.
X. L. N. T.—20,866. March 22, 1892. Wrapping for Electric Conductors. Thompson-Houston Electric Co., Boston, Mass.

THE SCIENTIFIC PUBLISHING CO.'S PUBLICATIONS.

The Mineral Industry, Its Statistics, Technology, and Trade, in the United States and other Countries, from the Earliest Times to the end of 1892. The Statistical Supplement of the Engineering and Mining Journal. Bound in Cloth, - - $2.50.

This is the most thorough and exhaustive work on the mineral productions and the industries of the world that has ever been issued, and no person at all interested in mining and metallurgy can afford to be without it.

Modern American Methods of Copper Smelting. *Peters.*	$4.00	Manual of Qualitative Blowpipe Analysis. *Endlich.*	$4.00
Mining Accidents and Their Prevention. *Abel.*	4.00	Phosphates of America. *Wyatt.*	4.00
Metallurgy of Steel. *Howe.*	10.00	Florida, Canadian, and South Carolina Phosphates. *Millar.*	2.50
Gems and Precious Stones of North America. *Kunz.*	10.00	Mining Laws of the Republic of Colombia. *Bullman.*	1.50
Chemical and Geological Essays. *Hunt.*	2.50	The Metallurgy of Lead. *Hofman.*	6.00
Mineral Physiology & Physiography. *Hunt.*	5.00	Ore Deposits of the United States. *Kemp.*	4.00
A New Basis for Chemistry. *Hunt.*	2.00	Parliamentary Practice. *Hoot.*	.50
Systematic Mineralogy. *Hunt.*	5.00		

Elaborate Classified Catalogue of Scientific and Technical Books will be forwarded free on application. Special discounts given to Libraries, Educational Institutions, and on important Cash Orders.

THE SCIENTIFIC PUBLISHING CO.
27 Park Place, New York.

TRADE-MARKS

FOR

Surgical and Electrical Appliances.

(CLASS 68.)

Designs showing essential feature claimed as Trade-Mark.

 430. August 22, 1871. Surgical Instrument. S. Maw, Son & Thompson, London, England.

 838. May 28, 1872. Vaginal Syringe. William Molesworth, New York, N. Y.

 1889. July 21, 1874. Electric and Galvanic Apparatus. Jerome Kidder, New York, N. Y.

 2728. July 6, 1875. Electro-Voltaic Bands. Volta Belt Co., Cincinnati, Ohio.

 3404. February 8, 1876. Surgical Appliances for the Body. W. H. Horn & Bro., Philadelphia, Pa.

 5794. March 19, 1878. Trusses for the Treatment of Hernia, etc. Isaac B. Seeley, Philadelphia, Pa.

 5795. March 26, 1878. Instruments for the Treatment of Hernia, etc. Isaac B. Seeley, Philadelphia, Pa.

 5796. March 26, 1878. Elastic Surgical Bandages. Isaac B. Seeley, Philadelphia, Pa.

 7234. April 22, 1879. Post Nasal Syringes. J. Irvin Carr & A. N. Williamson, Chicago, Ill.

 7962. July 6, 1880. Medicated Belts. Walsh & James, Brooklyn, N. Y.

 8324. June 7, 1881. Electrical Transfusing Battery. Wm. H. Brown, Boston, Mass.

 8824. November 8, 1881. Spirometers. Mathieu Souvielle, Montreal, Quebec, Canada.

SURGERY AND ELECTRICITY. 143

9295. April 18, 1882. Electro-Magnetic Appliances. Isaiah Baker, East Somerville, Mass.

9380. May 16, 1882. Magneto-Therapeutic Appliances. Hugh Thomas, New York, N. Y.

10,413. July 10, 1883. Electrical Medical Appliances. Geo. J. Baker, Hornsey, Middlesex, England.

10,846. January 8, 1884. Magnetic Medical Appliances, etc. August P. Lighthill, Boston, Mass.

13,456. June 29, 1886. Abdominal Supporters. Wm. Teufel, Stuttgart, Germany.

14,017. February 1, 1887. Electric or Galvanic Batteries. Harry B. Cox, Cincinnati, Ohio.

14,054. February 8, 1887. Electromotor Necklaces for Teething Children. Gebrüder Gehrig, Berlin, Germany.

17,043. September 17, 1889. Stomach Tubes, etc. Henry Bedford Sleeman, London, England.

17,172. November 5, 1889. Bandages. Geo. Staber, New York, N. Y.

17,204. November 19, 1889. Clinical Thermometers. Taylor Bros., Rochester, N. Y.

17,459. January 28, 1890. Composition for Electrical Insulators. Roxite Co., New York, N. Y.

17,746. April 8, 1890. Galvanic Batteries. Crosby Electric Co., New York, N. Y.

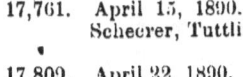
17,761. April 15, 1890. Surgical Instruments. Jetter & Scheerer, Tuttlingen, Wurtemberg, Germany.

17,809. April 22, 1890. Instruments for Cure of Diseases. Hercules Sanche, Detroit, Mich.

17,976. June 3, 1890. Clinical Thermometer. H. Hirschberg Optical Co., St. Louis, Mo.

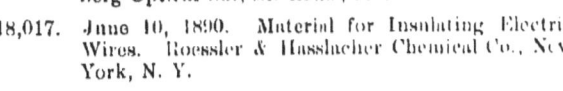
18,017. June 10, 1890. Material for Insulating Electric Wires. Roessler & Hasslacher Chemical Co., New York, N. Y.

18,024. June 10, 1890. Instruments for Cure of Diseases. Hercules Sanche, Detroit, Mich.

144   TRADE-MARKS.

 18,340. August 26, 1890. Insulated Electrical Wire. Benedict & Burnham Manufacturing Co., Waterbury, Conn.

 18,510. October 7, 1890. Electric Batteries. Leclanche Battery Co., New York, N. Y.

 19,111. March 3, 1891. Electric Insoles. Estella Wingren & Co., Burlington, Kansas.

 20,066. August 25, 1891. Electrical Appliances. Electrical Supply Co., Chicago, Ill.

 20,438. December 1, 1891. Splicing Tape for Insulating Purposes. E. S. Greeley & Co., New York, N. Y.

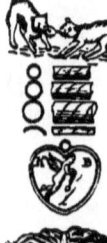 20,709. February 9, 1892. Electrical Conduit Tubes. Interior Conduit and Insulation Co., New York, N. Y.

20,898. March 29, 1892. Necklaces Made of Medicinal Substances. Franciska Korn, New York, N. Y.

 21,736. September 13, 1892. Electric Rings for Cure of Disease. Malcolm D. Peckham, New York, N. Y.

COMPILED BY
WALLACE A. BARTLETT,
Patent Attorney,
WASHINGTON, D. C.

TRADE-MARKS

FOR

TIME-KEEPING INSTRUMENTS.

(CLASS 70.)

Embracing watch cases and movements, clocks and parts thereof, &c. (See also Class 35, Jewelry and Plated-Ware; Class 40, Locks and Hardware.)

Words or Phrases Constituting the Marks Alphabetically Arranged.

Above All.—20,806. March 1, 1892. Watches, Watch Cases, and Ornaments. Byron L. Strasburger & Co., New York, N. Y.
Addison.—18,668. December 2, 1890. Watches. Waterbury Watch Co., Waterbury, Conn.
Adelphi.—14,608. July 19, 1887. Watches. Leopold S. Friedberger & Co., New York, N. Y.
Adjusted (and design).—14,733. September 6, 1887. Watch Movements. E. Howard Watch and Clock Co., Boston, Mass.
Agassiz.—4814. July 3, 1877. Watches. J. Eugene Roberts, Hoboken, New Jersey.
Age, The.—4994. August 7, 1877. 8415. June 28, 1881. Watches and Watch Movements. Elgin National Watch Co., Chicago, Ill.
Ajax.—18,171. July 15, . Watch Insulators. Metropolitan Watch Co., New York, N. Y.
Albatross.—2232. February 16, 1875. Clocks. Florence Kroeber, Hoboken, N. J.
Alpine.—10,594. September 18, 1883. Watches. Adolphe Schwob, New York, N. Y.
America.—20,614. January 19, 1892. Watch Cases. Fabys Watch Case Co., Sag Harbor, N. Y.
American Watch Co.—17,838. April 29, 1890. Watch Movements. American Waltham Watch Co., Waltham, Mass.
Americus Vespucius.—20,331. November 10,1891. Watch Cases. Crescent Watch Case Co., Newark, N. J.
Attleboro Watch Co.—19,046. February 17, 1891. Watch Cases and Movements. Byron L. Strasburger & Co., New York, N. Y.
Auburndale Rotary.—5016. August 7, 1877. Watches, Chronometers, and Timers. William B. Fowle, Auburndale, Mass.
B. A. & Co.—18,757. December 30, 1890. Watch Springs, Pin Tongues, etc. Benj. Allen, Chicago, Ill.
Bijou.—14,512. June 14, 1887. Watches. Adolph Schwob, New York. N. Y.
Bird's Eye.—6116. May 21, 1878. Clocks. Henry J. Davies, Brooklyn, N. Y.
B of L. 21,308. June 14, 1892. Watches and Clocks. Webster C. Ball, Cleveland, Ohio.

B of Lf.—21,625. August 16, 1892. Watches and Clocks. Webster C. Ball, Cleveland, Ohio.
B of Rt.—21,626. August 16, 1892. Watches and Clocks. Webster C. Ball, Cleveland, Ohio.
Bond St.—17,406. January 21, 1890. Watch Movements. American Waltham Watch Co., Waltham, Mass.
B. W. C. Co.—7199. April 15, 1879. Watch Cases. Brooklyn Watch Case Co., Brooklyn, N. Y.
B. W. Raymond.—1526. November 11, 1873. 8409. June 28, 1881. Watch Movements and Watches. Elgin National Watch Co., Chicago, Ill.
Centaur.—10,592. September 18, 1883. Watches. Adolphe Schwob, New York, N. Y.
Centennial.—1802. May 26, 1874. Watches. Lingg & Bro., Philadelphia, Pa.
Charming Boy's.—7864. March 30, 1880. Watches. Louis Strasburger & Co., New York, N. Y.
Chas. Fargo.—1558. December 2, 1873. 8414. June 28, 1881. Watch Movements and Watches. Elgin National Watch Co., Chicago, Ill.
Chicago Watch, The.—1562. December 2, 1873. Watches. National Watch Company, Elgin, Ill.
Chicago Watch Co.—1561. December 2, 1873. Watches. National Watch Company, Elgin, Ill.
College Queen.—22,181. December 20, 1892. Watches and Clocks. Webster C. Ball, Cleveland, Ohio.
Columbia.—18,366. August 26, 1890. Watch Cases. Essex Watch Case Co., Newark, N. J.
Columbian.—20,367. November 10, 1891. Watch Movements. Waterbury Watch Co., Waterbury, Conn.
Colombier.—8144. January 4, 1881. Watches. Louis Strasburger & Co., New York, N. Y.
Columbus.—20,381. November 17, 1891. Watch Cases. Crescent Watch Case Co., Newark, N. J.
Commander.—17,567. February 18, 1890. Watches. Illinois Watch Case Co., Chicago, Ill.
Congress.—9126. February 21, 1882. Watches. Adolphe Schwob, New York, N. Y.
Congress Watch, New York.—2979. September 21, 1875. Watches. Schwob Brothers & Co., New York, N. Y.
Continental.—7589. August 12, 1879. Watches. Leon L. Gallet, Chaux-de-Fonds, Switzerland.
Crescent.—12,841. December 15, 1885. Watch Cases. Crescent Watch Case Co., Brooklyn, N. Y.
Crystal Palace.—2102. December 1, 1874. Clocks. Henry J. Davies, New York, N. Y.
C. W. & Co.—1287. June 3, 1873. Watches. Courvoisier, Wilcox & Co., New York, N. Y.
Daisy B. W. C. Co.—13,283. May 11, 1886. Watch Cases. Brooklyn Watch Case Co., Brooklyn, N. Y.
Derby.—18,174. July 15, 1890. Watch Cases. Essex Watch Case Co., Newark, N. J.
Dexter St.—1557. December 2, 1873. 8413. June 28, 1881. Watches and Watch Movements. National Watch Co., Elgin, Ill.
Doric.—579. December 12, 1871. Clocks. E. Ingraham & Co., Bristol, Conn.
Echo.—8078. November 2, 1880. Clocks. Henry J. Davies, Brooklyn, New York.
Elgin.—3574. April 11, 1876. 9810. November 14, 1882. 21,462. July 19, 1892. Watches and Watch Movements. Elgin National Watch Co., Chicago, Ill.

TIME-KEEPING.   147

Elgin, Ill's.—9807. November 14, 1882. 21,461. July 19, 1892. Watch Movements and Watches. Elgin National Watch Co., Chicago, Ill.
Elgin National Watch Co.—9809. November 14, 1882. 21,464. July 19, 1892. Watch Movements and Watches. Elgin National Watch Co., Chicago, Ill.
Elgin Watch Co.—1560. December 2, 1873. 9808. November 14, 1882. 21,465. July 19, 1892. Watches and Watch Movements. National Watch Co., Elgin, Ill.
Eugene Mathey.—7617. August 26, 1879. Mainsprings for Watches. Cross & Beguelin, New York, N. Y.
Excelsior.—11,974. February 24, 1885. Filled Watch Cases. H. Muhr's Sons, Philadelphia, Pa.
Fashion.—3022. October 12, 1875. 10,497. August 7, 1883. Clocks. Southern Calendar Clock Co., St. Louis, Mo.
Father Time.—15,426. May 8, 1888. Watches. Elgin National Watch Co., Chicago, Ill.
F. C. (monogram).—2010. October 6, 1874. Watches. Courvoisier, Wilcox & Co., New York, N. Y.
Frances Rubie.—1556. December 2, 1873. 8407. June 28, 1881. Watches and Watch Movements. National Watch Co., Elgin, Ill.
Fredonia.—5720. March 12, 1878. Watches. E. D. & C. M. Howard, Fredonia, N. Y.
Gail Borden.—1555. December 2, 1873. 8411. June 28, 1881. Watch Movements and Watches. Elgin National Watch Co., Chicago, Ill.
Galena.—5417. December 11, 1877. Clocks. Florence Kroeber, Hoboken, N. J.
General Andrew Jackson, Exhibition Watch, 1876.—2820. August 10, 1875. Watches. Hugh Mulligan, Philadelphia, Pa.
Gen'l Geo. Wash., Exhibition Watch, 1876, Phila.—2535. May 18, 1875. Watches. Hugh Mulligan, Philadelphia, Pa.
Georges Favre-Jacot.—11,225. June 3, 1884. Watches. Georges Favre-Jacot, Locle, Switzerland.
Giant.—16,155. January 8, 1889. Watches. M. C. Eppenstein & Co., Chicago, Ill.
Globe, The.—15,304. March 20, 1888. Watches, Clocks, Jewelry, etc. S. F. Meyers & Co., New York, N. Y.
Globe Watch, The.—20,570. January 5, 1892. Watch Cases and Movements. S. F. Myers & Co., New York, N. Y.
G. M. Wheeler.—1549. December 2, 1873. 8406. June 28, 1881. Watches and Watch Movements. National Watch Co., Elgin, Ill.
Granger.—1943. August 18, 1874. Time Pieces. Fritz H. Mathez, West New Brighton, N. Y.
Granger (and sheaf).—2266. March 2, 1875. Watch. J. W. Tucker, San Francisco, Cal.
Granger (and design).—15,290. March 20, 1888. Watch Cases. Brooklyn Watch Case Co., Brooklyn, N. Y.
Granger (and design).—15,522. May 29, 1888. Watch Cases. Brooklyn Watch Case Co., Brooklyn, N. Y.
Gravier.—14,916. November 8, 1887. Mainsprings for Time Pieces. Jules Robert & Co., Chaux-De-Fonds, Switzerland.
Grecian.—576. December 12, 1871. Clocks. E. Ingraham & Co., Bristol, Conn.
Hartford Watch Co.—19,047. February 17, 1891. Watch Cases and Movements. Byron L. Strasburger & Co., New York, N. Y.
Heat and Cold (and design).—14,692. August 23, 1887. Watches. E. Howard Watch and Clock Co., Boston, Mass.
Hermetic.—3295. January 4, 1876. Watches and other Time Pieces. John Gordon, San Francisco, Cal.
H. H. Taylor.—1548. December 2, 1873. 8410. June 28, 1881. Watch Movements and Watches. Elgin National Watch Co., Chicago, Ill.

TRADE-MARKS.

H. L. Matile (and design).—4823. July 3, 1877. Watches. L. & A. Mathey, New York, N. Y.

Horse Shoe (and design).—11,578. October 14, 1884. Watches. Vacheron & Constantin, Geneva, Switzerland.

H. Z. Culver.—1547. December 2, 1873. 8405. June 28, 1881. Watch Movements and Watches. Elgin National Watch Co., Chicago, Ill.

Ideal, Philada. Watch C. Co.—16,617. May 21, 1889. Watch Cases. Philadelphia Watch Case Co., Philadelphia, Pa.

Independent.—5721. March 12, 1878. Watches. E. D. & C. M. Howard, Fredonia, N. Y.

Ionic.—578. December 12, 1871. Clocks. E. Ingraham & Co., Bristol, Conn.

I X L.—19,405. April 28, 1891. Watch Movements and Cases. Schild, Freres & Co., Grenchen, Switzerland.

James Picard, Geneva (and star).—2629. June 1, 1875. Watches. Louis Strasburger & Co., New York, N. Y.

Jay Gould.—8185. March 1, 1881. Watches. L. Strasburger & Co., New York, N. Y.

J. H. (monogram).—2011. October 6, 1874. Watches. Courvoisier, Wilcox & Co., New York, N. Y.

J. T. Ryerson.—1551. December 2, 1873. Watches. National Watch Co., Elgin, Ill.

J. T. Ryerson.—8408. June 28, 1881. Watch Movements. National Watch Co., Elgin, Ill.

Juniata.—1947. August 25, 1874. Clocks. Florence Kroeber, Hoboken, New Jersey.

Kansas.—2235. February 16, 1875. Clocks. Florence Kroeber, Hoboken, New Jersey.

Kenosha (and design).—20,266. October 27, 1891. Watch Cases. Kenosha Watch Case Co., Kenosha, Wis.

Kosmic (or) **Cosmic.**—14,224. March 29, 1887. Time-Piece Dials. Martin V. B. Ethridge, Boston, Mass.

Ladies' Friend (and design).—2632. June 1, 1875. Watches. John W. Tucker, San Francisco, Cal.

Lady Elgin.—1552. December 2, 1873. 8404. June 28 1881. 21,463. July 19, 1892. Watches and Watch Movements. National Watch Co., Elgin, Ill.

Lady Racine.—7587. August 12, 1879. Watches. Leon L. Gallet, Chaux-de-Fonds, Switzerland.

Lafayette.—20,332. November 10, 1891. Watch Cases. Crescent Watch Case Co., Newark, N. J.

Lake Shore.—6122. May 21, 1878. Watches. Lake Shore Watch Co., Fredonia, N. Y.

Leader.—4995. August 7, 1877. 8416. June 28, 1881. Watches and Watch Movements. Elgin National Watch Co., Chicago, Ill.

Leonville.—10,962. February 26, 1884. Watch Movements. Mathey Bros. & Mathey, New York, N. Y.

Leopold Hugenin (and locomotive).—2980. September 21, 1875. Watch. Schwob Bros. & Co., New York, N. Y.

Little Daisy.—10,593. September 18, 1893. Watches. Adolphe Schwob, New York, N. Y.

Longines.—997. September 17, 1872. 2597. May 25, 1875. Watches. J. Eugene Robert & Co., New York, N. Y.

Mariposa.—5409. December 11, 1877. Clocks. Florence Kroeber, Hoboken, N. J.

Mat Laflin.—1550. December 2, 1873. 8402. June 28, 1881. Watches and Watch Movements. National Watch Co., Elgin, Ill.

M. D. Ogden.—1554. December 2, 1873. 8401. June 28, 1881. Watches and Watch Movements. National Watch Co., Elgin, Ill.

Miner.—2507. May 11, 1875. Watches. John W. Tucker, San Francisco, Cal.

Monarch.—20,613. January 19, 1892. Watch Cases. Fahys Watch Case Co., Sag Harbor, N. Y.
Monitor.—14,014. February 1, 1887. Watch Cases, etc. Brooklyn Watch Case Co., Brooklyn, N. Y.
Montauk.—20,990. April 19, 1892. Watch Cases. Fahys Watch Case Co., Sag Harbor, N. Y.
Montauk (and design).—10372. June 26, 1883. Watches. Joseph Fahys & Co., New York, N. Y.
M. Paridis.—5634. February 12, 1878. 20,738. February 16, 1892. Watch Springs. Sussfeld, Lorsch & Co., New York, N. Y.
Napoleon.—8143. January 4, 1881. Watches. L. Strasburger & Co., New York, N. Y.
Nassau, The.—18,514. October 14, 1890. Watch Movements. Hippolyte Didisheim, New York, N. Y.
National Park.—18,842. January 13, 1891. Watches. Jules Racine & Co., New York, N. Y.
National Watch Co.—1559. December 2, 1873. 21,801. September 27, 1892. Watches. Elgin National Watch Company, Chicago, Ill.
Niagara.—2234. February 16, 1875. Clocks. Florence Kroeber, Hoboken, N. J.
Non-Pull-Out.—18,464. September 30, 1890. Watch Cases. Keystone Watch Case Co., Philadelphia, Pa.
Old Father Time.—15,425. May 8, 1888. Watches. Elgin National Watch Co., Chicago, Ill.
Old Time.—15,427. May 8, 1888. Watches. Elgin National Watch Co., Chicago, Ill.
Oneida.—2233. February 16, 1875. Clocks. Florence Kroeber, Hoboken, N. J.
O of R C.—21,309.—June 14, 1892. Watches and Clocks. Webster C. Ball, Cleveland, Ohio.
Oresilver.—12,693. October 20, 1885. Watch Cases. Joseph Fahys & Co., New York, N. Y.
Palace Car (and design).—2508. May 11, 1875. Watches. John W. Tucker, San Francisco, Cal.
Patriot.—16,494. April 16, 1889. Watches. Julien Gallett & Co., New York, N. Y.
Peep o' Day.—4763. June 26, 1877. Clocks. Henry J. Davies, Brooklyn, N. Y.
Pensacola.—5419. December 11, 1877. Clocks. Florence Kroeber, Hoboken, N. J.
P. H. Doret, Locle (and cross).—2630. June 1, 1875. Watches. Louis Strasburger & Co., New York, N. Y.
Ph. Doret, Locle (and crescent).—2631. June 1, 1875. Watches. Louis Strasburger & Co., New York, N. Y.
Phœnix.—16,540. April 30, 1889. Watch Cases. H. Muhr's Sons. Philadelphia, Pa.
Phœnix Philada. Watch C. Co.—16,615. May 21, 1889. Watch Cases. Philadelphia Watch Case Co., Philadelphia, Pa.
Polaris.—2236. February 16, 1875. Clocks. Florence Kroeber, Hoboken, New Jersey.
Progress.—7863. March 30, 1880. 8523. August 2, 1881. Watches. Louis Strasburger & Co., New York, N. Y.
Railroad. 7588. August 12, 1879. Watches. Leon L. Gallet, Chaux-de-Fonds, Switzerland.
Railway Dueber Silverine. 18,320. August 19, 1890. Watch Cases. Dueber Watch Case Manuf. Co., Canton, Ohio.
Railway Queen. 21,169. May 24, 1892. Watches and Clocks. Webster C. Ball, Cleveland, Ohio.
R. Lanier Geneva (arrow and stars). 2628. June 1, 1875. Watches. Lewis Strasburger & Co., New York, N. Y.

R. Lanier Geneva (and design).—19,045. February 17, 1891. Watch Movements and Cases. Byron L. Strasburger & Co., New York, New York.
Roanoke.—1957. September 1, 1874. Clocks. Florence Kroeber, Hoboken, N. J.
Roy.—17,112. October 15, 1889. Watch Cases. Roy Watch Case Co., New York, N. Y.
Safety.—17,518. February 11. 1890. Balance Staffs for Watches. Gustave Meiners, Hoboken, N. J.
Silverine.—11,647. November 11, 1884. Composition Watch Cases. John C. Dueber, Newport, Ky.
Silverine.—16,915. August 13, 1889. Composition Watch Cases. Dueber Watch Case Manuf. Co., Cincinnati, Ohio.
Silverex.—19,079. February 24, 1891. Watch Movements and Cases. Byron L. Strasburger & Co., New York, N. Y.
Success.—18,841. January 13, 1891. Watches. Jules Racine & Co., New York, N. Y.
S X.—18,186. July 15, 1890. Watch Cases. Essex Watch Case Co., Newark, N. J.
Symbol.—7991. August 3, 1880. Clocks. Henry J. Davies, Brooklyn, New York.
Tally-Ho.—7248. April 29, 1879. Clocks. Henry J. Davies, Brooklyn, New York.
Tiffany & Co.—4637. May 15, 1877. Jewelry and Watches. Tiffany & Co., New York, N. Y.
Time Telegraph.—9977. January 23, 1883. Electrical Time Indicators. Time Telegraph Co., New York, N. Y.
Tucker (and design).—4439. March 13, 1877. Watches. John Gordon, San Francisco, Cal.
Tuxedo.—22,070. November 29, 1892. Watches. Waterbury Watch Co., Waterbury. Conn.
Unique, Philada. Watch C. Co.—16,616. May 21, 1889. Watch Cases. Philadelphia Watch Case Co., Philadelphia, Pa.
Universal.—4491. March 27, 1877. 9127. February 21, 1882. Watches. Adolphe Schwob, New York, N. Y.
Vacheron.—9845. November 28, 1882. Watch Cases and Movements. Vacheron & Constantin, Geneva, Switzerland.
Vanderbilt.—6186. March 1, 1881. Watches. L. Strasburger & Co., New York, N. Y.
Venetian.—577. December 12, 1871. Clocks. E. Ingraham & Co., Bristol, Conn.
Victor.—10,301. May 22, 1883. Watches. Adolph Schwob, New York, N. Y.
Wabash.—1955. September 1, 1874. Clocks. Florence Kroeber, Hoboken, N. J.
Waltham (and design).—13,730. October 12, 1886. Watches, etc. American Waltham Watch Co., Waltham, Mass.
Waterbury, The.—11,163. May 6, 1884. Watches. Waterbury Watch Co., Waterbury, Conn.
Webster.—17,506. February 11. 1890. Foot Wheels for Watches. American Watch Tool Co., Waltham, Mass.
W. H. Ferry.—1553. December 2, 1873. Watches. National Watch Co., Elgin, Ill.
W. H. Ferry.—8403. June 28, 1881. Watch Movements. Elgin National Watch Co., Chicago, Ill.
Windsor.—19,203. March 14. 1891. Watch Cases. Brooklyn Watch Case Co., Brooklyn, N. Y.
Winona.—1956. September 1, 1874. Clocks. Florence Kroeber, Hoboken, N. J.
X. C.—8924. December 20, 1881. Watch-Case Springs. Orvis W. Bullock, Springfield, Mass.
X L N T.—9115. February 21, 1882. Ornamental Jewelry Chains. S. and B. Lederer, Providence, R. I.

TRADE-MARKS

FOR

TIME-KEEPING INSTRUMENTS.

(CLASS 70.)

Designs showing essential features claimed as mark.

 36. November 1, 1870. Watch. Hirsh & Oppenheimer, New York, N. Y.

 419. August 8, 1871. Jewelry and Watches. S. Landsberg, New York, N. Y.

 472. October 17, 1871. Watches and Jewelry. Aikin, Lambert & Co., New York, N. Y.

 474. October 17, 1871. 2796. August 3, 1875. Clock Spring. Wallace Barnes, Bristol, Conn.

 1187. April 1, 1873. Watches and Watch Materials. Bourquin Brothers, New York, N. Y.

 1444. September 9, 1873. 8601. August 30, 1881. Watch Cases. John C. Dueber, Cincinnati, Ohio.

 1656. March 3, 1874. 8412. June 28, 1881. 15,452. May 8, 1888. Watches. National Watch Co., The, Elgin, Ill.

 1774. May 12, 1874. Clocks. Angelus Clock Co., Philadelphia, Pa.

 2010. October 6, 1874. Watches. Courvoisier, Wilcox & Co., New York, N. Y.

 2011. October 6, 1874. Watches. Courvoisier, Wilcox & Co., New York, N. Y.

2266. March 2, 1875. Watches. J. W. Tucker, San Francisco, Cal.

2388. April 20, 1875. Watch Movements. L. & M. Kahn, New York, N. Y.

2508. May 11, 1875. Watches. John W. Tucker, San Francisco, Cal.

2628. June 1, 1875. Watches. Louis Strasburger & Co., New York, N. Y.

2629. June 1, 1875. Watches. Louis Strasburger & Co., New York, N. Y.

2630. June 1, 1875. Watches. 19,044. February 17, 1891. Watch Movements, etc. Louis Strasburger & Co., New York, N. Y.

2631. June 1, 1875. Watches. Louis Strasburger & Co., New York, N. Y.

2632. June 1, 1875. Watches. John W. Tucker, San Francisco, Cal.

2980. September 21, 1875. 8576. August 16, 1881. Watches. Louis Strasburger & Co., New York, N. Y.

3016. October 5, 1875. Watches. J. H. McMillan & Co., Chicago, Ill.

3470. February 29, 1876. Watch Cases, Lockets, and Medallions. T. B. Hagstoz & Co., Philadelphia, Pa.

4245. December 26, 1876. 10,984. March 4, 1884. Time-Keeping Instruments. Seth Thomas Clock Co., Thomaston, Conn.

4439. March 13, 1877. Watches. John Gordon, San Francisco, Cal.

4823. July 3, 1877. Watches. L. & A. Mathey, New York, N. Y.

6086. May 14, 1878. Watch Cases. Joseph Fahys, Brooklyn, N. Y.

7015. February 11, 1879. 19,581. May 26, 1891. Clocks. Ansonia Clock Co., Ansonia, Conn.

7596. August 19, 1879. Watches and Watch Movements. Augustus Saltzman, Plainfield, N. J.

8671. September 27, 1881. 9711. October 10, 1882. Watch Cases, Rings, etc. Dueber Watch-Case Manufacturing Co., Cincinnati, Ohio.

TIME-KEEPING. 153

 8784. October 25, 1881. Watches and Watch Movements. Leon L. Gallet, Chaux-de-Fonds, Switzerland.

 8995. January 10, 1882. Silver Watch Cases. Dueber Watch Case Manufacturing Co., Cincinnati, Ohio.

 9567. July 25, 1882. Watch Cases. Michael H. Cronin, Philadelphia, Pa.

 9609. August 15, 1882. Watch Movements. May & Son, New York, N. Y.

 9708. October 10, 1882. Eighteen Carat Gold Watch Cases. Dueber Watch Case Manufacturing Co., Chicago, Ill.

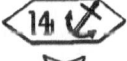 9709. October 10, 1882. Ten Carat Gold Watch Cases. Dueber Watch Case Manufacturing Co., Chicago, Ill.

 9710. October 10, 1882. Gold Rings. Dueber Watch Case Manufacturing Co., Chicago, Ill.

 9783. November 7, 1882. Watch Cases and Movements. Vacheron & Constantin, Geneva, Switzerland, and New York, N. Y.

 10,315. May 29, 1883. Watches. Louis Strasburger & Co., New York, N. Y.

 10,372. June 26, 1883. Watches. Joseph Fahys & Co., New York, N. Y.

 10,377. June 26, 1883. Rolled-Gold-Plate Watch Cases. Dueber Watch Case Manufacturing Co., Chicago, Ill.

 10,920. February 5, 1884. Watches and Clocks. Waterbury Watch Co., Waterbury, Conn.

 10,921. February 5, 1884. Watches and Clocks. Waterbury Watch Co., Waterbury, Conn.

 10,922. February 5, 1884. Watches and Clocks. Waterbury Watch Co., Waterbury, Conn.

 11,150. April 29, 1884. 11,578. October 18, 1884. Watches. Vacheron & Constantin, Geneva, Switzerland.

 11,457. September 2, 1884. Springs of Watches, etc. Charles Robert, Chaux-de-Fonds, Switzerland.

 12,079. April 7, 1885. Watches and Clocks. Eugene Naegele, Philadelphia, Pa.

 12,841. December 15, 1885. 13,816. November 23, 1886. Watch Cases, etc. Crescent Watch Case Co., Brooklyn, N. Y.

154   TRADE-MARKS.

12,862.   December 15, 1885. Filled Watch Cases.   H. Muhr's Sons, Philadelphia, Pa.

12,958.   January 19, 1886. Watch Cases.   H. Muhr's Sons, Philadelphia, Pa.

13,282.   May 11, 1886. Watch Cases.   Brooklyn Watch Case Co., Brooklyn, N. Y.

13,730.   October 12, 1886. Watches, Watch Cases, Watch Movements, etc.   American Waltham Watch Co., Waltham, Mass.

14,695.   July 19, 1887. Filled Cases for Watches.   Dueber Watch Case Manufacturing Co., Cincinnati, Ohio.

14,692.   August 23, 1887. Watch Movements.   E. Howard Watch & Clock Co., Boston, Mass.

14,732.   September 6, 1887. Watch Movements.   E. Howard Watch & Clock Co., Boston, Mass.

14,733.   September 6, 1887. Watch Movements.   E. Howard Watch & Clock Co., Boston, Mass.

15,046.   December 20, 1887. Watch Mainsprings.   Henry Zimmern, New York, N. Y.

15,200.   February 21, 1888. Mainsprings for Time Pieces.   L. Hammel & Co., New York, N. Y.

15,290.   March 20, 1888. Watch Cases.   Brooklyn Watch Case Co., Brooklyn, N. Y.

15,522.   May 29, 1888. Watch Cases.   Brooklyn Watch Case Co., Brooklyn, N. Y.

15,923.   October 2, 1888. Watches.   Non-Magnetic Watch Co. of America, New York, N. Y.

16,168.   January 8, 1889. Watches, Movements, and Cases.   Emile Quartier, Fils, Brenets, Switzerland.

16,328.   March 5, 1889. Watches and Their Parts.   Vacheron & Constantin, Geneva, Switzerland.

16,354.   March 5, 1889. Spiral or Volute Springs for Watches.   Usine Genevoise de Dégrossissage D'or, Geneva, Switzerland.

16,355.   March 5, 1889. Balance Wheels for Watches.   Usine Genevoise de Dégrossissage D'or, Geneva, Switzerland.

16,418.   March 26, 1889. Cased Watches.   Dubail, Monnin, Frossard & Co., Porentruy, Switzerland.

TIME-KEEPING.   155

   16,533.   April 30, 1889. Watches and Watch Cases. Crescent Watch Case Co., Brooklyn, N. Y.

   16,540.   April 30, 1889. Watch Cases. H. Muhr's Sons, Philadelphia, Pa.

   16,618.   May 21, 1889. Watch Cases. Philadelphia Watch Case Co., Philadelphia, Pa.

   16,679.   June 4, 1889. Watch Movements. American Waltham Watch Co., Waltham, Mass.

   16,874.   July 30, 1889. Watch Movements. American Waltham Watch Co., Waltham, Mass.

   17,105.   October 15, 1889. Watch Movements. American Waltham Watch Co., Waltham, Mass.

   17,579.   February 25, 1890. Watch Cases. American Waltham Watch Co., Waltham, Mass.

   18,101.   July 1, 1890. Watch Cases. American Waltham Watch Case Co., Waltham, Mass.

   18,267.   August 5, 1890. Watch Cases. Metropolitan Watch Co., New York, N. Y.

   18,509.   October 7, 1890. Watch Cases. Essex Watch Case Co., Newark, N. J.

   18,644.   November 18, 1890. Watch Cases. Metropolitan Watch Co., New York, N. Y.

   18,740.   December 23, 1890. Watch Springs. Louis Combremont, New York, N. Y

   19,045.   February 17, 1891. Watch Movements and Cases. Byron L. Strasburger & Co., New York, N. Y.

   20,266.   October 27, 1891. Watch Cases. Kenosha Watch Case Co., Kenosha, Wis.

   20,644.   January 26, 1892. Watch Cases. Dubois Watch Case Co., New York, N. Y.

   21,684.   August 23, 1892. Time Keeping and Recording Instruments. Seth E. Thomas, New York, N. Y.

   22,180.   December 20, 1892. Watches. Hampden Watch Co., Canton, Ohio.

TRADE-MARKS

FOR

TOOLS AND DEVICES.

(CLASS 73.)

Embracing hammers, saws, files, blacksmiths', wheelrights' and other tools, and articles of a miscellaneous character. (See also Class 17, Cutlery, &c.; Class 40, Hardware; Class 41, Machines.)

WORDS AND PHRASES CONSTITUTING THE MARK ALPHABETICALLY ARRANGED.

A A A.—11,518. September 30, 1884. Saws. E. C. Atkins & Co., Indianapolis, Ind.
Acme.—11,828. December 30, 1884. Carpet Stretchers. Cooper & Thompson, Chicago, Ill.
Alligator.—14,524. June 21, 1887. Wrenches. American Saw Co., New York, N. Y.
American (and design).—6514. August 27, 1878. Files. New American File Co., Lincoln, R. I.
Balloon.—6342. July 9, 1878. Wire Gauge Fly Traps. National Manufacturing Co., Boston, Mass.
Bee Gimlet (and design).—2753. July 20, 1875. Gimlets. Edward A. Goddard, Brooklyn, N. Y.
Best—R (and design).—5981. April 30, 1878. Saws and Saw Attachments. Christopher Richardson, Newark, N. J.
Bonanza.—7643. September 2, 1879. Machinists' Tools. Collins Company, Collinsville, Conn.
Boss Dog, The.—3647. May 2, 1876. Saw Mill Dogs. Filer, Stowell & Co., Milwaukee, Wis.
Boss.—11,014. March 18, 1884. Button Fasteners. J. K. Krieg & Co., New York, N. Y.
Brown's 3.—8864. November 15, 1881. Saws. Henry Disston & Sons, Philadelphia, Pa.
C. Bishop, 1.—8865. November 15, 1881. Saws. Henry Disston & Sons, Philadelphia, Pa.
Champion, The.—1733. April 21, 1874. 8440. July 5, 1881. Saws. Wheeler, Madden & Clemson Manufacturing Co., Middletown, N. Y.
Collins.—11,352. July 22, 1884. Machinists' Tools. Collins Co., Collinsville, Conn.
Collins & Co., Hartford.—7645. September 2, 1879. Machinists' Tools. Collins Company, Collinsville, Conn.
Columbia.—21,082. May 10, 1892. Can-Openers. A. F. Meisselbach & Bro., Newark, N. J.

Conqueror.—7495. July 8, 1879. 8398. June 21, 1881. Saw-Swages. Henry Disston & Sons, Philadelphia, Pa.
Cube.—16,387. March 19, 1889. Metal Working Tools, Metal Supplies, etc. Chas. H. Besly & Co., Chicago, Ill.
Cut-Cure.—January 9, 1883. Bucksaws. J. Barton Smith Co., Philadelphia, Pa.
Cutter Tooth—Crocker.—1168. 'March 18, 1873. Files. Crocker Cutter-Tooth File Co., Norwich, Conn.
Delusion.—5116. September 4, 1877. Animal Trap. Claudius Jones, Seward, Nebraska.
Dexter (and design).—8880. November 29, 1881. 18,030. June 17, 1890. Saws. Elias C. Atkins, Indianapolis, Ind.
Diamond.—1371. July 22, 1873. 9522. July 11, 1882. 17,275. December 17, 1889. 18,200. July 22, 1890. Saws. E. C. Atkins & Co., Indianapolis, Ind.
Diamond.—2813. August 10, 1875. Mop and Brush Holders. Clark & Co., Buffalo, N. Y.
Diamond.—15,721. July 24, 1888. Razor Strops. Union Cutlery Co., Chicago, Ill.
Diamondized.—13,052. February 23, 1886. Glass Cutters. Samuel G. Monce, Bristol, Conn.
Double Ender.—6034. May 7, 1878. Files. Nicholson File Co., Providence, R. I.
D8.—9641. September 5, 1882. Handsaws. Henry Disston & Sons, Philadelphia, Pa.
Eagle.—11,018. March 18, 1884. Files, Straw Knives, Grass Hooks, etc. Wm. K. & H. K. Peace, Sheffield, England.
Eclipse.—14,467. May 31, 1887. Mechanics and Farmers' Tools. Kansas City Hardware Co., Kansas City, Mo.
Electric.—341. June 20, 1871. 2722. July 6. 1875. Saws. Bissell & Moore Manufacturing Co., New York, N. Y.
Electric.—17,864. May 6, 1890. Razor Strops, Hones, Steels, etc. Electric Cutlery Co., New York, N. Y.
Flexo.—17,989. June 3, 1890. Files. Geo. L. Primrose, Syracuse, New York.
Forester.—9533. July 11, 1882. Crosscut Saws. E. C. Atkins & Co., Indianapolis, Ind.
Gilt Edge.—17,508. February 11, 1890. Saws. E. C. Atkins & Co., Indianapolis, Ind.
Goldschmidt I. P. G. Berlin.—16,629. May 28, 1889. Razor Strops. American Enamel Co., Providence, R. I.
Granger.—1745. April 28, 1874. Saws. E. C. Atkins & Co., Indianapolis, Ind.
Great American.—9664. September 12, 1882. Saws. Henry Disston & Sons, Philadelphia, Pa.
Green River.—8845. November 15, 1881. Blacksmith's and Machinist's Tools. Wiley & Russell Manufacturing Co., Greenfield, Mass.
Handy Saw.—1594. January 6, 1874. Saws. Wheeler, Madden & Clemson, Middletown, N. Y.
Hartshorn.—8385. June 21, 1881. Shade Rollers. Stewart Hartshorn, Millburn, N. J.
Hercules.—19,063. February 24, 1891. Wrencher, Screw-Drivers, etc. Capitol Manufacturing Co., Chicago, Ill.
Hub.—7576. August 12, 1879. Punch. C. H. Graves & Sons, Boston, Mass.
Improved Conqueror Saw.—1074. November 26, 1872. Saws. Wheeler, Madden & Clemson, Middletown, N. Y.
Interchangeable Wing Flange. 18,118. July 1, 1890. Screw-Drivers. Emile James, New York, N. Y.
Jackson Gorham. 29. 8863. November 15, 1881. Saws. Henry Disston & Sons, Philadelphia, Pa.

Kalmoid.—5164. September 25, 1877. Emery Wheels, etc. Edgar C. Burgess, Weissport, Pa.
Keystone.—1464. September 23, 1873. 9741. October 24, 1882. Saws, Tools, Steel, and Files. Henry Disston & Sons. Philadelphia, Pa.
Lightning.—3340. January 4, 1876. Screw Plates, Taps, Dies, etc. Wiley & Russell Manufacturing Co., Greenfield, Mass.
Magnetic.—22,237. December 27, 1892. Razor Strops. Wm. M. Bowes, New York. N. Y.
Monarch.—6777. November 5, 1878. 8439. July 5, 1881. Saws. Wheeler, Madden & Clemson Manufacturing Co., Middletown, N. Y.
Nancy Hanks.—21,902. November 1, 1892. Saws. Wm. B. Barry, Indianapolis, Ind.
Needle.—21,623. August 16, 1892. Saws. E. C. Atkins & Co., Indianapolis, Ind.
O. E. D.—16,408. March 19, 1889. Heel Shaves. Varanus Snell, Brockton, Mass.
Planer, The.—10,795. December 18, 1883. Saws Having Insertible Teeth. Jas. E. Emerson, Beaver Falls, Pa.
Pride of Texas.—8969. December 27, 1881. Hoes, Axes, Hatchets, Saws, etc. J. S. Brown & Co., Galveston. Texas.
Razor.—21,689. August 23, 1892. Saws. Shurly & Dietrich, Galt, Canada.
Salamander (and design).—7849. March 9, 1880. Plumber's Crucibles. Patent Plumbago Crucible Co., Battersea, England.
S. C. C.—19,668. June 9, 1891. Curry Combs. Spring Curry Comb Co., South Bend, Ind.
Secret.—21,688. August 23, 1892. Saws. Shurley & Dietrich, Galt, Canada.
Segment-Ground.—13,309. May 18, 1886. Saws. E. C. Atkins & Co., Indianapolis, Ind.
Shaker.—5879. April 16, 1878. Wrenches. Girard Wrench Manufacturing Co., Girard, Pa.
Silver Steel.—2636. June 8, 1875. 17,666. March 18, 1890. Saws. E. C. Atkins & Co., Indianapolis, Ind.
Silver Steel, Sheffield.—2733. July 13, 1875. Saws. E. C. Atkins & Co., Indianapolis, Ind.
Simonds, The.—7466. July 1, 1879. Saws. Simonds Manufacturing Co., Fitchburg, Mass.
Snell.—9047. January 24, 1882. Augers and Auger-Bits. F. F. Tennis, New York, N. Y.
Souvenir.—96. December 13, 1870. Razor Strop. Benj. F. Badger, Everett, Mass.
Special.—10,050. February 13, 1883. Saws. Simonds Manufacturing Co., Fitchburg, Mass.
Star Saw.—1620. February 3, 1874. Saws. Wheeler, Madden & Clemson Manufacturing Co., Middletown, N. Y.
Star Welt-Trimmer.—2007. October 6, 1874. Welt-Trimmers. Isaac A. Dunham, Brockton, Mass.
Steakgreith.—7597. August 19, 1879. Beefsteak Tenderers. Frank E. Clark, Westville, Conn.
Tanite.—17,884. May 6, 1890. Emery Weels, etc. Tanite Co., Stroudsburg, Pa.
T B.—16,095. December 11, 1888. Hammers. Simmons Hardware Co., St. Louis, Mo.
T. B. Taylor.—7540. July 22, 1879. Mop Holders. Henry H. Mason, Springfield, Vt.
Tested (and design).—1101. January 7, 1873. Files. Thos. Jowett & Sons, Sheffield, England.
The Genuine Coes Screw Wrench.—361. July 4, 1871. Wrenches. A. G. Coes & Co., Worcester, Mass.

Trenton (and lozenge).—3568. April 11, 1876. Mechanics' Tools. Hermann, Boker & Co., New York, N. Y.
Trimo.—19,637. June 2, 1891. Wrenches. Trimont Manufacturing Co., Portland, Me.
True Blue.—16,094. December 11, 1888. Hammers. Simmons Hardware Co., St. Louis, Mo.
Trusty (and design).—1350. July 1, 1873. Files, Rasps, and Steel. Sheffield File Works, Albany, N. Y.
T. Taylor, O.—8862. November 15, 1881. Saws. Henry Disston & Sons, Philadelphia, Pa.
Unbreakable Solid Wing Auger.—18,276. August 5, 1890. Augers. Cornelius Whitehouse & Sons, Bridgetown Cannock, England.
Union.—20,819. March 8, 1892. Tanners' and Curriers' Tools. Geo. D. Ellis & Sons Co., Philadelphia, Pa.
Union Made (and design).—17,962. May 27, 1890. Saws, Saw Sets, etc. Chas. Warren Boyd, Newark, N. J.
Victor.—3299. January 4, 1876. Carpenter's Planes. Leonard Bailey, Hartford, Conn.
Victor.—3670. May 16, 1876. Chucks for Drills. Victor Sewing Machine Co., Middletown, Conn.
V. T. W.—3317. January 1, 1876. Tool for Stone-Masons, Blacksmiths, etc. Metcalf, Paul & Co., Pittsburg, Pa.
Vulcabeston.—14,345. May 3, 1887. Rings, Knobs, Gaskets, etc. Johns Pratt Manuf. Co., Hartford, Conn.
Walworth's.—16,411. March 19, 1889. Die Plates for Threading Pipes. Walworth Manuf. Co., Boston, Mass.
Washoe.—8541. August 2, 1881. Pickaxes, Axes, Hatchets, etc. Henry H. Trenor, New York, N. Y.
W. Goodlad (and anchor design). 777. April 23, 1872. Files. W. and S. Butcher, Sheffield, England, and New York, N. Y.
Wisconsin Farmer. 4888. July 17, 1877. Axes and Saws. Wm. Frankforth & Co., Milwaukee, Wis.
Wolverine. 13,007. February 9, 1886. Hog Rings. Heesen Brothers & Co., Tecumseh, Mich.
X C D.—10,597. September 25, 1883. Files, Edgetools, Razors, and Cutlery. C. F. Butcher, Sheffield, England.
76.—9640. September 5, 1882. Hand-Saws. Henry Disston & Sons, Philadelphia, Pa.
7X.—8399. June 21, 1881. Razor Strops. Joseph R. Torrey, Worcester, Mass.

COMPILED BY
WALLACE A. BARTLETT,
Patent Attorney,
WASHINGTON, D. C.

THE CUTS

IN THIS WORK

WERE ENGRAVED

BY THE

Standard Engraving Co.

OF WASHINGTON, D. C.

TRADE-MARKS
FOR
TOOLS AND DEVICES.
(CLASS 73.)

Designs showing essential feature claimed as Trade-Mark.

 171. February 20, 1871. Cotton Bale Ties. James J. McComb, Liverpool, England.

 636. January 23, 1872. Saws. E. M. Boynton, New York, N. Y.

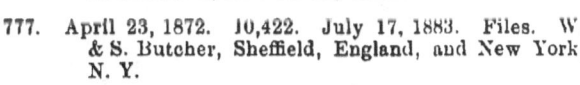 729. April 2, 1872. Metal Tools, Implements, etc. Thomas F. Hamilton, New Haven, Conn.

 777. April 23, 1872. 10,422. July 17, 1883. Files. W. & S. Butcher, Sheffield, England, and New York, N. Y.

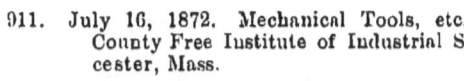 778. April 23, 1872. 10,596. September 28, 1883. Files, Edge Tools, Razors, etc. W. & S. Butcher, Sheffield, England, and New York, N. Y.

 911. July 16, 1872. Mechanical Tools, etc. Worcester County Free Institute of Industrial Science, Worcester, Mass.

 944. August 13, 1872. Razor Strap. Benj. F. Badger, Charlestown, Mass.

 990. September 10, 1872. Driven Well Points and Drills. William P. Smith, New Orleans, La.

 1101. January 7, 1873. Files. Thos. Jowitt & Son, Sheffield, England.

 1270. May 20, 1873. Flue for Draft, Ventilation, etc. Henry R. Farmer, Danville, Va.

1281. May 27, 1873. 8499. July 19, 1881. Files and Rasps. G. & H. Barnett, Philadelphia, Pa.

 1350. July 1, 1873. Files, Rasps, and Steels. Sheffield File Works, Albany, N. Y.

1382. July 22, 1873. Steam Gages and Fixtures. Utica Steam Gage Co., Utica, N. Y.

 1452. September 16, 1873. Saws, Tools, Steel, and Files. Henry Disston & Sons, Philadelphia, Pa.

 1499. October 14, 1873. Quicksilver Flasks. Quicksilver Mining Company, The, New Almaden, Cal.

 1696. March 31, 1874. Screw Wrenches. L. Coes & Co., Worcester, Mass.

 1898. July 21, 1874. Files and Steel. Walter Spencer & Co., Masbrough, England.

 2405. April 20, 1875. 8929. December 20, 1881. Rasps and Files. Heller & Brothers, Newark, N. J.

 2753. July 20, 1875. Gimlets. Edward A. Goddard, Brooklyn, N. Y.

 2791. July 27, 1875. Broom and Tool Holders. Hiram Carsley, Lynn, Mass.

 2903. September 7, 1875. Wood-Working Tools. Barley Tool Co., Woonsocket, R. I.

 2981. September 21, 1875. Carpenter's Planes. Stanly Rule and Level Co., The, New Britain, Conn.

 3038. October 12, 1875. Bevel and Try Squares. St. Johnsbury Tool Co., St. Johnsbury, Vt.

 3220. December 7, 1875. Clasps for Pocketbooks, Satchels, etc. Henry Silberman, Philadelphia, Pa.

 3341. January 4, 1876. Saws. Joseph Woodwell & Co., Pittsburg, Pa.

 3365. January 18, 1876. Clasps and Catches for Pocketbooks, Satchels, etc. Henry Silberman, Philadelphia, Pa.

 3403. February 8, 1876. Tools for Manufacturing Leather, etc. W. H. Horn & Bro., Philadelphia, Pa.

3406. February 8, 1876. Axes, Adzes, Augers, etc. 3407. February 8, 1876. Sledges, Hammers, Wrenches. Collins Co., Collinsville, Conn.

 3535. March 28, 1876. 9707. October 3, 1882. Band Saws and Strip-Knives. Perin, Panhard & Co., Paris France.

TOOLS AND DEVICES. 163

3550. April 4, 1876. Files. Warner File Co., Holyoke, Mass.

3568. April 11, 1876. Mechanics' Tools. Hermann, Boker & Co., New York, N. Y.

3679. May 16, 1876. Stencil Plates. Samuel G. Monce, Bristol, Conn.

4102. November 7, 1876. Pipe Tongs. Edward H. Ashcroft, Lynn, Mass.

4631. May 15, 1877, Stencil Plates. Anselm Neuwall, Chicago, Ill.

5876. April 16, 1878. Saws and Files. Emerson, Smith & Co., Beaver Falls, Pa.

5939. April 23, 1878. Files. Western File Co., Beaver Falls, Pa.

5940. April 23, 1878. Files. Western File Co., Beaver Falls, Pa.

5941. April 23, 1878. Files. Western File Co., Beaver Falls, Pa.

5981. April 30, 1878. Saws and Saw Attachments. Christopher Richardson, Newark, N. J.

6413. July 30, 1878. Cow Milker. Wm. Crozier, Northport, N. Y.

6514. August 27, 1878. Files. New American File Co., Lincoln, R. I.

6551. September 3, 1878. 8446. July 12, 1881. Jewelers' Tools and Files. Frederick W. Gesswein, Jersey City Heights, N. J.

6704. October 8, 1878. 8302. May 31, 1881. Tools and Devices for Ringing Hogs. H. W. Hill & Co., Decatur, Ill.

6932. January 7, 1879. Gimlets, Bits, etc. H. H. Mayhew & Co., Shelburne, Mass.

7111. March 18, 1879. Tackle or Pulley Blocks. Bagnall & Loud, Boston, Mass.

7165. April 8, 1879. Bellows. Young & Stern, New York, N. Y.

7849. March 9, 1880. Plumbago Crucibles, etc., for Chemical Purposes. Patent Plumbago Crucible Co., Battersea, England.

8005. August 17, 1880. Iron and Steel Files. Kearney & Foot, New York, N. Y.

8740. October 18, 1881. Saws. Henry Disston & Sons, Philadelphia, Pa.

8880. November 29, 1881. Crosscut Saws. Elias C. Atkins, Indianapolis, Ind.

9422. May 30, 1882. Hammers. Hartford Hammer Co., Hartford, Conn.

9742. October 24, 1882. Saws, Tools, and Files. Henry Disston & Sons, Philadelphia, Pa.

9976. January 23, 1883. Saddle and Harness Tools. C. S. Osborne & Co., Newark, N. J.

10,389. July 3, 1883. Cutting and Drilling Tools. Morse Twist Drill and Machine Co., New Bedford, Mass.

11,015. March 18, 1884. Files, Straw Knives, Grass Hooks, etc. Wm. K. Peace and H. K. Peace, Sheffield, England.

11,063. April 1, 1884. Lumber-Drivers' Calks. Lumber Drivers Calk Co., Bingham, Me.

12,263. May 26, 1885. Meat Saws, etc. Geo. N. Clemson, Middletown, N. Y.

13,111. March 16, 1886. Horse Rasps. Kearney and Foot Co., New York, N. Y.

13,607. August 24, 1886. Saws. John J. Parker, Aitkin, Minn.

14,899. November 8, 1887. Taps, Dies, and Chasers for Cutting Metal. Chas. Elterich, New York, N. Y.

15,675. July 10, 1888. Engraver's Plates, Dies, and Tools. John Sellers & Sons, New York, N. Y.

15,896. September 25, 1888. Tools used in Engraving on Metal. Antoine Glardon, Vallorbe, Canton of Vaud, Switzerland.

16,227. January 29, 1889. Razors and Razor Strops. Philip Hahn, New York, N. Y.

16,357. March 19, 1889. Metal-Working Tools, Metals, etc. Chas. H. Besly & Co., Chicago, Ill.

TOOLS AND DEVICES.

 16,431. April 2, 1889. Saws. Samuel I. Goodall, Philadelphia, Pa.

 17,630. March 11, 1890. Roll-Paper Holders and Cutters. American Roll Paper Co., St. Louis, Mo.

 17,858. May 6, 1890. Saws. E. C. Atkins & Co., Indianapolis, Ind.

 17,962. May 27, 1890. Saws, Saw Sets, and Trowels. Chas. Warren Boyd, Newark, N. J.

 18,118. July 1, 1890. Screw-Drivers. Emile James, New York, N. Y.

 18,166. July 15, 1890. Twist Drills. Thomas Hooker, Syracuse, N. Y.

 18,200. July 22, 1890. Saws. E. C. Atkins & Co., Indianapolis, Ind.

 19,951. July 28, 1891. Blacksmiths' and Machinists' Small Tools. J. M. Carpenter Tap and Die Co., Pawtucket, R. I.

 20,399. November 24, 1891. Razor Strops. William A. Shull, Philadelphia, Pa.

 20,986. April 19, 1892. Hones. Escher & Co., Sonneberg, Germany.

 21,073. May 3, 1892. Razor Strops. William A. Shull, Philadelphia, Pa.

 21,515. July 26, 1892. Saws, Tools, Files, and Steel. Henry Disston & Sons, Philadelphia, Pa.

 21,904. November 1, 1892. Files, Chisels, Scopers, etc. Grobet Freres, Vallorbe, Switzerland.

 21,969. November 8, 1892. Curry Combs. Spring Curry Comb Co., South Bend, Ind.

 22,147. December 6, 1892. Files, Chisels, Gouge-Chisels, etc. Sl. Vautier & Fils, Carouge, Switzerland.

TRADE-MARKS
FOR
VEHICLES.
(CLASS 76.)

Embracing cars, carriages, wagons, cycles, &c., and parts thereof.

WORDS OR PHRASES CONSTITUTING THE MARK ARRANGED ALPHABETICALLY.

Anchor.—2248. February 23, 1875. Shafts, Spokes, etc., for Vehicles. Jacob A. Lieppe, Lancaster, Pa.
Axtell.—20,663. February 2, 1892. Shaft and Pole Couplings for Vehicles. Henry A. Luttgens, Manchester, N. J.
B. B.—16,968. August 27, 1889. Carts. D. M. Sechler Carriage Co., Moline Ill.
Banner.—17,118. October 15, 1889. Side Spring Wagons. Harvey A. Moyer, Syracuse, N. Y.
Boss, The.—10 140. March 27, 1883. Wagon End Gates. Hagen H. Perkins, Kewanee, Ill.
Boudoir.—11,270. June 17, 1884. Sleeping Car. Mann's Boudoir Car Co., New York, N. Y.
B. S. B.—12,790. November 24, 1885. Wheel Hubs. Acme Hub Co., Dayton, Ohio.
Buck Jumper.—17,946. May 27, 1890. Bicycles, Tricycles, etc. Asser Jacob Samuels, Amsterdam, Netherlands.
Burlington, Boys' Own.—14.081. February 15, 1887. Coasting Sleds and Toboggans. Johnson, Emerson & Co., Burlington, Vt.
C. C. C. (in monogram).—2658. June 8, 1875. Carriage Hardware. C. Cowles & Co., New Haven, Conn.
Challenge.—12.598. September 22, 1885. Velocipedes and their Parts. Geo. Singer, Coventry, England.
Cleveland (and arrow).—3695. June 5, 1877. Carriage Axles. Cleveland Axle Manufacturing Co., Cleveland, Ohio.
Columbia.—6942. January 7, 1879. Bicycles. Pope Manufacturing Co., Boston, Mass.
Columbian.—21,837. October 4, 1892. Top Buggies. Chas. H. Palmer, Jr., Amesbury, Mass.
Comet.—19,296. April 7, 1891. Bicycles. Keefe and Becannon, New York N. Y.
Comfort.—21,101. May 10, 1892. Bicycle Saddles. Bretz & Curtis Manufacturing Co., Philadelphia, Pa.
Common Sense.—9992. January 30, 1883. Sleds and Sleighs. B. F. and H. L. Sweet, Fond du Lac, Wis.

VEHICLES. 167

Concord, N. H., Use.—2459. May 11, 1875. Wagon Axles. D. Arthur Brown & Co., Fisherville, N. H.
Credenda.—19,173. March 10, 1891. Bicycles and Tricycles. A. G. Spalding & Bros., Chicago, Ill.
Crescent.—6586. September 17, 1878. Car-Springs. Miller, Metcalf & Parkin, Pittsburg, Pa.
Cryogen.—5391. December 4, 1877. Railway Cars. John Gamgee, Washington, D. C.
Cushioned Axle.—5258. October 23, 1877. Axles and Axle-Boxes. Rubber-Cushioned Axle Co., New York, N. Y.
Daisy.—18,002. June 3, 1890. Buggies, etc. James H. Mahler, St. Paul, Minn.
Davis, Gould & Co.—11,856. January 13, 1885. Carriages, Phaetons, Buggies, etc. H. W. Davis & Co., Cincinnati, Ohio.
Delamater.—17,520. February 11, 1890. Propeller-Wheels. Samuel L. Moore & Sons Co., Elizabeth, N. J.
Dexter.—5080. August 21, 1877. Vehicles and Vehicle Springs. William W. Grier, Hulton, Pa.
Eagle.—19,220. March 24, 1891. Bicycles, Tricycles, etc. Eagle Bicycle Manufacturing Co., Stamford, Conn.
Ease-About.—18,481. September 30, 1890. Vehicle. A. N. Parry & Co., Amesbury, Mass.
Eclipse.—20,883. March 22, 1892. Bicycles. David L. Whittier, Indianapolis, Ind.
Empire.—11,740. December 2, 1884. Tire Bolts. Port Chester Bolt and Nut Co., Port Chester, N. Y.
Equalizing.—21,057. April 26, 1892. Tramway Trucks. Sheffield Velocipede Car Co., Three Rivers, Mass.
Essex Trap.—20,981. April 19, 1892. Carriages. Samuel R. Bailey & Co., Amesbury, Mass.
Eureka.—20,704. February 9, 1892. Motor Trucks for Street Cars. J. G. Brill Co., Philadelphia, Pa.
Evertite.—21,967. November 8, 1892. Pneumatic Tires for Bicycles. Boston Woven Hose and Rubber Co., Boston, Mass.
Four Hundred.—18,386. September 2, 1890. Buckboards. Biddle & Smart Co., Amesbury, Mass.
Gold Basis, S.—3352. January 11, 1876. Wagons and Carriages. Studebaker Bros. Manufacturing Co., South Bend, Ind.
Granger's Own.—3229. December 14, 1875. Wagons. William H. Garrett, St. Louis, Mo.
Grange Wagon, P. of H., The.—2496. May 11, 1875. Wagons. Wm. M. Price, St. Louis, Mo.
Green Jacket.—2306. March 23, 1875. Steel Springs and Axles. Fort Plain Spring and Axle Works, Fort Plain, N. Y.
Gurney.—18,405. September 9, 1890. Cabs. James T. Gurney, Boston, Mass.
Hammock.—20,213. October 13, 1891. Carts and Carriages. Slates D. Palmer, Marshalltown, Iowa.
Hammock.—20,735. February 16, 1892. Carts and Carriages. Ketchum Wagon Co., Marshalltown, Iowa.
Handy.—17,048. September 24, 1889. Vehicles. Bradley & Co., Syracuse, N. Y.
Hard Rubber Coated Mountings.—2218. February 9, 1875. Carriage Mountings. Andrew Albright, Newark, N. J.
Herdic.—12,022. March 17, 1885. Wheeled Vehicles for Passengers. Peter Herdic, Williamsport, Pa.
Humber, The (and design).—20,325. November 3, 1891. Velocipedes. Humber & Co., Coventry, England.
Ideal.—19,552. May 19, 1891. Bicycles and Tricycles. Gormully & Jeffrey Manufacturing Co., Chicago, Ill.
Imperial.—21,828. October 4, 1892. Velocipedes, etc. Ames & Frost Co., Chicago, Ill.

I X L.—1116. February 4, 1873. 2480. May 11, 1875. Anti-friction Metal and Journal Bearings. I. X. L. Metal Co., St. Louis, Mo., and Sacramento, Cal.

J. & W. Composition Bearings.—378. July 18, 1871. Composition Journal Bearings. Jackson & Wiley, Detroit, Mich.

Kangaroo.—12,406. July 14, 1885. Velocipedes. Hillman, Herbert & Cooper, Premier Works, Coventry, England.

Keystone.—11,741. December 2, 1884. Fire Bolts. Port Chester Bolt and Nut Co., Port Chester, N. Y.

La Belle.—3138. November 16, 1875. Wagons, Carriages, etc. Benjamin F. Moore, Fon du Lac, Wis.

League.—18,348. August 26, 1890. Velocipedes. Banker & Campbell Co., New York, N. Y.

M. C. B.—20,710. February 9, 1892. Car Couplers. Standard Car Coupling Co., Troy and New York, N. Y.

Monarch.—7543. July 22, 1879. Carriage Springs. A. A. Dart Company, New Haven, Conn.

Niagara.—21,458. July 19, 1892. Bicycles. Buffalo Wheel Co., Buffalo, N. Y.

Nonpareil.—19,172. March 10, 1891. Bicycles and Tricycles. A. G. Spalding & Bros., Chicago, Ill.

Old Hickory.—7474. July 1, 1879. Wagons. Kentucky Wagon Manufacturing Co., Louisville, Ky.

Ormonde.—18,349. August 26, 1890. Velocipedes. Banker & Campbell Co., New York, N. Y.

Overland.—20,884. March 22, 1892. Bicycles. David L. Whittier, Indianapolis, Ind.

Phantom.—22,223. December 20, 1892. Bicycles. Henry Sears Co., Chicago, Ill.

Polo.—3968. September 5, 1876. Carriages and Wagons. J. B. Brewster & Co., New York, N. Y.

Premier.—19,858. July 7, 1891. Velocipedes, etc. Hillman, Herbert & Cooper, Coventry, England.

Psycho.—16,702. June 4, 1889. Bicycles, Tricycles, etc. Starley Bros., Coventry, England.

Quadrant.—21,066. May 3, 1892. Bicycles and Tricycles. Quadrant Cycle Co., Birmingham, England.

Quality, not Quantity.—20,443. December 8, 1891. Carriages, Cutters, Sleighs, etc. Thomas Neville, Oshkosh, Wis.

Rambler.—19,553. May 19, 1891. Bicycles. Gormully & Jeffery Manufacturing Co., Chicago, Ill.

Ram's Horn.—13,218. April 20, 1886. Vehicle Springs. H. W. Moore & M. W. Barse, Olean, N. Y.

Referee Cycles.—19,157. March 10, 1891. Bicycles, Tricycles, etc. G. L. Morris & W. T. Wilson, London, England.

Rival.—19,953. July 28, 1891. Bicycles, Tricyles, etc. Warman & Hazlewood, Coventry, England.

Rudge.—12,961. January 19, 1886. Bicycles, Tricycles, etc. D. Rudge & Co., Coventry, England.

Runabout.—16,352. March 5, 1889. Road Wagons. Rufus M. Stivers, New York, N. Y.

Sandage.—20,389. November 17, 1891. Wagon Skeins. Sandage Steel Skein Co., South Bend, Ind.

Standard.—10,459. July 24, 1883. Cabs. D. P. Nichols & Co., Boston, Mass.

Standard.—11,659. November 11, 1884. Saddle-Bags and Buggy Cases. A. A. Mellier, St. Louis, Mo.

Star.—13,266. May 4, 1886. Toboggans. J. R. McLaren, Jr., Montreal, Quebec, Canada.

Steeled Wheel.—8. October 25, 1870. Car Wheel. Wm. G. Hamilton, New York, N. Y.

Sunol.—20,574. January 12, 1892. Bicycles, Velocipedes, etc. McIntosh-Huntington Co., Cleveland, Ohio.
Surre-yet.—17,531. February 11, 1890. Buggies and Light Carriages. Chas. M. Blydenburgh, Riverhead, N. Y.
Swift.—21,201. May 24, 1892. Bicycles. Coventry Machinists' Co., Coventry, England.
Tally-Ho.—6576. September 17, 1878. Toys and Toy Vehicles. Charles W. F. Dare, Brooklyn, N. Y.
Telegram.—21,014. April 19, 1892. Bicycles. Sercombe-Bolte Manufacturing Co., Milwaukee, Wis.
Tennessee.—4881. July 17, 1877. Road Wagons. Cherry, O'Conner & Co., Nashville, Tenn.
Tennessee.—17,436. January 28, 1890. Farm and Freight Wagons. Cherry, Morrow & Co., Nashville, Tenn.
Tourist.—19,886. July 14, 1891. Safety Bicycles. Geo. R. Bidwell Cycle Co., New York, N. Y.
Trade Wagon, The.—528. November 14, 1871. 2460. May 11, 1875. Wagons. S. N. Brown & Co., Dayton, Ohio.
Turnbull.—15,557. May 29, 1888. Freight or Farm Wagons. Turnbull Wagon Co., Defiance, Ohio.
Ulster.—4152. November 28, 1876. Sleds. Abel A. Crosby, Rondout, New York.
Union.—17,608. March 4, 1890. Bicycles. Union Cycle Manufacturing Co., Highlandville, Mass.
Victoria.—9629. August 29, 1882. Vehicle Springs. John M. Miller, Cincinnati, Ohio.
Vulcan.—4354. February 13, 1877. Wagon Axles. D. Arthur Brown & Co., Fisherville, N. H.
Vulcan.—8394. June 21, 1881. Wagon Axles. Concord Axle Co., Fisherville, N. H.
Vulcan.—10,585. September 18, 1883. Spiral Car Springs. French Spiral Spring Co., Pittsburg, Pa.
Vulcanized Fibre.—1965. September 8, 1874. Washers, Journal Bearings. Wm. Courtenay, Wilmington, Del.
Windsor.—2019. October 13, 1874. Carriages and Wagons. J. B. Brewster & Co., New York, N. Y.
Young America.—21,068. May 3, 1892. Bicycles. Bradshaw Manufacturing Co., Boston, Mass.

COMPILED BY
WALLACE A. BARTLETT,
Patent Attorney,
WASHINGTON, D. C.

TRADE-MARKS

FOR

VEHICLES.

(CLASS 76.)

Designs showing essential feature claimed as mark.

 97. December 13, 1870. Wagon Axle. D. Arthur Brown & Co., Fisherville, N. H.

 967. August 20, 1872. Carriage Bolts. Plumb & Burdict, Buffalo, N. Y.

 1095. December 31, 1872. Steel Springs and Axles. Fort Plain Spring and Axle Works. Fort Plain, N. Y.

 1521. November 4, 1873. Toy Wheels. Sam'l T. Wheelwright & Chas. L. Locke, Buffalo, N. Y.

 2248. Februray 23, 1875. Shafts, Spokes, etc., for Vehicles. Jacob A. Leippe, Lancaster, Pa.

 2658. June 8, 1875. Carriage Hardware. C. Cowles & Co., New Haven, Conn.

 3192. December 7, 1875. Railway Journal Bearings. Bowles & Wilkins, Chicago, Ill.

 3742. June 6, 1876. Carriage and Wagon Wood-Work. Hoopes, Bro. & Darlington, West Chester, Pa.

 4695. June 5, 1877. Carriage Axles. Cleveland Axle Manufacturing Co., Cleveland, Ohio.

 5682. February 26, 1878. Railroad Supplies. Nottingham Manufacturing Co., New York, N. Y.

 6524. August 27, 1878. Wagons, Carriages, and Sleighs. R. M. Stivers, New York, N. Y.

7893. May 4, 1880. Vehicle Wheels. Woodburn Sarven Wheel Co., Indianapolis, Ind.

VEHICLES. 171

7929. June 1, 1880. Velocipedes. Nahum S. C. Perkins, Norwalk, Ohio.

10,612. October 2, 1883. Farm and Spring Wagons, Buggies, Sleds, etc. Fish Bros. & Co., Racine, Wis.

11,741. December 2, 1884. Tire Bolts. Port Chester Bolt and Nut Co., Port Chester, N. Y.

12,060. March 31, 1885. Spokes, Rims, Hubs, etc., for Carriages. Crane & McMahon, New York, N. Y.

12,061. March 31, 1885. Wood-Ware for Vehicles. Crane & McMahon, New York, N. Y.

12,062. March 31, 1885. Wood-Ware for Vehicles. Crane & McMahon, New York, N. Y.

13,773. November 2, 1886. Carriages and Carriage Springs. James Harris Snodgrass, Mifflinburg, Pa.

14,726. September 6, 1887. Stock Cars. Geo. D. Burton, Boston, Mass.

14,925. November 15, 1887. Stock Cars. Geo. D. Burton, Boston, Mass.

15,365. April 17, 1888. Pleasure Carriages. Healey & Co., New York, N. Y.

15,677. July 10, 1888. Bicycles and Tricycles. St. George Engineering Co., Birmingham, England.

15,683. July 17, 1888. Railway Stock Cars. George D. Burton, Boston, Mass.

16,876. July 30, 1889. Vehicle Wheels. Jerome Bolick, Conover, N. C.

17,314. December 24, 1889. Wagon Brake Locks. Hurlbut Manuf. Co., Racine Junction, Wis.

19,881. July 14, 1891. Velocipedes. Raleigh Cycle Co., Nottingham, England.

19,889. July 14, 1891. Car-Couplings. Thurmond Car-Coupling Co., New York, N. Y.

20,084. August 25, 1891. Articles of Railway Equipment. The Q. & C. Co., Portland, Me.

172   TRADE-MARKS.

 29,172. September 29, 1891. Wagons. Parsons Low-Down Wagon Co., Earlville and New York, N. Y.

 29,325. November 3, 1891. Velocipedes. Humber & Co., Coventry, England.

  29,555. January 12, 1892. Bicycles and Parts. Parker H. Sercombe, Milwaukee, Wis.

 29,735. February 16, 1892. Carts and Carriages. Ketchum Wagon Co., Marshalltown, Iowa.

  29,832. March 15, 1892. Bicycles, Tricycles, etc. Chas. H. Pugh, Birmingham, England.

 29,883. March 22, 1892. Bicycles. Smith Wheel Manufacturing Co., Washington, D. C.

   21,602. August 9, 1892. Metallic Wheelbarrow. J. C. McNeil, Akron, Ohio.

  21,973. October 18, 1892. Bicycles, Velocipedes, etc. McIntosh Huntington Co., Cleveland, Ohio.

COMPILED BY
WALLACE A. BARTLETT,
Patent Attorney,
WASHINGTON, D. C.

FORM OF STATEMENT.

The following is the usual form of statement employed in registering a trade-mark under the present law:

To all whom it may concern:

Be it known that —— ——, a citizen of —— ——, residing at —— ——, and doing business at No. ——, —— street, in ——, have adopted for —— use a trade-mark for ——, of which the following is a full, clear, and exact specification.

Said trade-mark consists of the word Champion, and the representation of a Maltese Cross. This has generally been arranged as shown in the accompanying facsimile, in which the word Champion is printed in plain capital letters across the face of the representation of the maltese cross. But the style of lettering and the special arrangement thereof are unimportant, and may be changed at pleasure without materially affecting the character of the trade-mark, the essential feature of which is the word Champion and the representation of the Maltese Cross.

This trade-mark —— have used continuously in —— business since about —— —— ——.

The class of merchandise to which this trade-mark is appropriated is ——, and the particular description of goods comprised in said class on which —— use it is ——.

It is —— practice to apply said trade-mark to the goods by printing the same on the labels which are attached to the goods, but the mark may be branded or stenciled on, or otherwise applied to the goods or to the packages in which they are contained, or otherwise legitimately used in connection with —— business.

(Signed) —— ——.

Two witnesses:
—— ——.
—— ——.

FORM OF DECLARATION.

(TO ACCOMPANY STATEMENT.)

State of ——,
County of ——, } ss:

——— ———, being duly sworn, states that —— is the applicant named in the foregoing statement; that he verily believes that the foregoing statement is true; that said applicant at this time has a right to the use of the trade-mark therein described; that no other person, firm, or corporation has the right to such use, either in the identical form or in any such near resemblance thereto as might be calculated to deceive; that it is used by ——— ——— in commerce between the United States and foreign nations or Indian tribes, and particularly with ———, and that the description and facsimile presented for record truly represent the trade-mark sought to be registered.

(Signed.) ——— ———.

Sworn to and subscribed before me, a notary public, this —— day of ——, 18 —.

[SEAL.]

——— ———,
Notary Public.

NOTE.—The facsimile must be on a card 10 x 15 inches, with an inch margin all round; must be in black, of such character that photo-lithographic copies may be produced therefrom, and must be signed (within the margin at the bottom of the sheet) by the applicant or his attorney, and the signature attested by two witnesses.

ERRATA.

Page xiii, add class **Tools and Devices.**
Page 3, line 8, for **Chrystal** read Crystal.
Page 3, line 46, for **Creedmore** read Creedmoor.
Page 8, line 6, for Rockport read Brockport.
Page 23, to trade-mark 19,987, add the words "Brockton White" to the design.
Page 25, trade-marks 19,777, and 19,779, read "E. A. Whitney & Co." instead of E. A. Whiting & Co."
Page 31, last line, for "Joseph N. Gardner" read "Joseph W. Gardner."
Page 82, trade-mark "**Boss,**" for "Dryden Horseshoe Co.," read "Bryden Horseshoe Co."
Page 82, trade-mark "**Champion,**" No. 3,123, for "Buelde" read "Buckle."
Page 91, trade-mark 5,829, after 1878 insert "No. 8340, of June 14, 1881."
Page 101, trade-mark "**Little Giant,**" 6394, add date "July 23, 1878."
Page 103, trade-mark "**Swan,**" for "Middletown, N. Y.," read "Middletown, Ct."
Page 131, trade-mark "**Favorite,**" for "1890" read "1880."

INDEX.

	PAGE.
Copyrights	xv
Form of Statement for Trade-Mark	173
Form of Declaration for Trade-Mark	174
Errata	175
Index of Classes	xiii
Notes on Decisions and Practice	x
Patents	xiv
Prints and Labels	xvi
Trade-Mark Law	vii
Trade-Marks for Agricultural Implements	1–13
Cleaning and Polishing Preparations	14–23
Cutlery and Edge Tools	24–37
Fire-Arms, &c.	40–45
Household Articles	46–48
Iron, Steel, and other Metals	49–62
Jewelry and Plated Ware	65–73
Lamps and Lanterns	74–77
Laundry Articles	78–80
Locks and Hardware	81–96
Machines	97–110
Needles and Pins	112–116
Machine Packing, Belting, &c.	117–124
Sewing Machines, &c.	125–128
Stoves and Heaters	129–137
Surgery and Electricity	138–144
Time-Keeping Instruments	145–155
Tools and Devices	156–165
Vehicles	166–172
Treasury Order	x

www.ingramcontent.com/pod-product-compliance
Lightning Source LLC
Chambersburg PA
CBHW030821190426
43197CB00036B/713